BROOKINGS-WHARTON

PAPERS *on* FINANCIAL SERVICES
2003

ROBERT E. LITAN
and
RICHARD HERRING
Editors

BROOKINGS INSTITUTION PRESS
Washington, D.C.

030434

BROOKINGS-WHARTON
PAPERS *on*
FINANCIAL
SERVICES
2003

THE BROOKINGS-WHARTON PAPERS ON FINANCIAL SERVICES is an annual publication containing the articles, formal discussants' remarks, and highlights of the discussions from a conference held at the Brookings Institution and arranged by the editors. This year's forum and journal are financed in part by grants from ABN AMRO Bank, AEGON, Citigroup, First Data, Financial Services Roundtable, Fortis, GE Foundation, ING, Merrill Lynch, Morgan Stanley, Netherlands Ministry of Finance, New York Stock Exchange, Rabobank Nederland, UBS Warburg, and the USAA Foundation.

The annual forum and journal are the products of a collaboration between the Brookings Institution and the Financial Institutions Center at the Wharton School of the University of Pennsylvania. This year's volume was also done in collaboration with the Royal Netherlands Embassy. All of the papers and discussants' remarks represent the views of the authors and not necessarily the views of the staff members, officers, or trustees of the Brookings Institution or the Wharton School of the University of Pennsylvania, or of the institutions affiliated with the authors.

Ordering Information

Standing order plans are available by calling 1-800/275-1447 or 202/797-6258. Send subscription orders to the Brookings Institution, Department 037, 1775 Massachusetts Avenue, N.W., Washington, DC 20042-0037. Or call 202/797-6258 or toll free 1-800/275-1447. Or email bibooks@brookings.edu.

Visit Brookings online at www.brookings.edu.

Brookings periodicals are available online through both Online Computer Library Center (contact the OCLC subscriptions department at 1-800/848-5878, ext. 6251) and Project Muse (http://muse.jhu.edu).

Coeditors	Robert E. Litan	*Brookings Institution*
	Richard Herring	*University of Pennsylvania*

Staff	Elizabeth Forsyth	*Editorial Associate*
	Catherine Theohary	*Research Verifier*
	Kai Bode	*Research Verifier*

Authors	Arnoud W. A. Boot	*Universiteit van Amsterdam and Centre for Economic Policy Research*
	Stijn Claessens	*Universiteit van Amsterdam*
	Jeroen J. M. Kremers	*Ministry of Finance of the Netherlands*
	Andrew Kuritzkes	*Oliver, Wyman and Company*
	Arnold Schilder	*De Nederlandsche Bank*
	Dirk Schoenmaker	*Ministry of Finance of the Netherlands*
	Til Schuermann	*Federal Reserve Bank of New York and University of Pennsylvania*
	Peter P. Swire	*Ohio State University Law School*
	Iman van Lelyveld	*De Nederlandsche Bank*
	Ingo Walter	*New York University*
	Scott M. Weiner	*Alliance Capital*
	Lawrence J. White	*New York University*
	Peter J. Wierts	*Ministry of Finance of the Netherlands*

Advisers participating in the conference	Michael Brennan	*University of California, Los Angeles*
	Eugene Fama	*University of Chicago*
	Edward Kane	*Boston College*
	Jonathan Macey	*Cornell University*
	Robert Merton	*Harvard Business School*
	Geoffrey Miller	*New York University*
	Stewart Myers	*Massachusetts Institute of Technology*
	Robert Shiller	*Yale University*

Editors' Summary

RICHARD J. HERRING
ROBERT E. LITAN

In 1999, AFTER NEARLY TWENTY YEARS of debate, the United States finally enacted legislation permitting bank affiliations with all sorts of other financial enterprises and vice versa. In taking this step, the United States joined many other countries—especially in Europe and, more recently, Japan—in allowing the operation of financial conglomerates.

But are financial conglomerates the wave of the future in finance? And if so, how are they to be regulated? These were the two central questions addressed in the sixth annual conference on financial services, held in October 2002 at the Dumbarton House in Washington, D.C. We were joined in sponsoring this conference by the government of the Netherlands, with the benefit of financial support from financial institutions on both sides of the Atlantic.[1]

In this introduction, we briefly outline the main conclusions of the papers presented at the conference. To preview the answers to the questions just posed, the papers suggest that although the future may see more financial conglomerate activity than in the past, there still will be a role for specialist, or "monoline," financial companies. As for regulation,

1. We are grateful for the support of ABN AMRO Bank, AEGON, Citigroup, First Data, Financial Services Roundtable, Fortis, GE Foundation, ING, Merrill Lynch, Morgan Stanley, Netherlands Ministry of Finance, New York Stock Exchange, Rabobank Nederland, UBS Warburg, and the USAA Foundation.

there is no settled model: some nations will pursue consolidated supervision, with authority over entire conglomerates vested in a single authority (often the central bank), while others will continue to regulate the pieces of diversified financial enterprises along structural lines.

INGO WALTER ADDRESSES the threshold question about the future landscape of the financial industry, in the United States and abroad, by surveying what we know and don't know about the success of various business strategies in the financial services sector. In particular, are economies of scale and scope so compelling that the future must inevitably belong to the largest financial conglomerates?

Walter concludes that the answer to this conclusion is no. The available evidence, in his survey, suggests that firm performance in financial services is essentially unrelated to size and that the evidence of economies or diseconomies of scope is inconclusive. Instead, the key to explaining differences in firm performance seems to be variations in management effectiveness, or "X-efficiency." Much of the gain from mergers may derive from the extension of successful management of the acquiring firm to the acquired entity, not from an increase in scale or scope. So-called "revenue efficiencies" from cross-selling products and services across a conglomerate, meanwhile, appear to be firm-specific and cannot be generalized to all financial services firms. Walter cautions, however, that most studies investigating the effects of economies of scope were conducted during a period when many financial firms were incurring large, but transitory, set-up costs, which create a bias against finding such economies.

In principle, firms operating with market power should be able to charge higher prices and earn greater profits than firms operating in a competitive environment. Although Walter finds that banks doing business in concentrated markets do tend to charge higher rates for loans and provide lower rates for deposits, higher expenses appear to absorb the excess revenue generated by the larger spreads, so that banks in such markets do not systematically earn supranormal profits.

Again, in principle, an increase in the size and scope of a financial conglomerate should lower its risk and thereby lead to a higher stock price. The empirical evidence supports this view with respect to combinations of commercial banking and insurance, but not with respect to commercial banking and securities activities.

One key downside of the movement toward financial conglomerates, in Walter's view, is the increased opportunity for conflicts of interest. As the activities of conglomerates become more complex and varied, so do the number and nature of their conflicts. Correspondingly, it becomes more difficult for regulators to monitor and police them effectively.

Significantly, investors do not necessarily welcome financial firms' drive to be conglomerates or financial supermarkets. Walter reports that stock prices of (nonfinancial) multiproduct firms generally sell at some discount relative to firms with more narrowly drawn product or service lines. A major reason: conglomerates tend to use capital less efficiently than more focused firms. Walter suggests that the same tendency is true among financial services firms.

In sum, despite much of the hype surrounding the supposed inevitability of financial conglomerates taking increasing shares of the financial services market, the evidence, so far at least, does not appear to support this view. There is still a role to be played by firms of all sizes and specialties.

GIVEN THE PARTICIPATION by European experts and financial market actors at the conference, it was appropriate that one of the papers examine financial consolidation and strategy in Europe. This is the focus of the paper by Arnoud Boot.

Boot echoes the view expressed by Walter that neither scope nor scale economies are driving consolidation in the financial services sector, which Boot characterizes as "breathtaking" in both the United States and Europe. Instead, Boot believes that firms are moving toward the conglomerate model for various strategic reasons, notably, the desire for first-mover advantages and the quest for market power and thus supranormal profits. In addition, uncertainty about the source of future profits may lead firms to diversify their activities—as a way of hedging all bets. Deregulation and rapid technological change clearly contribute to this uncertainty. For this reason, Boot believes that much consolidation may be more defensive than offensive in nature.

Yet despite the growing consolidation across traditional industry lines, Boot finds that competitive pressures in financial services are growing, not receding. Margins are therefore eroding, threatening the viability of costly scope-expanding strategies.

These tendencies are especially apparent in banking, according to Boot. Running against the conventional wisdom that capital market financing will drive out bank lending, Boot finds that loans serve as a check against excessive risk-taking from borrowing firms, thereby lowering their overall cost of capital. Although securitization will continue, banking will restructure rather than disappear. Banks still offer valuable information as well as processing and credit enhancement services, even if they do not provide the bulk of financing.

Boot also claims that the widely reported demise of relationship banking is overblown. Precisely because cutting prices in response to eroding margins cannot be a recipe for success, banks can only survive by focusing more on clients and by customizing their services to client needs.

As for the lack of empirical evidence of scale and scope economies in banking, Boot notes that most of the studies reaching this conclusion rely on data that now look somewhat stale—from the 1980s and earlier. At the same time, various technological, regulatory, managerial, and political barriers may continue to prevent larger firms from realizing these economies. In principle, diversified firms may nonetheless be able to realize scope economies through information technology (which can be used to reduce costs for a broad range of services and products), reputational benefits, financial innovation, and risk diversification. Still, the jury is out on whether these sources of possible gains will justify the move toward financial conglomerates and "universal banking."

If Boot is right, then the recent move toward financial conglomerates may be temporary or at least about to peak. In a more competitive environment, narrowly focused business strategies may trump the financial supermarket model. Banks, in particular, may rely more heavily on alliances, which are inherently more flexible and can be changed more easily, as an alternative to outright consolidation.

THE INTEREST IN financial conglomerates is not confined to developed economies. Financial conglomerates are an important feature of the financial landscape in emerging markets as well, as Stijn Claessens reports in his paper.

Historically, banks have been regulated because of their inherent fragility—they are highly leveraged with highly liquid liabilities and illiquid assets—and because of their importance to the real economy. However, as banks' relative importance has waned, while the lines between bank and nonbank services have become blurred, new financial regulatory challenges have arisen.

Claessens reviews the financial landscape around the world and finds a broad and growing international consensus in favor of allowing banks to affiliate with other types of financial enterprises. Of the countries surveyed, only China still narrowly circumscribes the activities of banks and their affiliates (an attitude that may reflect the policy of the United States in this respect, at least until recently).

Claessens assesses both the benefits and costs of allowing integrated financial services (IFS) firms. On the benefit side, he too finds minimal evidence of economies of scope. In principle, however, diversified firms should be less risky because revenues from different lines of business may be uncorrelated or negatively correlated with each other.

On the cost side of allowing IFS firms—again, in principle—most prominent are the potential conflicts of interest, the difficulty of monitoring complex institutions, and the potential changes in the balance of competition and political power. From the extensive empirical literature applicable to developed economies, Claessens finds that universal banks have been largely successful in avoiding conflicts of interest, while little evidence exists of anticompetitive behavior by these diversified institutions. In developing countries, IFS firms may pose greater dangers of conflicts of interest, but there may also be greater opportunities to realize the benefits of diversification in those environments.

Claessens also reviews the cross-country studies that bear on the benefits and costs of IFS firms. He finds that countries that impose greater restrictions on the mingling of banking and securities activities have been substantially more likely to suffer banking crises than countries that allow these two activities to be pursued by a single entity. There is also some evidence that allowing IFS firms to operate improves financial sector efficiency, although it may also add to market concentration.

A key challenge for regulators in emerging markets is to ensure that their financial systems are open and contestable and to strictly enforce measures designed to prevent leakage from any publicly provided safety net to support the nonbanking activities of IFS firms.

WHETHER OR NOT they prove to be the most efficient form of financial institution, are financial conglomerates less or more risky than narrowly focused financial firms? In principle, risk should fall as firms diversify their services. If so, then financial conglomerates may need less capital than financial firms engaged in only one or a few lines of financial business.

This is among several questions that Andrew Kurtizkes, Til Schuermann, and Scott Weiner address in their paper. They also examine whether the typical regulatory approach toward financial conglomerates—attention to the individual lines of business within the firm rather than to the overall conglomerate or holding company—is appropriate. And using what they believe to be reasonable parameters, the authors estimate what combinations of financial business are likely to achieve the greatest reduction in risk.

Taking the last question first, the authors find that the most effective risk-reducing financial strategy is to combine banking with property and casualty insurance. As for the effects of size, the most risk reduction occurs among combinations of equal-size firms.

Meanwhile, the authors are critical of the so-called "silo" approach to regulation, which among other things, fails to take account of risk concentrations or diversification across different operating subsidiaries. In addition, when different regulators oversee different financial lines of business within the same diversified financial firm, the same or similar activities may be inconsistently treated depending on the line of business where they are located. Realizing this, opportunistic managers may be tempted to take advantage of or "game" the differences in regulation by booking business in subsidiaries or even shell companies facing the lightest regulation. Finally, the silo approach ignores capital at unlicensed subsidiaries and the parent holding company.

To address these problems, the authors propose that regulators supplement existing supervision of regulated financial subsidiaries with oversight and capital requirements enforced at the holding-company level. The authors also urge regulators to validate internal capital models, paying specific attention to "economic capital," which should take account of risks at each of the subsidiaries, as well as the correlations between the various lines of business that may increase, or more commonly reduce, the need for capital in the overall enterprise. The authors would like regulators to learn more from market judgments about the appropriate level of capital at the holding-company level, but these judgments can be relied on only with more disclosure of the risk and financial structure of financial conglomerates, which they advocate.

FINANCIAL REGULATORS ARE already grappling with how to supervise the risk of financial conglomerates in other countries. The following two papers—by Iman van Lelyveld and Arnold Schilder, and by Jeroen Kremers, Dirk Schoenmaker, and Peter Wierts—look to the Netherlands and use it as a case study in recommending how regulators around the world should address this challenge.

Financial conglomerates have become an important part of the financial system in the Netherlands, increasing significantly in scale over the past decade. In the authors' view, consolidation has been driven by the search for additional revenues and cost savings, all the while encouraged by improvements in information technology.

Regulators have a role to play in the financial services arena, not because of the size of the firms involved, but because of the need to protect the public against systemic risk and potentially unscrupulous activity. Both sets of authors argue that these objectives are applicable to the regulation of both banks and insurers.

In the Netherlands, financial regulation is both functional—aimed at supervising the individual components of a diversified entity—and consolidated (although as Kremers and his team point out, it was not always this way, with regulators before 1999 supervising along functional or sectoral lines only). The Board of Financial Supervisors now coordinates the responsibilities of each of the individual functional regulators (banking, insurance, and securities), with special attention paid to financial conglomerates.

A main aim of regulating financial conglomerates is to prevent "double leveraging"—the issuance of debt by a parent company to provide equity to its subsidiaries. In addition, regulators remain concerned about the potential reputational impacts of a failure of one part of a financial conglomerate on the rest of the enterprise.

As diversified financial institutions became more important features of the Dutch financial landscape, regulators responded by adopting new institutional arrangements that facilitated consolidated supervision. The Board of Financial Supervisors is the main such response. Its formation signals that the financial diversification in the marketplace had made the old, purely sectoral-based regulatory system obsolete. As both sets of authors recognize, other nations, too, are now grappling with this fact and, as in the Netherlands, are having to refine their approach toward supervising the large and growing financial conglomerates that make up their respective financial systems.

NOT ALL REGULATION of financial institutions is effected through government agencies. The market also regulates, or more accurately "disciplines," financial institutions by raising their cost of capital if they take on too much risk relative to the potential rewards.

Market discipline, in turn, can only work effectively if relevant information about institutions is made available on a timely basis. Although all firms have market-based reasons for providing disclosure, events in the past in the United States and elsewhere have underscored how unscrupulous managers, often with stock-based performance incentives, can withhold or distort necessary disclosures. Accordingly, if there were ever any doubts about the need for mandated disclosure for firms, the corporate accounting scandals of 2002 clearly have removed them.

Banks have long been under special obligations to disclose their financial status, although more so to regulators than to the public. In his paper, Lawrence White examines the adequacy of mandated bank disclosures and future directions for policy in this area, with special focus on the disclosure requirements for financial conglomerates under the latest proposed version of the revisions to the Basel Capital Accord.

As it is now, banks are required to release their balance sheet and income statements, both to the public and to regulators. As for other public corporations in the United States, U.S. bank financial disclosures are based on U.S. generally accepted accounting principles (GAAP). Yet GAAP, according to White, does not quickly reflect changes to a bank's *economic capital*, as measured by the market values of the assets and liabilities in its portfolio. For this reason, White strongly advocates the replacement of GAAP with market value accounting, wherever and whenever feasible. White would allow banks to use historical costs only where market values or estimates are not available.

Furthermore, since timeliness is critical for bank regulation—it being essential to know as soon as possible when a bank's economic capital has been significantly impaired so as to threaten the institution's solvency—White supports bank financial reporting on a weekly, if not daily, basis (rather than quarterly, as is the practice now). Since banks (and other financial institutions) already close their banks daily, White believes that more frequent public and regulatory reporting would be feasible and minimally burdensome.

Regulators also must supervise the risk assumed by banks and deal with it by demanding that banks maintain sufficient capital to absorb these risks, while proscribing activities by banks that are not easily susceptible to examination. To ensure that bank risk is properly supervised, White recommends that banks make available to regulators information relating to covariances between their assets as well as results from "stress tests" of how the bank performs under various, unwelcome scenarios. White also advocates that banks back a certain portion of their assets with long-term tradable subordinated debt, so that banks are subject to market discipline as well as regulatory oversight. The price of this debt in the marketplace would provide a key signal of the bank's financial well-being, while holders of the debt would be most concerned about bank solvency, the primary objective of bank regulators.

This is not the general approach taken so far in the proposed revisions to the Basel accord, however. The Basel committee has been resistant to both market value accounting and more frequent financial reporting. Instead, the revisions have adopted three approaches to risk. The "standardized" approach, based largely on the risk weights developed in the initial standards, explicitly eschews the use of stress tests, covariances, or market value accounting. The second approach, which relies on a bank's self-estimate of the likelihood of default, is more sophisticated than the first approach, but it too avoids the tools White advocates. The third "advanced internal-ratings" approach permits banks to make estimates of more risks than the second approach, but it is subject to the same criticisms, in White's view. Furthermore, none of the three approaches would mandate the use of subordinated debt to enhance market discipline. For all these reasons, White is highly critical of the Basel committee's latest approach to controlling bank risk and encouraging appropriate disclosure.

Finally, White argues that what is appropriate disclosure for a financial conglomerate should resemble the standard for any other public company, with two variations: the requirement that banks back a certain percentage of their assets with subordinated debt and a provision requiring securities affiliates to report the connections among their underwriting activities, analysts' recommendations, and bank lending to their clients.

ONE OF THE MORE controversial policy issues posed by the recent wave of financial consolidation relates to the use by diversified institutions of information about their customers. Specifically, how and under what circumstances should financial firms be able to use customer information to attract their business in other lines of activity, whether or not engaged in by affiliates of the same firm?

Peter Swire addresses this important topic in the final paper in this volume. Countering what he claims is the belief by many economists that the need for perfect information trumps the preference for privacy, Swire argues that maintaining the privacy of financial information is more efficient than economists generally suppose.

The resistance among some economists to the need for privacy, in Swire's view, stems from the perception or belief that perfect information is required for markets to operate efficiently. However, by definition, protecting privacy entails some limits on the sharing of information. The fact that in financial services privacy has been the norm for decades therefore seemingly runs counter to the economic intuition that limits on information can be a cause of market failure.

Swire surveys confidentiality in other areas to substantiate his position that limits on information flow to protect privacy can be efficient. The maxim "don't hand out the keys to the safe" is one example where everyone would agree that confidentiality is essential and efficient. The same logic applies to electronic passwords for bank and e-mail accounts: release of such information would entail very high costs and little social benefit (if not outright harm). In short, if parties cannot be secure in the secrecy of sensitive information, economic activity can be disrupted, not facilitated.

Despite consistent polling data showing the public's strong preference for privacy, economists seemingly discredit this evidence by noting that, in fact, customers generally do reveal sensitive information about themselves when asked. Swire responds to this view in several ways. First, he believes that economists often underestimate the value many individuals attach to privacy and ignore the fact that individuals place different values on privacy in the short and long runs. Second, market failures may exist due to individuals' inability to express their preferences in monetary terms. In particular, lack of privacy for sensitive information could have a chilling effect on some kinds of economic activity in the long run.

Swire supports his argument from recent polling data suggesting that consumers do in fact demonstrate strong preferences for privacy. The study indicates a strong correlation between the intensity of use of online banking and a bank's rating on privacy protection, as perceived by the public. Swire concludes by outlining a template for assessing the efficiency of confidentiality in a wide variety of contexts.

TAKEN AS A WHOLE, this collection of papers reflects the current understanding of why financial conglomerates are being formed, whether they are likely to dominate the financial landscape, and the policy issues that they present. Because this is a comparatively recent phenomenon in many countries, many of the empirical judgments must be tentative. It is simply too soon to rule out the importance of scale and scope economies definitively. But the early evidence certainly warrants a substantial measure of skepticism.

Similarly, the formation of consolidated regulators to deal with financial conglomerates is a very recent event. Fortunately, this approach to regulation has not yet been forced to withstand the test of a major financial crisis. But for the moment, it appears that the consolidated approach to regulation and supervision will stand alongside traditional functional approaches, which may complicate future attempts to harmonize financial regulation internationally.

Strategies in Financial Services, the Shareholders, and the System: Is Bigger and Broader Better?

INGO WALTER

T HE CLASSIC STRUCTURE-CONDUCT-PERFORMANCE approach to industrial organization centers on three questions. First, why does an industry look the way it does, in terms of numbers of competitors, market share distribution, and various other metrics? Second, how do firms actually compete, in terms of the formation of prices, quality of products and services, rivalry and collaboration within and across strategic groups, and other attributes of economic behavior? And third, how does the industry perform for its shareholders, employees, clients, and suppliers, and how does it perform within the context of the system as a whole, in terms of its impact on income and growth, stability, and possibly less clearly defined ideas about such issues as social equity? In the financial services industry, these same questions have attracted more than the normal degree of attention. The industry is "special" in a variety of ways, including the fiduciary nature of the business, its role at the center of the payments and capital allocation process with all the static and dynamic implications for economic performance, and the systemic nature of problems that can arise in the industry. So the structure, conduct, and performance of the financial services industry have unusually important public interest dimensions.

One facet of the discussion has focused on the size of financial firms, however measured, and the range of activities conducted by them. Figure 1 depicts a taxonomy of broad-gauge financial services businesses. What

1

Figure 1. Multifunctional Financial Linkages

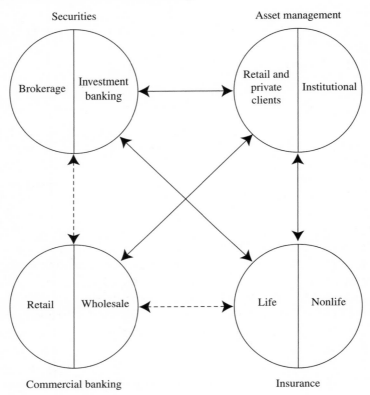

are the strategic opportunities and competitive consequences of deepening and broadening a firm's business within and between the four sectors and eight subsectors? Is size positively related to total returns to shareholders? If so, does this involve gains in efficiency or transfers of wealth to shareholders from other constituencies, or maybe both? Does greater breadth generate sufficient information-cost and transaction-cost economies to be beneficial to shareholders and customers, or can it work against their interests in ways that may ultimately impede shareholder value as well? And what about the "specialness," notably the industry's fiduciary character and systemic risk? Is bigger and broader also safer?

This paper begins with a simple strategic framework for thinking about these issues from the perspective of the management of financial firms. What should they be trying to do, and how does this relate to the issues of size and breadth? It then reviews the available evidence and reaches a set of tentative conclusions from what we know so far, both from the perspective of a shareholder and from that of the financial system as a whole.

A Simple Strategic Schematic

Financial firms want to allocate available financial, human, and technological resources to market segments that promise to throw off the highest risk-adjusted returns.[1] In order to do this, they have to appropriately attribute costs, returns, and risks to specific cells in a client-product-geography matrix. And the cells themselves have to be linked together in a way that maximizes what practitioners and analysts commonly call "synergies":

—Client-driven linkages exist when a financial institution serving a particular client or group of clients can, as a result, supply financial services either to the same client or to another client in the same group more efficiently in the same or different geographies. Risk mitigation results from spreading exposures across clients, and achieving more stable earnings, to the extent that income streams from different clients or segments of clients are not perfectly correlated.

—Product-driven linkages exist when an institution can supply a particular financial service in a more competitive manner because it is already producing the same or a similar financial service in different client or arena dimensions. Here again, there is risk mitigation to the extent that net revenue streams from different products are not perfectly correlated.

—Geographic linkages are important when an institution can serve a particular client or supply a particular service more efficiently in one geography as a result of having an active presence in another geography. Once more, the risk profile of the firm may be improved to the extent that business is spread across different currency, macroeconomic, and interest rate environments.

To extract maximum returns from the market matrix, firms need to understand the competitive dynamics of specific segments as well as the

---

1. Much of the following discussion relies on Walter (2003).

costs—including acquisition and integration costs in the case of merger and acquisition (M&A) initiatives—and the risks embedded in the overall portfolio of activities. Especially challenging is the task of optimizing the linkages between the segments to maximize potential joint cost and revenue economies. Firms that do this well can be considered to have a high degree of "strategic integrity" and should have a market capitalization that exceeds the stand-alone value of their constituent businesses.

So are bigger and broader better in the financial services industry? If so, why? And what is the evidence? Here we shall consider each of the major arguments, pro and con.

Economies and Diseconomies of Scale

Whether economies or diseconomies of scale exist in financial services has been at the heart of strategic and regulatory discussions about optimum firm size in the financial services industry. Are larger firms associated with increased scale economies and hence profitability and shareholder value? Can increased average size of firms create a more efficient financial sector? Answers are not easy to find, because they have to isolate the impact of pure size of the production unit as a whole from all of the other impacts of size on revenues and costs.

In an information- and transactions-intensive industry with frequently high fixed costs, such as financial services, there should be ample potential for scale economies. However, the potential for diseconomies of scale attributable to disproportionate increases in administrative overhead, management of complexity, agency problems, and other cost factors could also occur in very large financial services firms. If economies of scale prevail, increased size will help to create financial efficiency and shareholder value. If diseconomies prevail, both will be destroyed. Scale effects should be directly observable in the cost functions of financial services firms and in aggregate measures of performance.

Many studies of economies of scale have been undertaken in the banking, insurance, and securities industries over the years.[2] Unfortunately, examinations of both scale and scope economies in financial services are unusually problematic. The nature of the empirical tests used, the form of

---

2. See Saunders (2000) for a survey.

the cost functions, the existence of unique levels of optimum output, and the optimizing behavior of financial firms all present difficulties. Limited availability and conformity of data present serious empirical issues. And the conclusions of any study that has detected (or failed to detect) economies of scale or scope in a sample of financial institutions do not necessarily have general applicability. Nevertheless, the impact on the operating economics (production functions) of financial firms is so important that the available empirical evidence is central to the whole argument.

Estimated cost functions form the basis of most of the available empirical tests. Virtually all of them have found that economies of scale are achieved with increases in size among small commercial banks (below $100 million in assets). A few studies have shown that scale economies may also exist in banks falling into the $100 million to $5 billion range. There is very little evidence so far of scale economies in the case of banks larger than $5 billion. More recently, there is some scattered evidence of scale-related cost gains for banks up to $25 billion in assets.[3] But according to a survey of all empirical studies of economies of scale through 1998, there is no evidence of such economies among very large banks. Several studies have found the relationship between size and average cost to be U-shaped.[4] This suggests that small banks can benefit from economies of scale but that large banks seem to suffer from diseconomies of scale, resulting in higher average costs as they increase in size. The consensus seems to be that scale economies and diseconomies generally do not result in more than about a 5 percent difference in unit costs. Inability to find major economies of scale among large financial services firms is also true of insurance companies and broker-dealers.[5] Lang and Wetzel find diseconomies of scale in both banking and securities services among German universal banks.[6]

Except for the very smallest banks and nonbank financial firms, scale economies seem likely to have relatively little bearing on competitive performance. This is particularly true because smaller institutions sometimes are linked together in cooperatives or other structures that allow

3. Berger and Mester (1997).
4. Berger, Demsetz, and Strahan (1998); Berger, Hunter, and Timme (1993).
5. On insurance companies, see Cummins and Zi (1998); on broker-dealers, see Goldberg and others (1991).
6. Lang and Wetzel (1998).

them to harvest available economies of scale centrally or are specialists in specific market segments that are not particularly sensitive to the relatively small cost differences that seem to be associated with economies of scale in the financial services industry. A basic problem is that most of the available empirical studies focus entirely on firm-wide scale economies when the most important issues of scale are encountered at the level of individual businesses.

There is ample evidence, for example, that economies of scale are significant for operating economies and competitive performance in areas such as global custody, processing of mass-market credit card transactions, and institutional asset management. Economies of scale may be far less important in other areas such as private banking and M&A advisory services. Unfortunately, empirical data on cost functions that would permit identification of economies of scale at the product level are generally proprietary and therefore unavailable. Although disturbing, it seems reasonable that a scale-driven strategy may make a great deal of sense in specific areas of financial activity even in the absence of evidence that there is much to be gained at the firm-wide level. Still, the notion that some lines of activity clearly benefit from scale economies, while at the same time firm-wide economies of scale are empirically elusive, suggests that diseconomies of scale must exist in numerous lines of activity (or combinations of activities).

Cost Economies of Scope

Beyond pure scale effects, are there cost reductions to be achieved by selling a broader rather than a narrower range of products? On the one hand, cost economies of scope mean that jointly producing two or more products or services is accomplished more cheaply than producing them separately. "Global" scope economies become evident on the cost side when the total cost of producing all products is less than producing them individually, while "activity-specific" economies consider the joint production of particular pairs or clusters of financial services. Cost economies of scope can be harvested through the sharing of information technology platforms and other types of overhead, information and monitoring costs, and the like. Information, for example, can be reused and thereby avoid cost duplication, facilitate creativity in developing solutions to client problems, and leverage client-specific knowledge.[7] On the other hand, cost diseconomies of scope may arise from such factors as inertia and lack of responsiveness and creativity that may come with increased breadth, complexity, and bureaucratization of the firm, "turf" and profit-attribution conflicts that increase costs or erode product quality in meeting client needs, or serious cultural differences across the organizational "silos" that inhibit seamless delivery of a broad range of financial services.

Like economies of scale, cost-related scope economies should be directly observable in the cost functions of financial services suppliers and in aggregate measures of performance. Most empirical studies have failed to find significant cost economies of scope in the banking, insurance, or securities industries.[8] They suggest that some cost diseconomies of scope are encountered when firms in the financial services sector add new product ranges to their portfolios. Saunders and Walter, for example, find negative cost economies of scope among the world's 200 largest banks—as the product range widens, unit costs seem to go up, although not dramatically so.[9]

However, the period covered by many of these studies involves firms that were shifting away from a pure focus on banking or insurance and may thus have incurred considerable front-end costs in expanding the range of their activities. If these outlays were expensed in accounting statements during the period under study, then one might expect to see evidence of diseconomies of scope reversed in future periods. The evidence on the cost economies of scope so far remains inconclusive.

Operating Efficiencies

Besides economies of scale and cost economies of scope, financial firms of roughly the same size and providing roughly the same range of services can have very different cost levels per unit of output. There is ample evidence that such differences in performance exist, for example, in comparisons of cost-to-income ratios among banks, insurance compa-

---

7. Stefanadis (2002).
8. Stefanadis (2002).
9. Saunders and Walter (1994).

nies, and investment firms of comparable size. The reasons involve differences in production functions, reflecting efficiency and effectiveness in the use of labor and capital, sourcing and application of available technology, and acquisition of inputs, organizational design, compensation, and incentive systems—that is, in just plain better or worse management. These are what economists call X-efficiencies.

A number of studies have found rather large disparities in cost structures among banks of similar size, suggesting that the way banks are run is more important than their size or the selection of businesses that they pursue.[10] The consensus of studies conducted in the United States seems to be that average unit costs in the banking industry are some 20 percent above those of best-practice firms producing the same range and volume of services, with most of the difference attributable to operating economies rather than differences in the cost of funds.[11] Siems finds that the greater the overlap in branch networks, the higher the abnormal equity returns in U.S. bank mergers; no such abnormal returns are associated with other factors like regional concentration ratios, suggesting that gains in shareholder value in many of the U.S. banking mergers of the 1990s were associated more with increases in X-efficiency than with reductions in competition.[12] If true, this is good news for smaller firms, since the quality of management seems to be far more important in driving costs than raw size or scope. Of course, if very large institutions are systematically better managed than smaller ones (which may be difficult to document in the real world of financial services), then there may be a link between firm size and X-efficiency.

It is also possible that very large organizations may be more capable of the massive and "lumpy" capital outlays required to install and maintain the most efficient information technology and transactions processing infrastructures.[13] If extremely high recurring levels of technology spending result in greater X-efficiency, then large financial services firms will tend to benefit in competition with smaller ones. Smaller firms will then have to rely on pooling and outsourcing, if feasible.

In banking M&A studies, Berger and Humphrey find that acquiring banks tend to be significantly more efficient than acquired banks, sug-

---

10. Berger, Hancock, and Humphrey (1993); Berger, Hunter, and Timme (1993).
11. Akhavein, Berger, and Humphrey (1997).
12. Siems (1996).
13. Walter (2003).

gesting that the acquirer may potentially improve the X-efficiency of the target.[14] Akhavein, Berger, and Humphrey find that mega-mergers between U.S. banks increase returns by improving efficiency rather than increasing prices, suggesting also that acquiring banks use acquisitions as an occasion to improve efficiency within their own organization.[15] Houston and Ryngaert as well as DeLong find that the market rewards mergers where geographic overlap exists between acquirer and target, presumably due to expected gains in X-efficiency.[16]

Revenue Economies of Scope

On the revenue side, economies of scope attributable to cross-selling arise when the all-in cost to the buyer of purchasing multiple financial services from a single supplier is less than the cost of purchasing them from separate suppliers. This includes the cost of the services themselves plus information, search, monitoring, contracting, and other costs. And firms that are diversified into several types of activities or several geographic areas tend to have more contact points with clients. Revenue diseconomies of scope could arise from management complexities and conflicts associated with greater breadth.

Some evidence on revenue economies of scope comes from historical studies. Kroszner and Rajan find that U.S. bank affiliates typically underwrote better-performing securities than specialized investment banks during the 1920s, when U.S. commercial banks were permitted to have securities affiliates.[17] Perhaps commercial banks obtained knowledge about firms contemplating selling securities through the deposit and borrowing history of the firm. If so, they could then select the best risks to bring to market. Likewise, Puri finds that securities underwritten by commercial banks generated higher prices than similar securities underwritten by investment banks; this suggests lower ex ante risk for securities underwritten by commercial banks.[18]

---

14. Berger and Humphrey (1992).
15. Akhavein, Berger, and Humphrey (1997).
16. Houston and Ryngaert (1994); DeLong (2001).
17. Kroszner and Rajan (1994).
18. Puri (1996).

Table 1. Volume of Wholesale Banking among Top-Twelve Firms

Bank	Volume of wholesale banking (U.S. dollars)[a]		Market share (percent), 2001	Rank, 2001
	2000	2001		
Citigroup[b]	1,236,248	1,873,452	10.81	1
Goldman, Sachs	1,268,177	1,462,301	8.43	4
Morgan Stanley	1,283,288	1,422,292	8.20	5
Merrill Lynch	1,163,164	1,672.698	9.65	3
Credit Suisse First Boston[b]	1,085,050	1,212,275	6.99	6
Lehman Brothers	418,807	864,778	4.99	9
J. P. Morgan Chase[b]	1,295,220	1,794,838	10.35	2
Bank of America Securities[b]	483,986	664,468	3.83	10
UBS Warburg[b]	481,574	967,104	5.58	8
Deutsche Bank[b]	409,417	917,702	6.29	7
Dresdner Kleinwort Wasserstein[b]	448,538	540,445	3.12	11
Barclays[b]	162,425	406,207	1.41	12

Source: Thomson Financial Data Platinum.
a. Wholesale banking volume comprises loan syndications (full credit to lead manager), debt and equity underwriting (full credit to book runner), medium-term notes (full credit to dealer), and M&A advisories (full credit to lead adviser).
b. Wholesale banking unit of a universal bank or financial conglomerate.

Most empirical studies of cross-selling are based on survey data and are therefore difficult to generalize. The issue is whether companies are more likely to award M&A work to banks that are also willing lenders or whether the two services are separable—so that companies go to the firms with the perceived best M&A capabilities (probably investment banking houses) for advice and to others (presumably the major commercial banks) for loans. The responses suggest that companies view these services as a single value chain, so that banks that are willing to provide significant lending are also more likely to obtain M&A advisory work. Indeed, table 1 suggests that well over half of the major M&A firms (in terms of fees) in 2001 were commercial banks with substantial lending power. This is sometimes called "mixed bundling," meaning that the price of one service (for example, commercial lending) is dependent on the client also taking another service (for example, M&A advice or securities underwriting), although the search for immediate scope-driven revenue gains may have led to some disastrous lending by commercial banks in the energy and telecommunications sectors in recent years.

However, it is at the retail level that the bulk of the revenue economies

Figure 2. Prototype Online Personal Finance Platform

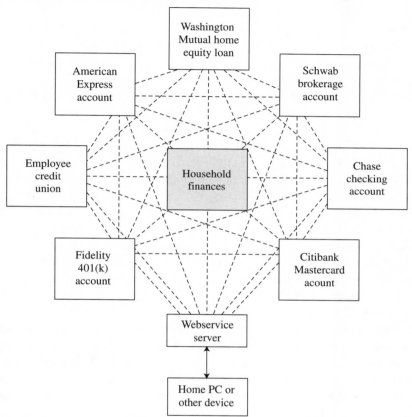

of scope are likely to materialize, since the search costs and contracting costs are likely to be higher for retail customers than for corporate customers. There is limited U.S. evidence on retail cross-selling due to the regulatory restraints in place until 1999, and evidence from Europe, where universal banking and multifunctional financial conglomerates have always been part of the landscape, is mainly based on cases and suggests highly variable outcomes as to the efficacy of *bancassurance* or *allfinanz*.

In any case, the future may see some very different retail business models. One example is depicted in figure 2. Here clients take advantage of user-friendly home interfaces to access web service platforms, which allow real-time linkages to multiple vendors of financial services. For the client, it could combine the "feel" of single-source purchasing with access to best-in-class vendors—the client "cross-purchases" rather than being "cross-sold." Absent the need for continuous financial advice, such a business model could reduce information costs, transactions costs, and contracting costs, while at the same time providing client-driven open-architecture access to the universe of competing vendors. Advice could be built into the model by suppliers who find a way to incorporate the advisory function into their downlinks or through independent financial advisers. If, in the future, such models of retail financial services delivery take hold in the market, then some of the rationale for cross-selling and revenue economies of scope could become obsolete.

Despite an almost total lack of hard empirical evidence, revenue econ-omies of scope may indeed exist at both the wholesale and retail level. But they are likely to be very specific to the types of services provided and the types of clients served. So revenue-related scope economies are clearly linked to a firm's specific strategic positioning across clients, products, and geographies. Even if the potential for cross-selling exists, the devil is in the details—mainly in the design of incentives and organi-zational structures to ensure that it actually occurs. And these incentives have to be extremely granular and compatible with the real-world behav-ior of employees. Without them, no amount of management pressure and exhortation to cross-sell is likely to achieve its objectives.

Network economies associated with multifunctional financial firms may be considered a special type of demand-side economy of scope.[19] Like telecommunications, relationships with end users of financial ser-vices represent a network structure wherein additional client linkages add value to existing clients by increasing the feasibility or reducing the cost of accessing them. So-called network externalities tend to increase with the absolute size of the network itself. Every link of the client to the firm potentially "complements" every other one and potentially adds value through either one-way or two-way exchanges. The size of network ben-efits depends on technical compatibility and coordination in time and location, which universal banks and financial conglomerates may be in a position to provide. And networks tend to be self-reinforcing in that they require a minimum critical mass and tend to grow in dominance as they increase in size, thus precluding perfect competition in network-driven

---

19. Economides and Encaoua (1996).

businesses. This characteristic may be evident in activities such as securities clearance and settlement, global custody, funds transfer, and international cash management and may serve to lock in clients insofar as switching costs tend to be relatively high.

What little empirical evidence there is suggests that revenue economies of scope seem to exist for specific combinations of products in the realm of commercial and investment banking as well as insurance and asset management. Empirical evidence concerning the existence of certain product-specific revenue economies of scope is beginning to materialize. For example, Yu shows that share prices of U.S. financial conglomerates as well as specialists responded favorably when the Financial Services Modernization Act of 1999 was announced.[20] The study finds that the market reacted most favorably for the shares of large securities firms, large insurance companies, and bank holding companies already engaged in some securities businesses (those with Section 20 subsidiaries allowing limited investment banking activities). The study suggests that the market expected gains from product diversification possibly arising from cross-product synergies. Another study—by Lown and others —similarly finds that both commercial and investment bank stocks rose when President Clinton announced on October 22, 1999, that passage of the Gramm-Leach-Bliley Act was imminent.[21]

Market Power

In addition to the strategic search for operating economies and revenue synergies, financial services firms also seek to dominate markets in order to extract economic returns. This is often referred to as economies of "size" as opposed to classic economies of "scale" and can convey distinct competitive advantages that are reflected in either volume of business or margins or both.

Market power allows banks to charge more (monopoly benefits) or pay less (monopsony benefits). Indeed, many national markets for financial services have shown a distinct tendency toward oligopoly. Supporters argue that high levels of market concentration are necessary in order

20. Yu (2001).
21. Lown and others (2000).

to provide a viable competitive platform. Without convincing evidence of scale economies or other size-related efficiency gains, opponents argue that monopolistic market structures serve mainly to extract rents from consumers or users of financial services and to redistribute them to shareholders, cross-subsidize other areas of activity, invest in wasteful projects, or reduce pressures for cost containment.

Indeed, it is a puzzle why managers of financial services firms often seem to believe that the endgame in their industry's competitive structure is the emergence of a few firms in gentlemanly competition with nice sustainable margins, whereas in the real world such an outcome can easily trigger public policy reaction leading to break-ups and spin-offs in order to restore more vigorous competition. Particularly in a critical economic sector that is easily politicized, such as financial services, a regulatory response to "excessive" concentration is a virtual certainty despite sometimes furious lobbying to the contrary. In the case of Canada, for example, regulators prevented two mega-mergers in late 1998 that would have reduced the number of major financial firms from five to three, with a retail market share of perhaps 90 percent between them. Regulators blocked the deals despite arguments by management that major U.S. financial services firms operating in Canada under the rules of the North American Free Trade Agreement would provide the necessary competitive pressure to prevent exploitation of monopoly power.

Financial services market structures differ substantially, as measured, for example, by the Herfindahl-Hirshman index. This metric of competitive structure is the sum of the squared market shares ($H = \Sigma s^2$), where $0 < H < 10,000$, and market shares are measured, for example, by deposits, by assets, or by other indicators of market share. H rises as the number of competitors declines and as market share concentration increases among a given number of competitors. Empirically, higher values of H tend to be associated with higher degrees of pricing power, price-cost margins, and returns on equity across a broad range of industries. For example, despite very substantial consolidation in recent years within perhaps the most concentrated segment of the financial services industry—wholesale banking and capital markets activities—there is little evidence of market power. With some 80 percent of the combined value of global fixed-income and equity underwriting, loan syndications, and M&A mandates captured by the top-ten firms, the Herfindahl-Hirshman index was still only 745 in 2001. This suggests a ruthlessly competitive market structure in most of these businesses, which is reflected in the returns to investors who own shares in the principal players in the industry—in fact, there has been a long-term erosion of return on capital invested in the wholesale banking industry.[22]

Another example is asset management, where the top firms comprise a mixture of European, American, and Japanese asset managers and at the same time a mixture of banks, broker-dealers, independent fund management companies, and insurance companies. Although market definitions clearly have to be drawn more precisely, at least on a global level asset management seems to be among the most contestable in the entire financial services industry, with a Herfindahl-Hirshman index of 540 among the top-forty firms in terms of assets under management. And it shows very few signs of increasing concentration in recent years.

In short, although monopoly power created through mergers and acquisitions in the financial services industry can produce market conditions that allow firms to reallocate gains from clients to themselves, such conditions are difficult to achieve or to sustain. Sometimes new players—even relatively small entrants—penetrate the market and destroy oligopolistic pricing structures. Or good substitutes are available from other types of financial services firms, and consumers are willing to shop around. Vigorous competition (and low Herfindahl-Hirshman indexes) seems to be maintained even after intensive M&A activity, in most cases as a consequence of relatively even distributions of market shares among the leading firms in many financial services businesses.

Berger and Hannan find that loan rates were higher and deposit rates were lower when banks operated in concentrated markets.[23] These higher revenues, however, did not result in higher profits—instead, the study shows evidence consistent with higher cost structures in banks in these markets than in their counterparts in less concentrated markets. Akhavein, Berger, and Humphrey find that banks that merge charge more for loans and pay less on deposits *before* they merge than other large banks—banks that merged charged 17 basis points more for loans than the average large bank prior to merging.[24] After the merger, however, this difference fell to about 10 basis points. This suggests that merging banks do not tend to

22. Smith and Walter (2003).
23. Berger and Hannan (1996).
24. Akhavein, Berger, and Humphrey (1997).

take advantage of their increased market power. The authors contend that antitrust policy is effective in preventing mergers that would create market power problems. Siems reaches a similar conclusion. In a study of nineteen bank mega-mergers (partners valued over $500 million) in 1995, he rejects the market power hypothesis, although he finds that in-market mergers create positive value for both the acquirer and the target on announcement.[25] There is no relationship between the resulting abnormal returns and the change in the Herfindahl-Hirshman index. Still, concentration seems to affect prices. Beatty, Santomero, and Smirlock find that the higher the market concentration of the banking industry in a given region, the higher the premium paid to acquire a bank in that area.[26]

Proprietary Information and Embedded Human Capital

One argument in favor of a large, diverse financial services industry is that internal information flows are substantially better and involve lower costs than external information flows that are accessible by more narrowly focused firms. Consequently, a firm that is present in a broad range of financial markets, functions, and geographies can find proprietary and client-driven trading and structuring opportunities that smaller and more narrow firms cannot.

A second argument has to do with technical know-how. Significant areas of financial services—particularly wholesale banking and asset management—have become the realm of highly specialized expertise that can be reflected in both market share and price effects. In recent years, large numbers of financial boutiques have been acquired by major banks, insurance companies, securities firms, and asset managers for precisely this purpose, and anecdotal evidence suggests that in many cases these acquisitions have enhanced shareholder value for the buyer.

Closely aligned is the human capital argument. Technical skills and entrepreneurial behavior are embodied in people, and people can and do move. Parts of the financial services industry have become notorious for the mobility of talent to the point of "free agency," and people or teams of people sometimes regard themselves as "firms within firms." There

---

25. Siems (1996).
26. Beatty, Santomero, and Smirlock (1987).

are no empirical studies of these issues, although there is no question about their importance. Many financial services represent specialist businesses that are conducted by specialists meeting the requirements of specialist clients. Know-how embodied in people is clearly mobile, and the key is to provide a platform that is sufficiently incentive compatible to make the most of it. It seems unclear whether size or breadth has much to do with this.

Diversification of Business Streams, Credit Quality, and Financial Stability

Greater diversification of earnings attributable to multiple products, client groups, and geographies is often deemed to create more stable, safer, and ultimately more valuable financial institutions. The lower the correlations among the cash flows from the firm's various activities, the greater the benefits of diversification. The consequences should include higher credit quality and higher debt ratings (lower bankruptcy risk) and therefore lower costs of financing than those faced by narrower, more focused firms, while greater earnings stability should bolster stock prices. In combination, these effects should reduce the cost of capital and enhance profitability.

It has also been argued that shares of universal banks and financial conglomerates embody substantial franchise value due to their nature as conglomerates and importance in national economies. Demsetz, Saidenberg, and Strahan suggest that this guaranteed franchise value serves to inhibit extraordinary risk-taking.[27] They find substantial evidence that the higher a bank's franchise value, the more prudent management tends to be. Such firms should therefore serve shareholder interests, as well as stability of the financial system—and the concerns of regulators—with a strong focus on risk management as opposed to financial firms with little to lose. This conclusion is, however, at variance with the observed, massive losses incurred recently by financial conglomerates and universal banks exposed to highly leveraged firms and special-purpose entities, real estate lending, and emerging market transactions.

Studies that test risk reduction often look at how hypothetical combi-

---

27. Demsetz, Saidenberg, and Strahan (1996).

nations could have reduced risk using actual industry data. In an early study, Santomero and Chung find that bank holding companies that existed from 1985 to 1989 could have reduced their probability of failure had they been permitted to diversify into insurance and securities.[28] Of the ten combinations the authors examined, the best combination is the bank holding company linking to both insurance and securities firms. The only combination that would have increased the probability of bankruptcy over a stand-alone bank holding company is one encompassing a large securities firm. Boyd, Graham, and Hewitt test whether hypothetical mergers between bank holding companies and nonbanking financial firms decrease risk.[29] In their sample of data from 1971 to 1987, they find that mergers between bank holding companies and insurance firms could have reduced risk, while mergers between bank holding companies and securities firms or real estate firms could have increased risk. Saunders and Walter carry out a series of simulated mergers between U.S. banks, securities firms, and insurance companies in order to test the stability of earnings of the pro forma "merged" firm as opposed to separate institutions.[30] The opportunity set of potential mergers between existing firms and the risk characteristics of each possible combination are examined. The findings suggest that there are indeed potential risk reduction gains from diversification in multiple-activity financial services organizations and that these increase with the number of activities undertaken. The main risk reduction gains appear to arise from combining commercial banking with insurance activities rather than with securities activities.

Too-Big-to-Fail Guarantees

Given the unacceptable systemic consequences of institutional collapse, large financial services firms that surpass a given threshold will be bailed out by taxpayers. In the United States, this policy became explicit in 1984 when the Comptroller of the Currency testified to Congress that eleven banks were so important that they would not be permitted to fail.[31] It was clearly present in the savings and loan collapses around that time.

28. Santomero and Chung (1992).
29. Boyd, Graham, and Hewitt (1993).
30. Saunders and Walter (1994).
31. O'Hara and Shaw (1990).

In other countries, the same policy tends to exist and seems to cover even more of the local financial system.[32] There were numerous examples in Finland, France, Japan, Norway, Sweden, and Switzerland during the 1990s. Implicit too-big-to-fail (TBTF) guarantees create a potentially important public subsidy for major financial firms.

TBTF support was arguably extended to nonbank financial firms in the rescue of Long-term Capital Management in 1998, brokered by the U.S. Federal Reserve (despite the fact that a credible private restructuring offer was on the table) on the basis that the firm's failure could cause systemic damage to the global financial system. J. P. Morgan made the same argument in 1996 about the global copper market and one of its then-dominant traders, Sumitomo. Morgan suggested that collapse of the copper market could have serious systemic effects. The speed with which the central banks and regulatory authorities reacted to that crisis signaled the possibility of safety net support of the copper market in light of major banks' massive exposures in highly complex structured credits to the industry. And there were even mutterings of systemic effects in the collapse of Enron in 2001. Most of the time, such arguments are self-serving nonsense, but in a political environment under crisis conditions, they could help to throw a safety net sufficiently broad to limit damage to the shareholders of exposed banks or other financial firms.

It is generally accepted that the larger the bank, the more likely it is to be covered under TBTF support. O'Hara and Shaw detail the benefits of TBTF status: Without state assurances, uninsured depositors and other liability holders demand a risk premium.[33] When a bank is not permitted to fail, the risk premium is no longer necessary. Furthermore, banks covered under the policy have an incentive to increase their risk in order to enjoy higher equity returns. Kane investigates the possibility that large banks enjoy access to the TBTF guarantees in a study of merger effects, although he does not distinguish between the stock market reaction to increased TBTF guarantees or the likelihood of increased profitability.[34] He suggests further study to determine whether acquiring banks increase their leverage, uninsured liabilities, nonperforming loans, and other risk exposures, all of which would suggest that they are taking advantage of TBTF guarantees.

32. U.S. General Accounting Office (1991).
33. O'Hara and Shaw (1990).
34. Kane (2000).

One problem with the TBTF argument is to determine precisely when a financial institution becomes too big to fail. Citicorp was already the largest bank holding company in the United States before it merged with Travelers in 1998. Therefore, the TBTF argument may be a matter of degree. That is, the benefits of becoming larger may be marginal if a firm already enjoys TBTF status.

Conflicts of Interest

The potential for conflicts of interest is endemic in all multifunctional financial services firms.[35] Classic conflict of interest arguments include the following:

—When firms have the power to sell affiliates' products, managers may no longer dispense "dispassionate" advice to clients and may have a salesman's stake in pushing "house" products, possibly to the disadvantage of the customer.

—A financial firm that is acting as an underwriter and is unable to place the securities in a public offering may seek to limit losses by "stuffing" unwanted securities into accounts over which it has discretionary authority.

—A bank with a loan outstanding to a client whose bankruptcy risk has increased, to the private knowledge of the banker, may have an incentive to encourage the borrower to issue bonds or equities to the general public, with the proceeds used to pay down the bank loan.[36]

—In order to ensure that an underwriting goes well, a bank may make below-market loans to third-party investors on condition that the proceeds are used to purchase securities underwritten by its securities unit.

—A bank may use its lending power activities to encourage a client to use its securities or securities services.

—By acting as a lender, a bank may become privy to certain material inside information about a customer or its rivals that can be used in set-

---

35. Saunders and Walter (1994).

36. One example is the 1995 underwriting of a secondary equity issue of the Hafnia Insurance Group by Den Danske Bank. The stock was distributed heavily to retail investors, with proceeds allegedly used to pay down bank loans even as Hafnia slid into bankruptcy (Smith and Walter 1997). The case came before the Danish courts in a successful individual investor litigation supported by the government.

ting prices, advising acquirers in a contested acquisition, or helping in the distribution of securities offerings underwritten by its securities unit.[37] More generally, a financial firm may use proprietary information regarding a client for internal management purposes that, at the same time, harms the interests of the client.

The potential for conflicts of interest covers various degrees and intensities. Some are serious and basically intractable. Others can be managed by appropriate changes in incentives or compliance initiatives. And some are not sufficiently serious to worry about. But using a matrix approach to mapping conflicts of interest demonstrates that the broader the range of clients and products, the more numerous are the potential conflicts of interest and the more difficult is the task of keeping them under control—and avoiding possibly large franchise losses.

Shareholders of financial firms have a vital stake in the management and control of conflicts of interest. They can benefit from the exploitation of conflicts in the short term, to the extent that business volumes or margins are higher as a result. On the one hand, preventing conflicts of interest is an expensive business—compliance systems are costly to maintain, and various types of walls between business units can have high opportunity costs because they give rise to inefficient use of information within the organization. On the other hand, costs associated with civil or criminal action and reputation losses due to conflicts of interest can weigh on shareholders very heavily indeed, as demonstrated by a variety of such problems in the financial services industry during 2000–02. Some have argued that conflicts of interest may contribute to the price to book value ratios of the shares of financial conglomerates and universal banks falling below those of more specialized financial services businesses.

Conflicts of interest can also impede market performance. For example, inside information accessible to a bank as lender to a target firm would almost certainly prevent that bank from acting as an M&A adviser to a potential acquirer. Entrepreneurs may not want their private banking affairs handled by a bank that also controls their business financing. A mutual fund investor is unlikely to have easy access to the full menu of available equity funds through a financial conglomerate offering competing in-house products. These issues may be manageable if most of the competition is coming from other financial conglomerates. But if the

37. Smith and Walter (1997).

playing field is also populated by aggressive insurance companies, independent broker-dealers, fund managers, and other specialists, these issues tend to be a continuing strategic challenge for management (and a source of comfort for clients).

Should a major conflict of interest arise, the repercussions for a firm's reputation can be quite detrimental.[38] Recent well-reported examples include equity analyst conflicts of interest in the late 1990s and early 2000s. Analysts working for multifunctional financial firms wear several hats and are subject to multiple conflicts of interest. They are supposed to provide unbiased research to investors. But they are also expected to take part in the securities origination and sales process centered in their firms' corporate finance departments. The firms argue that expensive research functions cannot be paid for by attracting investor deals and brokerage commissions, so that corporate finance has to cover much of the cost. This fact, and the astronomical compensation packages commanded by top analysts (occasionally exceeding $20 million a year), is the best demonstration of which of the two hats dominates. Prosecution of investment banks by the attorney general of the state of New York in 2002, a $1.4 billion settlement, and a frantic scramble by all securities firms to reorganize how equity research is organized and compensated simply validated facts long known to market participants.

More broadly, both Citigroup and J. P. Morgan Chase in 2001 and 2002 were touched by just about every U.S. corporate scandal that was revealed, often involving conflicts of interest, and both lost well over a third of their equity value in a matter of months, no doubt in part as a consequence of conflicts of interest.

Conglomerate Discount

It is often argued that the shares of multiproduct firms and business conglomerates tend to trade at prices lower than shares of more narrowly

---

38. For example, J. P. Morgan simultaneously served as commercial banker, investment banker, and adviser to Banco Español de Crédito (Banesto) in Spain, as well as an equity holder and fund manager for co-investors in a limited partnership holding shares in the firm. Additionally, Morgan's vice chairman served on Banesto's supervisory board. When Banesto failed and the conflicts of interest facing J. P. Morgan were revealed, the value of the firm's equity fell 10 percent. See Smith and Walter (1995, 1997).

focused firms (all else being equal). There are two basic reasons why this "conglomerate discount" is alleged to exist.

First, it is argued that, on the whole, conglomerates tend to use capital inefficiently. Thus the potential benefits of diversification must be weighed against the potential costs, which include greater management discretion to engage in value-reducing projects, cross-subsidization of marginal or loss-making projects that drain resources from healthy businesses, misalignments in incentives between central and divisional managers, and the like. For a sample of U.S. corporations during the period 1986–91, Berger and Ofek demonstrate an average value loss in multiproduct firms on the order of 13–15 percent, as compared to the stand-alone values of the constituent businesses.[39] They attribute the erosion of value in conglomerates largely to over-investment in marginally profitable activities and cross-subsidization. This loss of value was smaller in cases where the multiproduct firms were involved in closely allied activities within the same industrial sector. In other empirical work, John and Ofek show that the sale of assets by corporations results in significantly improved shareholder returns on the remaining capital employed, both as a result of greater focus in the enterprise and gains in value through high prices paid by the buyers of assets.[40] The evidence suggests that the internal capital market within conglomerates functions less efficiently than the external capital market.

Such empirical findings across broad ranges of industry may well apply to diverse activities carried out by financial firms as well. If retail banking, wholesale banking, and property and casualty (P&C) insurance are evolving into highly specialized, performance-driven businesses, for example, one may ask whether the kinds of conglomerate discounts found in industrial firms may not also apply to financial conglomerates— especially if centralized decisionmaking is becoming increasingly irrelevant to the requirements of the specific businesses.

A second possible source of conglomerate discount is that investors in shares of conglomerates find it difficult to "take a view" and add purely sectoral exposures to their portfolios. Investors may want to avoid such stocks in their efforts to construct efficient asset allocation profiles. This is especially true of performance-driven managers of institutional equity

39. Berger and Ofek (1995).
40. John and Ofek (1995).

portfolios who are under pressure to outperform their cohorts or equity indexes. Why would a fund manager want to invest in yet another (closed-end) fund in the form of a conglomerate—one that may be active in retail banking, wholesale commercial banking, middle-market lending, private banking, corporate finance, trading, investment banking, asset management insurance, and perhaps other businesses as well?

Both the capital misallocation effect and the portfolio selection effect may weaken investor demand for shares of universal banks and financial conglomerates, lower their equity prices, and produce a higher cost of capital than if the conglomerate discount were absent. This higher cost of capital would have a bearing on the competitive performance and profitability of the enterprise. It may wholly or partially offset some of the benefits of conglomeration, such as greater stability and lower bankruptcy risk, through diversification across business lines.

From Book Value of Equity to Market Value of Equity

From a shareholder perspective, all of the pluses and minuses of size and breadth among financial services firms can be captured in a simple valuation formula:

$$NPV_f = \sum_{t=0}^{n} \frac{E(R_t) - E(C_t)}{(1 + i_t + \alpha_t)^t}$$

NPV_f denotes the risk-adjusted discounted present value of a firm's after-tax earnings, $E(R_t)$ represents the expected future revenues of the firm, $E(C_t)$ represents expected future operating costs including charges to earnings for restructurings, loss provisions, and taxes. The net expected returns in the numerator are then discounted to the present using a risk-free rate i_t and a composite risk adjustment α_t—which captures the variance of expected net future returns resulting from credit risk, market risk, operational risk, and reputational risk and at the same time captures the correlations between such risks associated with the firm's various activities.

Strategic initiatives in financial firms increase shareholder value if they generate: (1) top-line gains that show up as increases in $E(R_t)$ due, for example, to market extension, increased market share, wider profit

Figure 3. Valuation Gains and Losses Attributable to Size and Scope

Potential market value of equity (PMVE)

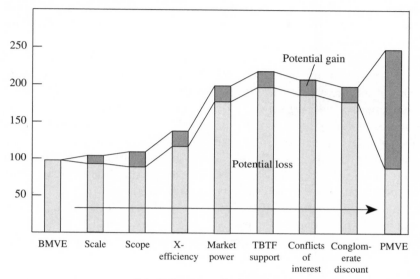

Principal sources of value gain or loss

margins, or successful cross-selling; (2) bottom-line gains related to lower costs due to economies of scale or improved operating efficiency—reduced $E(C_t)$—usually reflected in improved cost-to-income ratios as well as better tax efficiency; or (3) reductions in risk associated with improved risk management or diversification of the firm across business streams, client segments, or geographies whose revenue contributions are imperfectly correlated and therefore reduce the composite α_t.

This relationship can be depicted in a different way, as in figure 3. The left-hand bar represents the baseline market value of equity (BMVE). This starts with the book value of equity (BVE)—the sum of (1) the par value of shares when originally issued; (2) the surplus paid in by investors when the shares were issued; (3) retained earnings on the books of the bank; and (4) reserves set aside for loan losses.[41] BVE must be written up or written down by unrealized capital gains or losses associated with the mark-to-market values of all balance sheet items. This cal-

41. Saunders (2000).

culation yields the adjusted book value of equity (ABVE). Its value may depart significantly from BVE for banks and insurance companies due to a general absence of market value accounting across major categories of balance sheet items, although it may come pretty close for securities firms and asset managers.

After all balance sheet values have been taken into account and marked to market, there may still be a material difference between ABVE and the actual BMVE. This difference represents the market's assessment of the present value of the risk-adjusted future net earnings stream, capturing all known or suspected business opportunities, costs, and risks facing the firm and captured in the above equation—the "franchise value" of the firm. This value then increases or decreases in accordance with the size and scope effects discussed previously to ascertain the potential market value of equity (PMVE) in figure 3.

A simpler version is "Tobin's Q," defined as the ratio of the market value of a firm's equity divided by a firm's book value. If the Q ratio is significantly below 1, for example, breaking up the firm may serve the interests of shareholders if the book value of equity can be monetized. The Q ratio for well-run financial firms having a positive franchise value should normally be well in excess of 1 and is clearly susceptible to enhancement through managerial action.

In figure 3, each of the factors related to the size and breadth of financial services firms is identified in successive bars—scale and scope effects, operating and tax efficiencies, stability and TBTF premiums, conglomerate discount, and the rest—in building to the value of equity observed in the market, MVE. The difference between book value or market-adjusted book value could be highly positive, as it has been in the case of AIG in the insurance sector, for example. Or it could be significantly negative, with the firm's stock trading well below book value or even notional market-adjusted book value (its presumptive liquidation value). For example, J. P. Morgan Chase stock was trading below book value in late September 2002, reflecting concerns of large exposures (especially in the telecommunications sector) and questions about the bank's strategy and its execution.[42]

When strategic initiatives are undertaken, such as mergers or acquisitions, it is possible to add some empirical content to this kind of con-

---

42. "Strategy Worries Hit JP Morgan Share Price," *Financial Times*, September 19, 2002.

struct. During a period of intense M&A activity in the 1980s and early 1990s, U.S. commercial bank acquisitions occurred at price to book value ratios of about 2.0, sometimes as high as 3.0 or even more. In eight of the eleven years covered by one study, the mean price to book value ratio for U.S. commercial banking acquisitions was below 2.0, averaging 1.5 and ranging from 1.1 in 1990 to 1.8 in 1985.[43] In two years, the price to book value ratio exceeded 2.0—in 1986 it was 2.8, and in 1993 it was 3.2. These values presumably reflect the opportunity for the acquired institutions to be managed differently and to realize the incremental value needed to reimburse the shareholders of the acquiring institutions for their willingness to pay the premium in the first place. If in fact the potential to capture value for multifunctional financial firms exceeds that for the traditional U.S.-type separated commercial banks reflected in such studies, this should be reflected in higher merger premiums outside the United States as well as within the United States after the 1999 liberalization of line-of-business restrictions. Table 2 shows a decidedly mixed track record of a number of mergers during the 1998–2001 period.

Event study methodology can also be used to determine investor reaction to events such as the announcement of a presumably value-enhancing merger that adds either size or scope.[44] The technique controls for conditions in the general market and tries to determine the relationship that a particular stock has with the market under "normal" conditions—that is, before the event occurs. This relationship can be established by regressing the returns of the stock on the market index and a constant.[45] One then determines what the stock "should" have earned (total return) given the state of the general market as well as the stock's past relationship with that market. These hypothetical returns are compared with actual returns to determine the *abnormal returns*—that is, how much more or less the stock actually earns as a result of the announcement.[46]

Abnormal returns are added together over various time periods, usually several days before the announcement to several days after. One needs to look at a few days before the event in case any news about the

---

43. Walter and Smith (2000).

44. Brown and Warner (1985).

45. We obtain the following relationship: $\alpha_i + \beta_i R_{Mt}$ where R_{Mt} = the return on the market at time t; α_i = regression result on the constant; β_i = relationship between the market and stock i, also known as the beta of stock i.

46. That is, $AR_{it} = R_{it} - (\alpha_i + \beta_i R_{Mt})$, where AR_{it} = abnormal return for stock i at time t; R_{it} = return on stock i at time t; and R_{Mt} = the return on the market at time t.

Table 2. Post-acquisition Returns in Select U.S. Financial Sector Mergers

Acquirer	Target	Date	Value[a]	Premium (percent)[b]	Returns (percent)[c]		
					Seller, 1 week[d]	Buyer, 1 week[d]	Buyer, 1 year[e]
Travelers	Citicorp	April 1998	70.0	10.4	8	6	2
NationsBank	Bank of America	April 1998	59.3	48.4	2	4	4
Chase	Morgan	September 2000	36.3	59.7	24	–19	14
Norwest	Wells Fargo	June 1998	33.6	0.9	–3	–11	10
Conseco	Greentree	April 1998	7.1	85.9	35	–15	–55
M&T Bank	Keystone	May 2000	1.0	41.6	29	–4	54
Star Banc	Firstar	July 1998	7.0	44.1	32	–2	44
New York Community	Richmond	March 2001	0.8	7.2	11	7	43

Source: Standard and Poor's, Mergerstat, Boston Consulting Group, Thomson Financial.
a. Value of offer when announced.
b. Difference between offer price and market price one week before offer.
c. Percentage point differences over specified periods relative to Standard and Poor's 500 peers.
d. Price change one week pre- and post-announcement.
e. Price change one week pre-announcement to one year post-announcement.

event has leaked and affected the value of the stock. Looking at the abnormal returns for a few days after the announcement allows one to take "second thoughts" into account. The market may be so surprised by an announcement that it may need a few days to digest the news. One cannot know for sure the ideal length of the pre- or post-event periods. Extending either period leads to problems, since other events such as earnings reports or changes in management could have occurred and the market could be reacting to them instead of the one being examined.

As an example of how the event study approach can be used, we apply it to the seven strategic M&A deals undertaken by UBS AG and its predecessor organizations during the period 1992–2000. These include the Swiss Bank Corporation (SBC) acquisition of O'Connor (January 9, 1992), the SBC acquisition of Brinson (August 31, 1994), the SBC acquisition of S.G. Warburg (May 2, 1995), the SBC takeover of Dillon Read (May 15, 1997), the merger of Swiss Bank Corporation and Union Bank of Switzerland (UBS) to form the present UBS AG (December 8, 1997), the UBS acquisition of Global Asset Management (GAM) announced in September 13, 1999, and the UBS acquisition of PaineWebber announced on July 11, 2000. The first four deals were undertaken by Swiss Bank Corporation and can therefore be viewed in terms of the impact on the share price of SBC, the SBC-UBS merger in 1997 can be examined in terms of both SBC and UBS cumulative abnormal returns, while the GAM and PaineWebber deals can be viewed in terms of the impact on shares of the new UBS AG.

We estimate alpha and beta using daily returns from 500 to ten days before the merger announcement by regressing the returns of the stock on the returns of the Swiss SMI index. To determine the extent to which a particular merger was perceived by the market to have created or destroyed value, we cumulate the abnormal returns for various event windows for each SBC and UBS transaction beginning with O'Connor in 1992 and ending with PaineWebber in 2000. As mentioned, no scientific way of determining the ideal event window exists. No confounding events (earnings reports, changes in management, other major mergers) occurred around the time of the merger announcements. We therefore conclude that the market was reacting only to the announcement of the particular merger. The respective calculated abnormal returns are shown in table 3.

No regularity is obvious from the market's reactions to the SBC or UBS merger or acquisition announcements based on the seven cases

Table 3. Abnormal Returns for Acquirer

Percent

Merger	Date	Event date	[−1,+1] window	[−3,+3] window	[−5,+5] window
SBC O'Connor	January 9, 1992	0.444	0.930	−2.587	0.902
SBC Brinson	August 31, 1994	−0.713	1.084	−3.704	−5.205
SBC Warburg	May 2, 1995	−0.012	−2.515	−5.170	−7.127
SBC Dillon Read	May 15, 1997	−0.413	−1.551	−1.842	5.231
SBC-UBS (for SBC)	December 8, 1997	4.108	7.756	5.929	4.936
SBC-UBS (for UBS)	December 8, 1997	9.368	13.133	12.813	10.256
UBS-GAM	September 13, 1999	−0.082	0.977	1.452	−0.899
UBS-PaineWebber	July 11, 2000	−0.244	−7.306	−2.795	−3.509

examined here. That is, the market appears to judge each merger on its own merits. Market reaction to the merger of UBS and SBC, for example, was highly positive for shareholders of both firms, possibly reflecting cost cuts (especially in the domestic banking business) that could be made possible by the merger together with the presumably stronger competitive position of the new UBS AG in its various lines of activity, notably private banking and investment banking. This is in line with earlier event study research, such as that of DeLong and that of Houston, James, and Ryngaert, which finds that in-market (focusing) mergers tend to create value on announcement based on the flow of U.S. financial services deals—targets of in-market mergers gain and acquirers do not lose.[47] In contrast, market reaction to the UBS acquisition of PaineWebber was strongly negative, probably in large part due to the dilutive effect of the high price paid.

To obtain an alternative, rough assessment of whether bigger is better in commercial banking from the standpoint of firm valuation, we conduct a nonparametric Spearman rank correlation analysis between asset footings, as a measure of size, and market valuation as reflected in price-earnings ratios for each year during 1992–2001—a Spearman coefficient of +1 indicates a perfect correlation between size and valuation, −1 indicates a perfect negative correlation, and 0 indicates no correlation. We hypothesize that there is no correlation. Indeed, the Spearman coefficient is 0.1249, which is not significantly different from zero at the 1 and 5

47. DeLong (2001); Houston, James, and Ryngaert (1999).

percent levels of significance (two-tailed) in any year. In the case of insurance, however (measuring size by premium flow), the same is true at the 0.01 level of significance, although the Spearman coefficient of 0.3791 is significant at the 0.05 level of significance in four of the ten years. The same test for broker-dealers and asset managers is not meaningful because the number of independent firms with listed equities is insufficient.

Conclusions

Assessing the potential effects of size and scope in financial services firms is as straightforward in concept as it is difficult to calibrate in practice. The positives include economies of scale, improvements in operating efficiency (including the impact of technology), cost economies of scope, revenue economies of scope, impact on market structure and pricing power, improved financial stability through diversification of revenue streams, improvements in the attraction and retention of human capital, and possibly TBTF support. The negatives include diseconomies of scale, higher operating costs due to increased size and complexity, diseconomies of scope on either the cost or revenue sides (or both), the impact of possible conflicts of interest on the franchise value of the firm, and a possible conglomerate discount in the share price. Bigger and broader is sometimes better, sometimes not. It all depends.

The evidence so far suggests rather limited prospects for firmwide cost economies of scale and scope among major financial services firms in terms of overall cost structures, although they certainly exist in specific lines of activity. Operating economies (X-efficiency) seem to be the principal determinant of observed differences in cost levels among banks and nonbank financial institutions. Revenue economies of scope through cross-selling may well exist, but they are likely to apply very differently to specific client segments and product lines. Conflicts of interest can pose major risks for shareholders of multifunctional financial firms, which may materialize in civil or even criminal litigation and losses in franchise value. There is plenty of evidence that diversification across uncorrelated business streams promotes stability, although unexpected spikes in correlation (as between insurance and investment banking) may arise from time to time.

Table 4 shows the most valuable financial services in the United States, Europe, and the rest of the world by their market capitalization. Two observations can be made. First, the largest firms, by whatever measures are used in the major industry segments, are not necessarily the most valuable. Indeed, rank correlations between size and market value are low. And second, both lists are highly diverse. Generalists and specialists co-habitate at the top of the financial services league in both regions of the world. Both observations suggest that the key is in "how" things are done rather than in "what" is done. Although the burden of proof tends to fall on bigger and broader firms, a few cases like GE Capital Services (a conglomerate within a conglomerate) show that specialist businesses run by specialists on a highly rated capital platform—subject to unrelenting pressure to sweat the equity by a demanding corporate owner insisting on market dominance together with benchmark attention to service quality, cost control, and risk control—can be done and that it can be done on a sustained basis. However, even here the issue of transparency eventually forced a breakup of GE Capital's organizational structure in 2002.

In a way, the absence of clear signs of "strategic dominance"—generalists gaining the upper hand over specialists or the other way round—is encouraging. Any number can play, and there are no magic formulas. The devil remains in the details, and there is a premium on plain old good management. From a systemic perspective as well, diversity in the financial system is probably a good thing, as firms competing across strategic groups as well as within them put a premium on both efficiency in financial allocation and innovation in the evolution of financial products and processes.

Table 4. Top-Fifteen Global Financial Services Firms Ranked by Market Value, September 30, 2002

	United States		Europe		Rest of world	
Rank	Firm	Market value	Firm	Market value	Firm	Market value
1	Citigroup	150.1	HSBC plc	95.7	Mitsubishi Tokyo (Japan)	41.9
2	AIG	142.8	RBS Group plc	54.6	Sumitomo (Japan)	31.5
3	GE Capital[a]	99.3	UBS AG	52.1	NAB (Australia)	27.9
4	Berkshire Hathaway	97.4	Lloyds TSB plc	41.2	Nomura (Japan)	25.7
5	Bank of America	95.9	Barclays plc	39.6	UFJ (Japan)	23.3
6	Wells Fargo	81.8	HBOS Group plc	34.9	Royal Bank (Canada)	22.4
7	Wachovia	44.9	BNP Paribas	29.1	Mizuho (Japan)	22.0
8	BancOne	43.8	Deutsche Bank AG	28.2	Commonwealth (Australia)	20.4
9	American Express	41.4	ING Group	27.6	ANZ (Australia)	14.4
10	J. P. Morgan Chase	37.9	Grupo Santander	24.3	Scotiabank (Canada)	14.2
11	Morgan Stanley	37.1	BBVA	23.8	Westpac (Australia)	13.3
12	Fifth Third Bancorp	36.7	Crédit Suisse	23.3	Kookmin (Korea)	11.6
13	U.S. Bancorp	35.6	Unicredito Italiano	22.5	Bank of Montreal (Canada)	11.4
14	Goldman Sachs	31.8	Allianz AG	22.2	Toronto Dominion (Canada)	11.2
15	Washington Mutual	30.4	Munich Re	18.8	CIBC (Canada)	9.3

Source: Bloomberg.
a. Earnings volatility-adjusted GE Capital Services contribution to General Electric multiplied by General Electric market capitalization.

References

Akhavein, Jalal D., Allen N. Berger, and David B. Humphrey. 1997. "The Effects of Mega-mergers on Efficiency and Prices: Evidence from a Bank Profit Function." *Review of Industrial Organization* 12 (1, February): 95–139.

Beatty, Randolph, Anthony Santomero, and Michael Smirlock. 1987. *Bank Merger Premiums: Analysis and Evidence.* Monograph Series on Economics and Finance 3. New York University, Salomon Center for the Study of Financial Institutions.

Berger, Allen N., Rebecca S. Demsetz, and Philip E. Strahan. 1998. *The Consolidation of the Financial Services Industry: Causes, Consequences, and Implications for the Future.* New York: Federal Reserve Bank of New York.

Berger, Allen N., Diana Hancock, and David B. Humphrey. 1993. "Bank Efficiency Derived from the Profit Function." *Journal of Banking and Finance* 17 (April): 317–47.

Berger, Allen N., and Timothy H. Hannan. 1996. "Using Measures of Firm Efficiency to Distinguish among Alternative Explanations of the Structure-Performance Relationship." *Managerial Finance* 23 (October): 6–31.

Berger, Allen N., and David B. Humphrey. 1992. "Mega-Mergers in Banking and the Use of Cost Efficiency as an Antitrust Defense." *Antitrust Bulletin* 37 (Fall): 541–600.

Berger, Allen N., William C. Hunter, and Stephen J. Timme. 1993. "The Efficiency of Financial Institutions: A Review and Preview of Research Past, Present, and Future." *Journal of Banking and Finance* 17 (April): 221–49.

Berger, Allen N., and Loretta Mester. 1997. "Inside the Black Box: What Explains Differences in the Efficiencies of Financial Institutions?" *Journal of Banking and Finance* 21 (July): 895–947.

Berger, Philip G., and Eli Ofek. 1995. "Diversification's Effect on Firm Value." *Journal of Financial Economics* 37 (1): 39–65.

Boyd, John, Stanley Graham, and R. S. Hewitt. 1993. "Bank Holding Company Mergers with Non-bank Financial Firms: Effects on the Risk of Failure." *Journal of Financial Economics* 17 (1): 43–63.

Brown, Stephen J., and Jerold B. Warner. 1985. "Using Daily Stock Returns: The Case of Event Studies." *Journal of Financial Economics* 14 (1): 3–31.

Cummins, J. D., and H. Zi. 1998. "Comparisons of Frontier Efficiency Methods: An Application to the U.S. Life Insurance Industry." *Journal of Productivity Analysis* 10 (2): 131–52.

DeLong, Gayle. 2001. "Stockholder Gains from Focusing Versus Diversifying Bank Mergers." *Journal of Financial Economics* 59 (2): 221–52.

Demsetz, Rebecca S., Marc R. Saidenberg, and Philip E. Strahan. 1996. "Banks with Something to Lose: The Disciplinary Role of Franchise Value." *Federal Reserve Bank of New York Economic Policy Review* 2 (2, October): 1–4.

Economides, Nicholas, and David Encaoua. 1996. "The Economics of Networks." *International Journal of Industrial Organization* 14 (6): 673–99.

Goldberg, Lawrence G., Gerald A. Hanweck, Michael Keenan, and Allen Young. 1991. "Economies of Scale and Scope in the Securities Industry." *Journal of Banking and Finance* 15 (February): 91–107.

Houston, Joel, Chris James, and Michael Ryngaert. 1999. "Where Do Merger Gains Come from? Bank Mergers from the Perspective of Insiders and Outsiders." *Journal of Financial Economics* 60 (2-3): 285–331.

Houston, Joel, and Michael Ryngaert. 1994. "The Overall Gains from Large Bank Mergers." *Journal of Banking and Finance* 18 (December): 1155–76.

John, Kose, and Eli Ofek. 1995. "Asset Sales and Increase in Focus." *Journal of Financial Economics* 37 (1): 105–26.

Kane, Edward. 2000. "Incentives for Banking Megamergers: What Motives Might Regulators Infer from Event-Study Evidence?" *Journal of Money, Credit, and Banking* 32 (August): 671–701.

Kroszner, Randall, and Raghuram Rajan. 1994. "Is the Glass-Steagall Act Justified? A Study of the U.S. Experience with Universal Banking before 1933." *American Economic Review* 84 (4): 810–32.

Lang, Gunter, and Peter Wetzel. 1998. "Technology and Cost Efficiency in Universal Banking: A Thick Frontier Approach." *Journal of Productivity Analysis* 10 (1): 63–84.

Lown, Cara S., Carol L. Osler, Philip E. Strahan, and Amir Sufi. 2000. "The Changing Landscape of the Financial Services Industry: What Lies Ahead?" *Federal Reserve Bank of New York Economic Policy Review* 6 (4, October): 39–55.

O'Hara, Maureen, and Wayne Shaw. 1990. "Deposit Insurance and Wealth Effects: The Value of Being 'Too Big to Fail.'" *Journal of Finance* 45 (5): 1587–600.

Puri, Manju. 1996. "Commercial Banks in Investment Banking: Conflict of Interest or Certification Role?" *Journal of Financial Economics* 40 (3): 373–401.

Santomero, Anthony, and Eek-June Chung. 1992. "Evidence in Support of Broader Bank Powers." *Financial Markets, Institutions, and Instruments* 1 (1): 1–69.

Saunders, Anthony. 2000. *Financial Institutions Management: A Modern Perspective*, 3d ed. Burr Ridge, Ill.: Irwin.

Saunders, Anthony, and Ingo Walter. 1994. *Universal Banking in the United States*. New York: Oxford University Press.

Siems, Thomas F. 1996. "Bank Mergers and Shareholder Wealth: Evidence from 1995's Mega-Merger Deals." *Federal Reserve Bank of Dallas Financial Industry Studies* (August): 1–26.

Smith, Roy C., and Ingo Walter. 1995. "JP Morgan and Banco Español de Crédito: Teaching Note." In *Case Studies in Finance and Economics*, 2d ed. Case Study C53. New York University, Salomon Center.

———. 1997. *Street Smarts: Linking Professional Conduct with Shareholder Value in the Securities Industry*. Boston: Harvard Business School Press.

———. 2003. *Global Banking,* 2d ed. New York: Oxford University Press.

Stefanadis, Chris. 2002. "Specialist Securities Firms in the Gramm-Leach-Bliley Era." Working Paper. Federal Reserve Bank of New York.

U.S. General Accounting Office. 1991. "Deposit Insurance: Overview of Six Foreign Systems." GAO/NSIAD-91-104.

Walter, Ingo. 2003 (forthcoming). *Mergers and Acquisitions in Banking and Finance—What Works, What Does Not, and Why?* New York: Oxford University Press.

Walter, Ingo, and Roy C. Smith. 2000. *Investment Banking in the Euro-Zone.* London: Financial Times/Prentice-Hall.

Yu, Li. 2001. "On the Wealth and Risk Effects of the Glass-Steagall Overhaul: Evidence from the Stock Market." Working Paper. New York University.

Consolidation and Strategic Positioning in Banking with Implications for Europe

ARNOUD W. A. BOOT

T HE UNPRECEDENTED RESTRUCTURING and consolidation that are occurring around the globe are probably best characterized as a financial services sector in flux. Transactions are particularly numerous and breathtaking in the United States and Western Europe, but restructuring is also occurring in Asia. Most striking is the escalating scale of mergers in banking. In just the last few years, in the United States mergers have led to a consolidation of money center banks (for example, the Chase Manhattan and Chemical Bank merger, prior to their subsequent merger with J. P. Morgan) and the emergence of regional powerhouses (for example, the expansion strategies of BankOne and Nationsbank and their mergers with, respectively, First Chicago/NBD and BankAmerica). In Europe mergers have also been prominent. Although cross-border mergers are relatively infrequent—with exceptions in Scandinavia and the acquisitions across the Dutch-Belgian border,[1] such as the acquisition of the Belgian Bank BBL by the Dutch financial conglomerate ING—domestic mergers typically involve large universal banks and are often spectacular. Noteworthy examples include the marriage of the Union

The comments of Dick Herring, Bob Litan, Stijn Claessens, David Voute, Tineke Bahlmann, and other participants are gratefully acknowledged.

1. A noteworthy cross-border merger that goes beyond these culturally aligned regions is HSBC's purchase of Credit Commercial de France.

Bank of Switzerland with Swiss Bank Corporation and the acquisition of Paribas by Banque National de Paris. In Japan spectacular mega-mergers have put the Japanese banks among the largest banks in the world ranked by book value of assets.

A parallel phenomenon is the continued broad, if not broadening, scope of many banks. Even banks that traditionally followed well-motivated, focused strategies have given in to this trend. For example, Bankers Trust, with its activities aimed at the corporate market, has put itself in the arms of a scope-expanding universal bank (Deutsche Bank). Scope expansion also originates from investment banks. Major investment banks are redefining their domain by offering traditional commercial banking products like commercial and industrial loans and by moving into retail brokerage. The union of Salomon Brothers (investment bank) and Smith Barney (brokerage) within Travelers underscores the scope expansion in the industry. Similarly, Credit Suisse bought the U.S. stockbroker DLJ, and UBS bought Paine-Webber. The spectacular cross-industry merger by Citicorp and Travelers also brings insurance activities together with bank-oriented financial services. This concept is not really new, however. Some European banks—for example, ING in the Netherlands and the Belgian-Dutch conglomerate Fortis—already engage in *bancassurance*—that is, the combination of banking and insurance activities. Similarly, Credit Suisse expanded into insurance by acquiring the insurance corporation Winterthur. But in the United States, until passage of the Gramm-Leach-Bliley Act of 1999 many restrictions remained on combining banking, securities underwriting, and insurance.

One question is then immediate. Why are banks consolidating so much and expanding scope? The popular financial press points to the increasingly competitive environment of banking as the culprit. As commercial banking becomes more competitive, banks need to examine all possible ways to wring inefficiencies out of their cost structures. One way to do this is to merge with other banks and to realize efficiencies of scale through elimination of redundant branches and back-office consolidation. Moreover, the diminishing margins in commercial banking invite banks to look outside their traditional domain. Some nonbanking activities may offer higher margins and make scope expansion attractive.

However, these popular explanations are inadequate. The empirical evidence on scale and scope economies in banking is far from conclusive. It is questionable whether these economies are large enough to justify consolidation and scope expansion on the scale that we have observed.[2] Moreover, ample research in corporate finance points to the existence of a "diversification discount." On average, diversification seems to destroy value. There is substantial evidence that firms that have refocused have experienced improvements in operating performance and stock returns.[3] Therefore, the important question is why so many mergers and acquisitions are taking place in the industry. This question becomes even more relevant considering the media and analyst reports that increasingly challenge the broad focus of most financial institutions.[4]

This study aims to address this question and other related issues. I examine the existing empirical evidence on scope and scale economies in banking. In a recent survey paper, Berger, Demsetz, and Strahan evaluate the extensive, primarily U.S., evidence.[5] Their findings are, if anything, quite sobering about scope and scale economies. However, most studies that they report on are quite dated. An important question, therefore, is whether this empirical evidence is suitable for explaining the current wave of consolidation. Although I conclude that the existing evidence is of some value (and I cite some newer evidence that is of greater value), I doubt that it is really helpful for understanding the current restructuring in banking. Several issues play a role here. Apart from econometric and sample-selection issues, and possibly fundamental changes in underlying "state variables," in my view *the* important issue is that *strategic* considerations are *the* driving force behind the current wave of consolidation. As I argue, these considerations may have little to do with true scale or scope economies. Rather, learning, first-mover advantages, and strategic advantages of market power and associated "deep pockets" may explain the current wave of consolidation and the broad scope of many players in the industry.

Strategic positioning might, for the moment, be the rule of the game and an optimal response to the uncertainties and rapid (and unpredictable) changes facing financial institutions today. Consolidation might

---

2. See Berger (1998); Berger, Hunter, and Timme (1993).
3. See John and Ofek (1995); Comment and Jarrell (1995).
4. See, for example, a recent report by Oliver, Wyman and Company in collaboration with Morgan-Stanley that has the illuminating title "The Need to Differentiate." Oliver, Wyman and Company (2002).
5. Berger, Demsetz, and Strahan (1999).

then be an evolutionary phenomenon and be followed by a new type of repositioning when the uncertainties become more manageable. However, as I argue, the competitive pressures are growing in the financial services industry. Margins are eroding, and costly scope-expanding strategies may become unsustainable. The viability of a broad "wait and see" strategy may soon be over.

This paper is organized as follows. I start with a discussion of the growing research in the field of financial intermediation. This research—mainly theoretical in nature—sheds light on the costs and benefits of bank funding vis-à-vis direct funding in the financial market. Although primarily focused on the funding role of banks and financial markets, it provides valuable insights into the economics of banking. In this context, I also discuss the growing importance of securitization and the impact of competition on the value of relationship banking. These insights provide a foundation for understanding the role of financial institutions in the future. Subsequently, I discuss the extensive empirical literature on scale and scope economies in banking. Here, I focus on scale and scope considerations that may become important in the future. An issue in this context is that the literature needs to differentiate more between the various activities (services and products) of financial intermediaries. Scale and scope economies have been looked at too generically. Next I introduce strategic considerations—in particular, the importance of *strategic positioning*—and discuss in some detail the relevance of these insights for the ongoing restructuring in the European financial services industry. Finally, I conclude by offering some thoughts on the (to be expected) disaggregation of the value chain, with a more prominent role for alliances and joint ventures. I also discuss some political considerations, particularly in the European context, that may have an important impact on the future path of the ongoing restructuring.

Fundamentals: The Economics of Banking

What does economic theory tell us about the role of financial institutions? The relevant field of financial intermediation offers some guidance in uncovering the added value of financial institutions. The literature has focused primarily on three issues: the role of banks in funding real activities, the value of relationships in intermediated finance versus transactions in financial markets, and the prospects of liquefying bank assets (for example, securitization).

In this section, I examine what economic theory has to say on each of these issues. Of particular interest also is the impact of the ever more competitive environment on the value of relationship banking. This sheds some light on the competitive positioning of financial institutions and their possibly changing role. Although these insights are primarily theoretical, they provide a valuable foundation for understanding the ongoing restructuring in the financial services industry.

Traditional Versus Modern Banking

Traditional commercial banks hold nonmarketable or illiquid assets that are funded largely with deposits. There is typically little uncertainty about the value of these deposits, which often can be withdrawn on demand. The liquidity of bank liabilities stands in sharp contrast to that of bank assets, reflecting the banks' raison d'être. By liquefying claims, banks facilitate the funding of projects that might otherwise be infeasible.

The banks' assets are illiquid largely because of their information sensitivity. In originating and pricing loans, banks develop proprietary information. Subsequent monitoring of borrowers yields additional private information. The proprietary information inhibits the marketability of these loans. The access to information is the key to understanding the comparative advantage of banks. In many of their activities, banks exploit their informational advantages and the related network of contacts. This relationship-oriented banking is a characteristic of value-enhancing financial intermediation. The relationship and network orientation applies not only to traditional commercial lending but also to many areas of "modern banking."

One might be tempted to interpret modern banking as transaction oriented. An investment bank—generally considered a prime example of modern banking—facilitates a firm's access to public capital markets. The role of the investment bank could be interpreted as that of a broker: matching buyers and sellers for the firms' securities. In this interpretation, investment banks just facilitate transactions, which would confirm the transaction orientation of modern banking. The investment banks' added value would then be confined to their networks—that is, their ability to economize on search or matching costs. As a characterization of modern banking, this describes their economic role too narrowly. Investment banks do more. They—almost without exception—*underwrite* those public issues; that is, they absorb credit and placement risk. This brings the role of an investment bank much closer to that of a commercial bank engaged in lending; the processing and absorption of risk are typical intermediation functions similar to those encountered in traditional bank lending.[6]

In lending, a bank manages and absorbs risk (for example, credit and liquidity risks) by issuing claims on its total assets with different characteristics than those encountered in its loan portfolio. In financial intermediation theory, this is referred to as *qualitative asset transformation*.[7] The underwriting of an investment bank can be interpreted analogically; risk is (temporarily) absorbed and is channeled through to the claimholders of the investment bank. The role of investment banks is therefore more than just purely brokerage. Underwriting requires the acquisition of information about the borrower, which is supported by a relationship orientation. A relationship orientation will therefore still be present in investment banking, in the direction of both investors (placement capacity) and borrowing firms.

What is also true, however, is that relationships in investment banking depend much less on local presence. Nevertheless, public debt issues are *relatively* hands-off, with few interactions between financiers and borrowers over time.[8] The full menu of financing options for borrowers includes many other products with varying degrees of relationships. For example, syndicated loans are found in the continuum between bank loans and public debt issues. These are offered by investment banks and commercial banks alike and typically involve several financiers per loan. Generally, only the lead banks have a relationship with the borrower, and the relationship intensity is somewhere between a bank loan and a public debt issue.[9]

6. From this perspective, it is not surprising that several European banks are integrating their debt capital market activities with their corporate lending operations. Previously, they had the debt capital market activities typically linked to equity capital market operations (within their investment banking divisions). The commitment to equity-linked investment bank activities is being reduced or even dismantled by many players in the industry.

7. See Greenbaum and Thakor (1995).

8. Berlin and Mester (1992).

9. See Dennis and Mullineaux (2000).

It is important that the relationship aspect involves not only funding but also various other financial services, such as letters of credit, deposits, check clearing, and cash management services. I do not focus on these services per se, but one should keep in mind that these services can expand the information available to the intermediary. As some have argued, the information that banks obtain by offering multiple services to the *same* customer may be of value in lending.[10] For example, the use of checking and deposit accounts may help the bank to assess a firm's loan repayment capability. Thus the scope of the relationship may affect a bank's comparative advantage.

Are Bank Loans Special?

Some see public capital market financing as a potentially superior substitute for bank lending, but, stated as such, this is unwarranted. Bank lending has distinct comparative advantages. In particular, it may support enduring close relationships between debtor and financier that may mitigate information asymmetries. This has several components. A borrower might be prepared to reveal proprietary information to its bank, while it never would have disseminated this information to the financial markets.[11] A bank might also be more receptive to information because of its role as enduring and dominant lender. This amounts to observing that a bank might have better incentives to invest in the acquisition of information. While costly, the substantial stake that it has in funding the borrower and in maintaining an enduring relationship—with the possibility of reusing information over time—increases the value of information.[12]

The bank-borrower relationship is also less rigid than those normally encountered in the financial market. The general observation is that a better flow of information facilitates more informative decisions. In particular, relationship finance could allow for more flexibility and possibly value-enhancing discretion. This is in line with the important ongoing discussion in economic theory on rules versus discretion, where discre-

---

10. Degryse and Van Cayseele (2000).
11. Bhattacharya and Chiesa (1995).
12. Diamond (1984) introduces intermediaries as delegated monitors. See Chan, Greenbaum, and Thakor (1986) for a discussion on information reusability and James (1987) and Lummer and McConnell (1989) for empirical evidence. For a nice illustration supporting the special role of banks, see Berlin (1996).

tion allows for decisionmaking based on more subtle—potentially non-contractible—information.[13] Two dimensions can be identified. One dimension is related to the nature of the bank-borrower relationship; the other involves the structure of contracts. The first emphasizes that the bank-borrower relationship is in many ways a mutual commitment based on trust and respect.. This allows for *implicit*—non-enforceable—long-term contracting. An optimal flow of information is crucial for sustaining these "contracts." Information asymmetries in the financial market and the non-contractibility of various pieces of information may rule out long-term access to alternative sources of capital market funding as well as *explicit* long-term commitments by banks. Therefore, both bank and borrower may realize the added value of their relationship and have an incentive to foster the relationship.[14]

Another feature is that relationship banking could accommodate an intertemporal smoothing of contract terms, including accepting losses for the bank in the short term that are recouped later in the relationship. Petersen and Rajan show that credit subsidies to young or de novo corporations may reduce the moral hazard problems and information frictions that banks face in lending to such borrowers.[15] However, subsidies impose losses on the bank. Banks may nevertheless provide funding if they can expect to offset these losses through the long-term rents generated by these borrowers. The point is that without access to subsidized credit early in their lives, de novo borrowers would pose adverse selection and moral hazard problems so serious that *no* bank would lend to them. Relationship lending could make such subsidies and accompanying loans feasible because the proprietary information generated during the relationship produces rents for the bank later in the relationship and permits the early losses to be offset.[16] Berlin and Mester show that rate-insensitive core deposits allow for intertemporal smoothing in lending rates.[17] This suggests a complementarity between deposit taking and

13. See, for example, Simons (1936); Boot, Greenbaum, and Thakor (1993).

14. Mayer (1988) and Hellwig (1991) discuss the commitment nature of bank funding. Boot, Thakor, and Udell (1991) address the *credibility* of commitments. Schmeits (2002) formally considers the impact of discretion (flexibility) in bank loan contracts on investment efficiency.

15. Petersen and Rajan (1995).

16. The importance of intertemporal transfers in loan pricing is also present in Berlin and Mester (1998).

17. Berlin and Mester (1998).

lending. Moreover, the loan commitment literature has emphasized the importance of intertemporal tax-subsidy schemes in pricing to resolve moral hazard and also the complementarity between deposit taking and *commitment* lending.[18]

The other dimension is related to the structure of the explicit contracts that banks can write. Bank loans are generally easier to renegotiate than bond issues or other public vehicles for capital market funding. The renegotiation allows for a qualitative use of flexibility. Sometimes this is a mixed blessing because banks may suffer from a soft budget constraint (the borrowers may realize that they can renegotiate ex post, which could give them perverse ex ante incentives). In reality, bank loans often have *priority* to resolve this problem. With priority a bank may strengthen its bargaining position and thus become tougher.[19] The bank could then credibly intervene in the decisionmaking process of the borrower when it believes that its long-term interests are in danger. For example, the bank might believe that the firm's strategy is flawed or a restructuring is long overdue. Could the bank push for the restructuring? If the bank has no priority, the borrower may choose to ignore the bank's wishes. This is because the borrower realizes that the bank cannot credibly enforce its demands. The bank could threaten to call the loan, but the borrower, anticipating the dreadful consequences not only for himself but also for the bank, realizes that the bank would not carry out such a threat. However, when the bank has priority, the prioritized claim may insulate the bank from these dreadful consequences. It could now *credibly* threaten to call the loan and enforce its wishes on the borrower. This then identifies an important advantage of bank financing: *timely intervention.*[20]

These observations highlight the complementarity of bank lending and capital market funding. Prioritized bank debt facilitates timely intervention. This feature of bank lending is valuable to the firm's bondholders as

18. On the importance of intertemporal tax-subsidy schemes in pricing to resolve moral hazard, see Boot, Thakor, and Udell (1991). On the complementarity between deposit taking and commitment lending, see Kashyap, Rajan, and Stein (1999).

19. See Dewatripont and Maskin (1995) on the issues of soft budget constraints. Diamond (1993), Berglöf and von Thadden (1994), and Gorton and Kahn (1993) address the priority structure.

20. One could ask whether bondholders could be given priority and allocated the task of timely intervention. Note that bondholders are subject to more severe information asymmetries and are generally more dispersed (that is, have smaller stakes). Both characteristics make them ill suited for an "early" intervention task.

well. They might find it optimal to grant bank debt priority over their own claims and, in doing so, delegate the timely intervention activity to the bank.[21] Consequently, the borrower may reduce its total funding cost by accessing both the bank credit market and the financial market.

Diamond as well as Hoshi, Kashyap, and Scharfstein further develop arguments highlighting the complementarity of bank lending and capital market funding.[22] Hoshi, Kashyap, and Scharfstein show that bank lending exposes borrowers to monitoring, which may serve as a certification device that facilitates simultaneous capital market funding.[23] Diamond shows that borrowers may want to borrow first from banks in order to establish sufficient credibility *before* accessing the capital markets. Again banks provide certification and monitoring. Once the borrower is "established," it switches to capital market funding. In this explanation, there is a *sequential* complementarity between bank and capital market funding. In related theoretical work, Chemmanur and Fulghieri show that the quality of the bank is of critical importance for its role in certification.[24] This suggests a positive correlation between the value of relationship banking and the quality of the lender. The overall conclusion is that bank lending potentially facilitates more informative decisions based on a better exchange of information.[25] Although not universally valuable, this suggests a benefit of relationship-oriented banking.[26]

---

21. The bondholders will obviously ask to be compensated for their subordinated status. This—ignoring the timely intervention effect—is "a wash." In other words, the priority (seniority) or subordination features can be priced out. That is, as much as senior debt may *appear* cheaper (it is less risky), junior or subordinated debt will appear more expensive.

22. Diamond (1993); Hoshi, Kashyap, and Scharfstein (1993).

23. Empirical evidence provided by James (1987) and Slovin, Sushka, and Hudson (1988) support the role of banks in certification. Other evidence can be found in Houston and James (1995).

24. Chemmanur and Fulghieri (1994).

25. See, for example, Petersen and Rajan (1994) and Houston and James (1995) for empirical evidence.

26. The relationship feature of (primarily commercial) banking also has drawbacks. There are two primary costs to relationship banking: the soft budget constraint problem and the hold-up problem. The soft budget constraint problem has to do with the potential lack of toughness on the bank's part in enforcing credit contracts that may come with relationship banking proximity. The problem is that borrowers who realize that they can renegotiate their contracts ex post like this may have perverse incentives ex ante (Bolton and Scharfstein 1996; Dewatripont and Maskin 1995). The seniority structure of bank loans may mitigate this. The hold-up problem has to do with the information monopoly the bank generates in the course of lending, which may allow it to make loans at noncompetitive

Securitization: A Threat to Bank Lending?

Securitization is an example of a financial innovation—or an innovation in funding technology—that suggests a potential gain of (transaction-oriented) markets at the expense of bank lending. Is this true? Let me first evaluate the economics of securitization.[27]

Securitization is an example of the unbundling of financial services. It is a process whereby assets are removed from a bank's balance sheet. More specifically, banks no longer permanently fund assets; instead the investors buying the asset-backed securities provide funding. Asset-backed securities rather than bank deposits then fund dedicated pools of bank-originated assets. As I emphasize, securitization does not signal the demise of banks, even if it becomes an economically important innovation (and thus substantially reduces the banks' on-balance-sheet assets). To see this point, I analyze the traditional lending function in some detail.

The lending function can be decomposed into four more primal activities: origination, funding, servicing, and risk processing. Origination subsumes screening prospective borrowers and designing and pricing financial contracts. Funding relates to the provision of financial resources. Servicing involves the collection and remission of payments as well as the monitoring of credits. Risk processing alludes to hedging, diversification, and the absorption of credit, interest rate, liquidity, and exchange rate risk. Securitization decomposes the lending function such that banks no longer fund the assets but continue to be involved in the primal activities.

The economics of securitization dictate that the originating bank *credit enhances* the issue. Credit enhancement is typically achieved through the provision of excess collateral, guarantees, or a letter of credit. Effectively this means that the originating bank continues to bear

---

terms in the future to the borrower. More specifically, the proprietary information about borrowers that banks obtain as part of their relationships may give them an information monopoly. In this way, banks could charge (ex post) high interest rates on loans (see Sharpe 1990; Rajan 1992). The threat of being "locked in," or informationally captured by the bank, may make the borrower reluctant to borrow from the bank. Potentially valuable investment opportunities may then be lost. Alternatively, firms may opt for multiple bank relationships. This may reduce the information monopoly of any one bank, but possibly at a cost. Ongena and Smith (2000) show that multiple bank relationships indeed reduce the hold-up problem and worsen the availability of credit.

27. Gorton and Pennacchi (1995) provide an economic rationale for bank loan sales and securitization. See also Stone and Zissu (2000).

part of the consequences (losses) if the securitized assets do not perform. The credit enhancement reduces the riskiness of the asset-backed claims from the investors' perspective, but, which is more important, it addresses conflicts of interest rooted in the originating bank's proprietary information. With private information in possession of the originating bank, the market requires assurances that the bank will truthfully reveal the quality of the assets it seeks to sell. As with a warranty in product markets, credit enhancement discourages misrepresentation by requiring the originator to absorb a portion of the losses owing to default. Similarly, credit enhancement signals the market that the originator will perform a thorough credit evaluation and an undiminished monitoring effort. Credit enhancement therefore reduces the information sensitivity of securitized claims by enhancing their marketability.[28]

This implies that securitization could lead to a *reconfiguration* of banking. Banks would continue to originate and service assets, while also processing the attendant risk in order to sustain these activities. Banks would still screen and monitor borrowers, design and price financial claims, and provide risk management services. As such, securitization would preserve the incremental value of banks.[29]

How important will securitization become? I can only offer a very tentative answer. So far, the securitization market is still small in Europe, but it is growing. The U.S. market is much more developed. For example, the total volume of mortgage-linked securitization issues in Europe amounts to just 8 percent of that in the United States, where it stands at $1.6 trillion.[30] In the United States, securitization has spread rapidly in the last two decades, but mainly for car loans, mortgages, and credit card receivables. The standardization and modest size of these credits allow diversification of idiosyncratic risks on pooling. Private information distortions—as discussed in the context of credit enhancement—are thought to be less severe for these standardized credits.

---

28. The reputation of the originating bank will be equally important. Moreover, accreditation by credit-rating agencies could also add to the marketability of the securitized claims.

29. See also Boyd and Gertler (1995). They argue that a substitution from on-balance-sheet to off-balance-sheet banking may have (falsely) suggested a shrinking role for banks. As in the description of securitization in the text, much of the bank's value added in the primal activities would be preserved.

30. Figures from the Bond Market Association.

What can be said about the larger, more customized, and more hetero-geneous commercial loans? These tend to be more information sensitive. Their quality is therefore more dependent on the rigor of initial screening and subsequent monitoring. Hence the pooling of commercial loans does less to dissipate their information sensitivity, attenuating the benefits of securitization. These considerations, however, do not preclude the securitization of business credits. They merely elevate the cost. For example, with more information-sensitive assets, the originating bank may need to retain a larger portion of the credit risk; credit enhancement becomes more important. If the information sensitivity is too severe, credit enhancement, short of total recourse, may not overcome the private-information problem. Thus the potential advantages of securitization would largely be lost, and traditional bank lending would continue to dominate. However, for an increasing array of moderately information-sensitive assets, securitization might become the preferred intermediation technology.

In fact, over the last few years several successful examples of transactions involving the securitization of business credits have emerged. Including synthetic transactions (default swaps), the European volume of CDOs (securitization of business credits) has grown from €40 billion in 1999 to €128 billion in 2001. Moreover, a new market for the securitization of working capital (via asset-backed commercial paper conduits) is rapidly coming to maturity.[31]

As my discussion of the economics of securitization suggests, even if securitization becomes prevalent, banks could continue to play an important role for most of the primal activities that were previously combined together in bank lending. More important, the comparative advantage of banks rooted in proprietary information about their clientele could be preserved. However, the message is not totally comforting for banks. In particular, the securitization of loans may greatly benefit from standardization in the origination (lending). This may weaken the bank-borrower relationship somewhat. The securitization trend also forces banks to think about their market positioning. A key question is whether securitization skills (structuring, but also placement capacity with end investors) need to be developed. In other words, can the commercial bank continue

31. As a caveat, some of this activity in securitization is undoubtedly induced by capital arbitrage, and the new Basel II capital requirements may mitigate this somewhat.

just to originate assets (and let others bring in the securitization skills), or do securitization skills need to be developed in-house? For most commercial banks, it would be very difficult to develop placement capacity. Also their sheer size would make this a difficult proposition. Some structuring skills, however, and a better feeling for the financial markets might become indispensable.

Is Relationship Banking at Risk?

I have argued that relationships may facilitate a continuous flow of information between debtor and creditor that could guarantee uninterrupted access to funding. Some, however, believe that more competition threatens these relationships, while others argue the exact opposite. The question then is how elevated interbank competition or more intense competition from the financial market affect relationship banking.[32]

I first consider the viewpoint that more competition means less relationship banking. The argument here is that with more competition borrowers might be tempted to switch to other banks or to the financial market. When banks anticipate a shorter lifespan for their relationships, they may respond by reducing their relationship-specific investments. More specifically, anticipated shorter relationships inhibit the reusability of information and thus diminish the value of information.[33] Banks may then find it less worthwhile to acquire costly proprietary information, and relationships will suffer. Shorter or weaker relationships may then become a self-fulfilling prophecy.

A complementary negative effect of competition on relationship banking may come from the impact that competition has on the intertemporal pricing of loans. Increased credit market competition could impose constraints on the ability of borrowers and lenders to share surpluses intertemporally. In particular, it would become more difficult for banks to "subsidize" borrowers in earlier periods in return for a share of the rents in the future. Thus the funding role for banks that Petersen and Rajan see in the case of young corporations may no longer be sustainable

---

32. A second trend is the better dissemination of information. This, by itself, could reduce the value of (previously) proprietary information in the hands of banks and possibly reduce the value of relationship banking.

33. Chan, Greenbaum, and Thakor (1986).

in the face of sufficiently high competition.[34] This indicates that excessive interbank competition ex post may discourage bank lending ex ante.[35]

An alternative view is that competition may elevate the importance of a relationship orientation as a distinct competitive edge. It may mitigate somewhat the negative effect that pure price competition would otherwise have on bank profit margins. Boot and Thakor show that a relationship orientation can alleviate these competitive pressures because a relationship banking orientation can make a bank more *unique* relative to competitors.[36] A more competitive environment may then encourage banks to become more client driven and to customize services, thus focusing more, rather than less, on relationship banking.[37]

The impact of competition on relationship banking is complex; several effects need to be disentangled. What has emerged, though, is that greater interbank competition may very well elevate the value of relationship banking. Pure price competition is an unattractive alternative. However, truly creating an added value in relationship banking may require skills that many banks do not (yet) have. Without those skills, a retreat from relationship banking (including, for example, downsizing of the branch network) might be unavoidable.

Conclusions

The overall picture emerging from this overview of economic theory is that banks play an important role in the process of financial intermedi-

34. Petersen and Rajan (1995).

35. Berlin and Mester (1998) provide a related, albeit different, argument. Their analysis suggests that competition forces banks to pay market rates on deposits, which may complicate the potentially value-enhancing smoothing of lending rates. An extensive empirical literature focuses on the effect of consolidation in the banking sector on small business lending. This consolidation may in part be a response to competitive pressures. The effects on small business lending are, however, not clear-cut.

36. Boot and Thakor (2000).

37. Boot and Thakor (2000) distinguish generic (information-extensive) transaction lending by banks from relationship lending. Transaction lending is most similar to direct funding in the financial market. Boot and Thakor's analysis attaches two dimensions to relationship lending: volume and intensity or quality. That is, banks can choose to offer more relationship loans (at the expense of transaction loans) but also have to decide on the *intensity* of their relationship loans. Intensity points, for example, to sector specialization: How much does a bank invest in specific knowledge of a firm or industry? The more the bank invests, the better it can fine-tune its services to the needs of its relationship borrow-

ation. Banks process information, often proprietary, and will continue to have a distinct role in lending. Securitization of bank loans has some impact, but it will not fundamentally affect the relationship-oriented role of banks. However, obtaining some capabilities in the market for debt capital might become necessary.

Although most of the arguments in this section focus on the role of banks in lending, the applicability of the analysis is broader. Banks facilitate a fine-tuning of intermediation services and capitalize in this way on their relationships. The growing competitive pressures in the industry will more than ever force banks to search for comparative advantages. Offering tailored, relationship-oriented financial services is only possible for those institutions that can capitalize on distinct skills. The optimal scale and scope have not been addressed. I discuss this topic next.

Issues of Scale and Scope in Banking

Scale and scope economies are often cited as one of the main reasons behind the current wave of mergers and acquisitions in banking. But are scale and scope economies truly present? And could they rationalize the current restructuring in the industry? In this section, I first summarize the empirical evidence on scale and scope economies. Existing empirical evidence is quite generic. The existing studies do not differentiate between which activities in combination could offer scope benefits, nor do they focus on which activities generate economies of scale.

After discussing the empirical evidence and the main barriers to realizing scope and scale economies, I identify the main sources of scope and scale economies. I conclude with some observations on the activities that I consider most susceptible to scale and scope economies.

Early Empirical Evidence on Scale and Scope Economies

Scale and scope economies in banking have been studied extensively. A recent survey paper by Berger, Demsetz, and Strahan concludes that, in general, the empirical evidence cannot readily identify substantial

---

ers. Boot and Thakor's main finding is that competition induces banks to make more relationship loans at the expense of (generic) transaction loans. However, the quality (or intensity) of the relationship loans is lower when interbank competition heats up.

economies of scale or scope.[38] Scale economies are not readily found in banks beyond a relatively small size as measured by total assets (that is, beyond $100 million up to $10 billion in total assets). The story on scope economies is even more negative. Diseconomies of scope are quite prevalent. An important caveat is that this research largely involves U.S. studies only. Contrary to banking in many other countries, U.S. banking has historically been quite fragmented.[39] The mergers and acquisitions that were included in most studies took place in an environment where severe constraints existed on the type and geographic dispersion of activities. It is conceivable that these restrictions made it difficult to benefit from scale and scope economies.[40] Moreover, most studies use data from the 1970s and 1980s. Since the structure, technology, and environment of banking have changed dramatically over the last decade, it is not clear whether insights from those studies readily apply today.

In any case, most empirical researchers in the area of industrial organization will acknowledge that scale and scope economies are very difficult to measure. So, at best, very modest conclusions could ever be drawn from these empirical studies. The presence of largely inconclusive results should then not be surprising. Moreover, inefficiencies in managing larger organizations may mitigate possible benefits of scale and scope. This would be in line with the sizable literature on the "diversification discount." Berger offers an illustration by observing that managerial ability to control costs creates a differentiation in bank performance that may well dominate the potential scale economies.[41] The difference between an "average bank" and the "best-practice bank" is about 20 percent (of the costs of the average bank), while cost scale economies in the 1980s were not more then 5 percent but possibly are more today. Berger also argues that managerial ability may have an equally big impact on revenue efficiency.

---

38. Berger, Demsetz, and Strahan (1999). See also Shaffer and David (1991); Cornett and Tehranian (1992); Mester (1992); Clark (1996); and Mitchell and Onvural (1996).

39. This is not really surprising. U.S. banks faced substantial regulatory constraints on their activities concerning both the type of their activities (for example, banks could engage in commercial banking or investment banking, not both) and their location (for example, limits on interstate banking). More recently, however, regulatory constraints have become less binding. This undoubtedly partially explains the surge in mergers and acquisitions.

40. See also Calomiris and Karceski (2000).

41. Berger (2000).

A complication in the empirical studies is also that increasing scale and scope may facilitate market power and thus elevate profitability in the *absence* of scale and scope economies. This effect might be less important in intergeographic market mergers. Moreover, alternative distribution networks (for example, direct banking) and the proliferation of financial markets may have reduced the effective market power of locally concentrated financial institutions and elevated the contestability of markets. This points at a more general issue: the level of concentration may no longer be a good proxy for the (non-) competitiveness of a market.

Another issue is that the level of aggregation in most studies is high and may obscure the benefits of scale and scope. In particular, one should look at what *type* of mergers and acquisitions involve scale and scope benefits. For example, Flannery points at recent research suggesting that mergers with both a geographic and an activity focus are most value enhancing.[42] Similarly, in analyzing scope and scale issues, one should focus on the type of activities. What are the scale economies in each activity? And what mix of products offers true scope economies?[43]

A final concern relates to the effect of mergers on the valuation of financial institutions. A popular methodology is to look at the announcement effect of a merger. A problem with this approach is that mergers may change the structure and dynamics of the industry. If this were the case, the announcement effect could measure all kinds of other effects, including changes in expectations. Some of these and other concerns are summarized in table 1.

Further Evidence on Scope and Scale Economies

Let me first focus on scope economies. In "earlier" work (up to the mid-1990s), scope economies were measured by comparing the costs of a

---

42. Flannery (1999). An important issue is whether this only points at market-power benefits or whether true efficiency gains could be at work as well.

43. It is surprising that this type of research is still hard to find. A lot of research has been done on potential conflicts of interest in universal banking. To some extent, this is activity specific (investment banking versus commercial banking). However, this research is of limited interest for this study because it ignores the question of complementarity between activities. This is not surprising because the literature is motivated solely by the obscure Glass-Steagall regulation in the United States (see Kroszner and Rajan 1994; Puri 1996). See Ramirez (2002) for some evidence on the scope economies in U.S. banking before the Glass-Steagall Act.

Table 1. Some Problems with the Existing Empirical Studies on Scale and Scope Economies

Subject	Issues
Market power analysis: effect on prices and profits	
Static	Is concentration the right measure? What about contestability of markets?
Dynamic (effect of M&A)	The effects of changes in market power and efficiency are difficult to disentangle: (a) profitability ratios are affected by market power, (b) cost ratios via costs of deposits are linked to market power, (c) operational costs are affected by the relative importance of deposits versus purchased funds.
	Event studies are affected by "signaling." That is, the immediate effect of a merger announcement on stock prices incorporates all types of changes in expectations.
Efficiency consequences	
Static	What is the best way to measure scope economies? Data points are lacking for mega-institutions.
Dynamic	There is little differentiation between the type of mergers and the type of activities.

specialized single-product financial institution to a financial institution producing multiple financial services. Ferrier, Grosskopf, Hayes, and Yaisawarng offer a typical study along these lines.[44] They consider possible scope benefits of five closely related bank services—demand deposits, time deposits, real estate loans, installment loans, and commercial loans. Their sample includes 575 banks that participated in the Federal Reserve's functional cost analysis (FCA) program in 1984. Comparing the costs of the more specialized corporations to those of the more diversified corporations, they conclude that less than 3 percent of the banks in the sample showed scope economies, while 79 percent had scope diseconomies. Other contemporary studies come to similar conclusions.[45] Ferrier, Grosskopf, Hayes, and Yaisawarng also show that diseconomies of scope were most likely for the larger banks in the sample.[46]

More recent studies have focused on different efficiency concepts—in particular, profit efficiency. Again the results are inconclusive at best. In

44. Ferrier and others (1993).
45. Berger, Hanweck, and Humphrey (1987); Pulley and Humphrey (1993).
46. Ferrier and others (1993).

a typical study, Berger, Humphrey, and Pulley focus on the joint "consumption" benefits of deposits and loans—in a sense the benefits of one-stop banking.[47] Theoretically, various benefits could be envisioned, such as lower transaction and search costs and lower information costs. However, no profit efficiency enhancement could be discovered. This does not necessarily imply that scope economies do not exist. It is (theoretically) possible for competition between financial institutions to prevent banks from retaining the benefits. That is, the surplus that scope expansion creates might be passed through to the consumers. But in general scope economies are hard to realize. Illustrative in this respect is a study by Saunders in which, of twenty-seven studies, thirteen find diseconomies of scope, six find economies of scope, and eight are neutral.[48]

However, also in these studies "old" data dominate. Recently, DeLong looked at the shareholder gains—that is, the immediate announcement effects—from focused versus diversifying bank mergers in the United States between 1988 and 1995.[49] He found that focused mergers had positive announcement effects both in the level of activity and in geography. Moreover, focus in activities was more important than geographic focus, albeit the latter was important as well.[50] Activity-diversifying mergers had no positive announcement effects. These results point at the presence of scale rather than scope economies.

Although this paper (again) focuses on relatively small U.S. banking institutions (market cap of approximately $2 billion for the acquirer and less than $100 million for the target), recent European evidence on much larger institutions confirms the desirability of geographic focus. Beitel and Schiereck, analyzing mergers between European financial institutions between 1985 and 2000, show that domestic (intrastate) mergers on average have significantly positive combined (bidder plus target) announcement effects, but that these were weaker in the last few years (1998–2000).[51] They also find that diversifying domestic mergers (partic-

47. Berger, Humphrey, and Pulley (1996).
48. Saunders (2000).
49. DeLong (2001).
50. Geographic expansion in the United States often involves buying up neighboring (focused) retail banks, which allows for economies on information technology systems, management processes, and product offerings. Relative to the European scene, where geographic expansion often implies buying up big universal banks across the border, fewer barriers to an effective integration exist. This may explain the more favorable U.S. evidence.
51. Beitel and Schiereck (2001).

ularly between banks and insurers) had on average a positive value impact. In line with this evidence, the Citigroup-Travelers merger resulted in an increase in the stock prices of both merger partners.[52] The latter insight is also confirmed in other European studies on mergers between banks and insurers; for example, Cybo-Ottone and Murgia find a positive effect on combined value.[53] However, the distribution of the value gains is often tilted against bidders. Especially in cross-border bank mergers, bidding banks suffer a severe loss in value (and targets come out extremely well).

The importance of geographic focus may point at problems with managing (and improving) foreign acquisitions but also highlights the market power effect. Domestic consolidation often facilitates market power, and this is present with both scale- and scope-expanding mergers and acquisitions.[54]

These (and related) studies focus on stock market responses to acquisition announcements. While these announcement effects reveal the market's expectation of future cash flow, actual performance may differ from market expectations. As DeLong puts it, "Although the prior conditions to predict successful mergers may exist, their presence may be difficult to discern."[55] This is particularly true for some of the mega-mergers observed today. A lack of data points and potentially radical and unprecedented shifts in the structure of banking give us (and the market) little guidance in interpreting the consequences of these mergers for value. As an example, the reported significant positive announcement effects associated with bank-insurance mergers may be difficult to reconcile with the current market sentiment.

An alternative approach for analyzing scale and scope economies is to focus on structural differences between financial conglomerates and specialized institutions. Several studies look at the relative cost and profit

---

52. Michael Siconolfi, "Big Umbrella: Travelers and Citicorp Agree to Join Forces in $83 Billion Merger," *Wall Street Journal*, April 7, 1998.

53. Cybo-Ottone and Murgia (2000).

54. In an interesting recent paper, Focarelli, Panetta, and Salleo (2002) contrast the motivation for mergers to that of acquisitions. They conclude, based on Italian data, that mergers often have a strategic, revenue-enhancing objective (cross-selling), while acquisitions often aim at improving the credit policy (and thus the loan book quality) of the target.

55. DeLong (2001), p. 250.

efficiency.[56] Vander Vennett examines this in the European context.[57] He finds somewhat higher cost and profit efficiency for conglomerates and universal banks. This may seem surprising in light of earlier comments. However, these efficiency differences cannot be translated readily in scale and scope economies. The banking industry is changing rapidly, and the (traditional) inefficiencies in banking are coming under attack from competitive pressure and technological advances. Differences in efficiency may just reflect differences in the state of adjustment of these institutions, translating into temporarily diverging levels of X-efficiency rather than scale or scope economies.

Problems with Realizing Economies of Scope and Scale

Technological and regulatory frictions affect the potential realization of scope (and scale) economies. For example, a merger between two financial institutions may not readily lead to scale and scope economies because the integration of computer systems may take time. An interesting account on this very issue is the integration of Citicorp and Travelers. A quote from the *New York Times*:

> Citibank and Travelers say their deal is mainly about finding ways to grow rather than cutting costs. But the challenge will be finding common ground between Citicorp's traditional emphasis on advanced technology and Travelers' preference for low-cost, no frills systems.[58]

The same article states that Citicorp has to resolve a backlog of past integration issues before it can even think of making its systems compatible with those of Travelers. These issues point at the potential frictions that severely hamper the realization of scale and scope benefits. For example, ultimately, technological benefits might also include the cross-use of databases from the insurance and banking side. The realization of this scope benefit might have to wait until systems are finally made compatible. The bottom line is that technological frictions may severely hamper the realization of scope (and scale) benefits.

A similar argument can be made with respect to regulatory constraints. If regulations force banking and insurance activities to be oper-

---

56. For example, Berger and Mester (1997).
57. Vander Vennet (2002).
58. "Business Day Section," *New York Times,* April 13, 1998.

Table 2. Possible Barriers to Realizing Economies of Scope and Scale

Barrier	*Examples*
Technological barrier	Incompatible computer systems, conflicting distribution channels
Regulatory barrier	Explicit limitations on activities, regulatory-induced Chinese walls
Managerial barrier	Lack of leadership, cultural differences
Political considerations	"National flagship" attitude

ated separately, potential scope economies may suffer. This problem was most acute in the United States, where up to recently insurance and banking activities could not be combined under one corporate roof. In many other countries, regulations are (were) less stringent but could still have a major impact on the feasibility of realizing scope economies.

In the end, implementation issues are crucial as well. As the earlier reported evidence shows, there are enormous differences between the best-practice and average-practice financial institutions. Managerial ability may play a crucial role.

A final barrier may come from political considerations. Many countries seek to protect their domestic financial institutions and, if needed, help to create "national champions" to preserve domestic ownership and control. Table 2 summarizes the main barriers to realizing scope and scale economies.

Sources of Scope and Scale Economies

Having presented the mixed empirical evidence, I now examine the main sources of scale and scope economies:
—Information technology–related economies,
—Reputation- and marketing- or brand name–related benefits,
—Financial innovation–related economies,
—Benefits of diversification.

INFORMATION TECHNOLOGY–RELATED ECONOMIES. The first source, information technology, is most likely of great importance. Recent developments in information technology facilitate a more efficient and effective use of databases over a range of services and customers. That is, client-specific information may allow for scope economies and facilitate a competitive advantage to financial institutions that can offer a range of services to their clientele. Similarly, the possibilities for reusing information across customers may have increased.

Information technology helps in identifying related client needs. Scope economies therefore apply to all products that could be sold to the same group of clients. Examples for bank-insurance conglomerates include life insurance features in mortgages, asset management or private banking services combined with life insurance, commercial credits in combination with industrial risk insurance, and export financing together with export credit insurance.

This also points at distribution network–related benefits. These benefits may be rooted in information technology developments. In particular, information technology developments may facilitate scale economies in running a sizable distribution network. Simultaneously, scope economies might become much more visible. For example, information technology facilitates an increasing array of financial products and services to be offered through the same distribution network. Customers may attach value to "one-stop shopping," which encourages some financial institutions to offer a broader package of financial services tailored to particular categories of customers.

The developments in information technology also may affect the scope of control; information technology could facilitate the management of a bigger organization. This means that information technology could result in scale and scope economies. The implication is also that sizable investments in information technology are needed to truly benefit from scale and scope economies.

REPUTATION AND BRAND NAME MARKETING. The second source of scale and scope economies is linked to reputation and to brand name and marketing. Scope benefits may be present in the joint marketing of products to customers. Brand image is partially related to marketing but is also linked to the notions of trust, reputation, and confidence. These notions play an important role in the financial services industry. Increasingly, financial service providers are offering services that crucially depend on their reputation. For example, the growing importance of off-balance-sheet claims puts great emphasis on the ability of financial institutions to honor these *contingent* liabilities. But also the success of modern "virtual" distribution channels (the Internet) may depend crucially on reputation. Under certain conditions, increasing scale and scope allow financial institutions to capitalize more on their reputation. That is, a wider scope (or scale) may help a financial institution to put its reputational capital at work.[59]

A concrete example is the Dutch bank-insurance conglomerate ING, which offers direct banking services in, for example, Spain. The name ING is linked in advertisements explicitly to the Nationale Nederlanden brand name, its insurance subsidiary, which is a well-known and respected institution in Spain. This type of branding "externality" is also used by players entering the financial services arena from other industries (for example, supermarkets that leverage their brand name for financial services offerings).[60]

FINANCIAL INNOVATION. The next source of potential scale and scope economies is financial innovation–related economies. Financial innovation as a source of scope and scale economies is a two-edged sword. Some suggest that larger institutions are less likely to innovate due to the inherent bureaucracy. This might be true, but that is a governance issue. Ceteris paribus, larger institutions could better recoup the fixed costs of financial innovations. Innovations could be marketed to a larger customer base or introduced in a wider set of activities. For financial innovations, scale and scope might be particularly important given the rapid imitation by competitors. Only for a short period of time does a true competitive advantage exist. A wider scope and larger scale may help to recoup the fixed costs in this short period of time. Financial innovation–related economies could also be directly related to product and client databases. Wider product and client databases can provide superior information for the design of financial innovations.

Bank-insurance combinations could potentially be successful in leveraging each other's product skills. For example, insurance subsidiaries could benefit from derivative innovations coming from the banking arm. Similarly, securitization skills developed in banking are heavily cross-used, and, more recently, several securitization innovations have been motivated by particular needs in the insurance operation.

DIVERSIFICATION. The fourth potential source of scale and scope economies is the benefit of diversification. Several products might be

59. See Boot, Greenbaum, and Thakor (1993).
60. The ING example also shows the possible sharing of marketing expertise between insurance and banking subsidiaries. Banking subsidiaries have generally benefited from the extensive direct marketing expertise of the insurance arm. In the case of ING, the Postbank (an ING subsidiary) skills in direct banking were also relevant.

close substitutes—for example, pension, life insurance, and saving products. Combining these products and services within one organization mitigates the effects of demand substitution over these products and activities. This *could* be interpreted as a diversification benefit but may also point to cross-selling benefits.

From a corporate finance perspective, diversification is a controversial argument. After all, investors (shareholders) could diversify, and why would a financial institution itself need to do this (unless, of course, there are synergies and thus scope benefits)? However, various frictions may explain the value of diversification. For example, diversification facilitates an internal capital market where businesses that generate cash flow could help to fund other activities that need funding. If raising external funds is costly, this may add value. Nevertheless, this might be a mixed blessing. Often the presence of internal capital markets invites cross-subsidization of marginal or loss-making activities that could wipe out potential benefits. This is also the finding of Berger and Ofek, who see an average diversification discount of 13–15 percent.[61] Having said this, it is true that a low volatility in returns is considered very important in banking. This points to some benefit of diversification.

A link can also be made to the proliferation of off-balance-sheet banking. These activities involve all kinds of guarantees that lead to contingent liabilities. For such activities, the credibility of the bank in being able to honor such guarantees is crucially important. One measure of this is a bank's credit rating. With the proliferation of off-balance-sheet banking, ratings have become more important. If diversification helps in getting a better rating, a stronger argument for diversification can be made.

Further Observations and Conclusions

The various sources that I have discussed point to potential *revenue* (output) and *cost* (input) synergies.

Table 3 summarizes the discussion so far. Most potential sources of economies of scale and scope are related to distribution. The importance of the distribution network is clear and should be considered a primary source of scope and scale benefits.

The possibility for scope economies is generally present. For example,

---

61. Berger and Ofek (1995).

Table 3. Revenue and Cost Synergies

Source and type of synergy	Example
Information technology–related economies	
Revenue	Cross-selling potential
Cost	Fixed cost of information technology; reusability of information (cross-sectional and intertemporal); scale economies in running distribution network
Reputation- and marketing- or brand name–related benefits	
Revenue	Acceptance of new distribution channels (Internet); cross-selling potential
Cost	Fixed cost of marketing, branding
Financial innovation–related benefits	
Revenue	Superior innovations based on broader set of information; better extraction of rents due to bigger network
Cost	Fixed cost of innovation
Benefits of diversification	
Revenue	Avoidance of loss of turnover to substitutes; benefits linked to off-balance-sheet activities
Cost	Internal capital market and subsidies

on the demand side, the proliferation of savings products and their link to pensions, mutual funds, and life insurance clearly push for joint distribution and thereby facilitate economies of scope. However, a word of caution is warranted. Consider, for example, investments in information technology. Developments in information technology might have made it possible to better exploit potential scope economies by offering multiple products to a particular group of customers, using new direct distribution channels with relatively easy access to (formerly) distant customers. However, developments in information technology offer very good possibilities for focused single-product players as well. Also interfaces (may) come up that help to bundle the product offerings of specialized providers, thereby becoming a substitute for an integrated provider. Only very well-managed financial services firms may realize positive scope economies. The execution (X-efficiency) is probably more crucial than ever before, since inefficiencies will be exploited by single-product players. This means that it is very unlikely that (ultimately) a single strategy will dominate in the financial services sector.

The same arguments apply to vertical disintegration of the value chain. Specializing in one segment of the value chain might, for now, be too risky a strategy. Banking is too much in turmoil, and specialization within the value chain may lead to an overly vulnerable dependence on the other players. But ultimately it seems realistic to expect the emergence of, for example, product specialists without a distribution network.[62] This would fit a situation where financial intermediaries become supermarkets that sell products from a variety of suppliers.[63]

The scale economies and benefits coming from focus could be substantial.

In the particular context of bank-insurer mergers, several other comments can be made. An important issue concerns the potential benefits coming from asset management. Some argue that the income stream from asset management is relatively stable and hence a welcome addition to the otherwise erratic revenue stream of financial institutions. There might be some truth in this, but this benefit, at least from a corporate finance perspective, cannot be really big. That is, diversification for purely financial reasons could also be accomplished by investors individually in the financial market. Thus, unless the synergies with other business lines are substantial (and possibly they are), an independent asset management operation is a credible alternative.

Similarly, people argue that bank-insurance combinations have a distinct benefit on the funding side. Diversification may allow for a more effective use of equity capital. Also direct funding synergies may apply. The mismatch between assets and liabilities on the bank's balance sheet (short-term funding, long on the asset side) might be the reverse from that of an insurer (long-term obligations). Again, corporate finance theory is skeptical about the validity of these arguments.

Another argument for combining life insurance and banking is that it could augment the total asset management pool and thus offer scale economies. Although this might be true, more recently banks and insurers have learned that the asset management operation requires distinct skills and is not "automatically" profitable as a passive spin-off from other

62. See also Hamoir and others (2002).
63. On the benefits of vertical (dis)integration in the financial services industry, there is little empirical work. An interesting exception is a recent paper by Berger and others (2002), which looks at profit scope economies in combining life and non-life in the insurance industry. They find that conglomeration (and hence scope) *might* be optimal for larger institutions that are primarily retail or consumer focused and have vertically integrated distribution systems.

(feeding) activities. Thus synergies are present, but not necessarily dominant. This is not say that combining banking and insurance with an appropriate customer focus could not be value enhancing. As stated earlier, combining banking and insurance could offer synergies in distribution. This builds on the discussion of distribution network–related benefits.

However, other factors may undermine the possibility for realizing scope benefits. For example, due to national tax regulations, life insurance needs to be tailored to each specific country. Also other differences exist between countries in terms of (corporate) culture, law, and so forth. These complications make it important to have well-focused operations outside the home market and to abstain from scope-expanding strategies that would complicate the operation even more. In some cases, this also means that one should abstain from broad cross-border acquisitions and only choose to go cross-border where the specific activity at hand requires this.

These observations help to understand the reconfiguration of many European financial institutions. In particular, it becomes increasingly questionable to rationalize a universal banking strategy based on some company-wide synergy argument. Scope economies need to be carefully examined and linked directly to specific market segments across clients, products, and geographic areas of operation.[64]

Scope as a Strategic Advantage

The analysis so far has focused solely on scope and scale economies. This in itself is inadequate for predicting or explaining the positioning of financial institutions. The actual positioning will depend on quite a few other factors as well. In particular, a financial institution that has to position itself today will take the following factors into account:

—What are my core competencies? And what is my current position and financial strength?

—How do I expect the market for financial services to develop? Can I distinguish various scenarios?

—What market structure do I expect in the various scenarios? In particular, what do I expect the competition will do?

64. See also Smith and Walter (1997).

Only at this stage, the potential for scope and scale economies enters:

—What are the scope and scale economies in the delivery of financial services?

This implies that scope and scale economies are just one input, albeit an important one, for the positioning today. It is also worth noting that the decision about scale and scope (involving choices about clients, products, and geographic presence) is not final. For example, the choices being made today could seek to keep options open, anticipating further restructuring once more information becomes available. This is important for interpreting the restructuring that we observe. The current restructuring is motivated by strategic considerations (for example, positioning) and may not give a good indication about what the future structure of the financial services sector will be. Current decisions might be "posturing" vis-à-vis competitors that might be undone in the future. In this section, I develop this strategic rationale for restructuring in the financial services sector.

General Framework

The explanation developed in this section is that strategic uncertainty about future exploitable core competencies may dictate broadening of scope. The basic idea is as follows. Suppose a financial institution knows that—perhaps due to deregulation—it can participate in another market at some time in the future. The problem is that this is a new market, so the financial institution is highly uncertain about whether it has the skills to compete effectively in it.[65] The institution has two choices. It can wait until that future time to find out whether it has the capabilities and "core competencies" (as defined by Hamel and Prahalad) for this new market.[66] Or it can enter the market "early" and discover what its skills are prior to making costly resource allocation decisions. The advantage of the second approach is that it permits the institution to "experiment" with a new business and learn whether it has the skills to compete in that business. This learning permits better decisions when

---

65. These are strategic investments in activities that are "uncertain." What I mean by this is that the investment is in an activity with uncertain profit potential or that the fit between the new activity and the existing activities is uncertain. In both interpretations, the profit potential is "uncertain."

66. Hamel and Prahalad (1990).

competition commences. In particular, having better knowledge about its own skills allows the institution to be more aggressive in its decisions regarding output and to gain market share when it knows that its skills are superior to those of its competitors and to exit the market when its skills are inferior.

One could explain scope expansion as the financial institution reserving the right to play in a variety of "new" activities. By making incremental investments today, the institution puts itself in a privileged position through the acquisition of superior information by learning. This allows it to wait until the environment becomes less uncertain before determining whether to compete in the new market and, if so, how aggressively.[67] In a recent paper, Boot, Milbourn, and Thakor develop a model that formalizes these ideas and incorporates scope as a potential competitive advantage.[68] Their framework is as follows. It starts out with a financial services sector with narrowly defined existing activities and asks whether financial institutions should expand into a "new" activity. A key feature of the analysis is that there is strategic future uncertainty about the demand for this new activity—that is, the activity has prospects only in the long run, and demand may not materialize. The institution must decide whether or not to expand in this activity and, if so, whether to enter early or late. Early entry is costly because the activity becomes important only later. Demand may not materialize, and entering early requires investments to be made prior to the resolution of demand uncertainty. Moreover, the scope expansion associated with investing in strategic options could reduce the competitiveness of existing operations (say, due to dilution of focus). However, early entry offers potential strategic advantages. In particular, early entry could lead to the discovery of skills that would allow for a more efficient delivery of the new activity and hence make the financial institution a more credible competitor once the prospects of this activity become clear.

The question is, When will the benefits of early entry outweigh the costs? The uncertainty about skills plays a key role here. If this uncertainty is substantial, early entry may be beneficial. The other key factor is the competitive environment of the financial services sector and the

---

67. See also Courtney, Kirkland, and Viguerie (1997) for the link between strategy and uncertainty.

68. Boot, Milbourn, and Thakor (2002).

anticipated competition for the new activity. Suppose that the new activity can also be offered by a specialized provider (a "boutique" specializing in this activity). If the financial institution enters (early or late), one could consider the market for this activity as a Cournot duopoly game. Early entry is beneficial because it would then learn its skills in the new activity. This allows the institution to compete more aggressively when it has favorable information about its skills and more cautiously when it has poor information about its skills. The benefits of early entry also depend on the likelihood that a specialized provider will come along. Whether early entry is optimal will thus crucially depend on the competitive environment.

Importance of the Competitive Environment

Also the competitive environment of the existing activities enters the analysis because of the investment and risk associated with early entry in the new activity. If the existing activities face "too much" competition, financial institutions will be unable to absorb the investment and risk that come with early entry in the new activity. An immediate implication is that investments in strategic options and thus the adoption of broader, less focused strategies will be observed in less competitive industries, whereas firms in competitive industries will embrace more focused strategies. This could explain why continental European financial institutions generally follow broad strategies. Their local market power allows them to afford the "widening of scope" strategy and to benefit from its potential future strategic advantages.

Moreover, the anticipated future competitive environment for the new activity matters as well. If the financial institution anticipates facing little or no competition in this activity in the future, early entry—with its accompanying cost and dilution of focus—is unnecessary because a competitively unchallenged institution can operate successfully in this market without the benefit of early entry. At the other extreme, when the anticipated competition for the new activity is very intense (perhaps due to many potential future competitors), early entry is not an attractive proposition and is once again suboptimal. The analysis thus leads to the prediction that moderate anticipated competition in the new activity together with not "too much" competition in the existing activities facilitate early entry. Table 4 summarizes the main insights.

Table 4. Optimal Scope as a Function of the Competitive Environment

Anticipated competitive environment in the strategic option (new activity)	*Current competitive environment in existing financial services activities*[a]	
	Little to moderate competition	*High competition*
Little competition	Narrow	Narrow
Medium competition	Broad	Narrow
High competition	Narrow	Narrow

a. Narrow—no early investment in new activity. Broad—early investment in new activity.

The analysis shows that starting from a situation with strategic uncertainty, the competition the financial institution faces in its current activities together with the competition it anticipates in the future in the new activity lead to predictions about early entry and hence optimal scope. Scope expansion is seen to be optimal when there is high strategic uncertainty, moderate competition expected in the new activity, and low-to-moderate competition in the existing activity.

In this context the benefits of consolidation also could be explored. Now assume that there are multiple competing institutions at the outset. Consider two of these contemplating a merger. The question before them is whether consolidation (merging) today gives them a competitive advantage in undertaking the new activity tomorrow. The answer is affirmative. Merging helps to create "deep pockets" and possibly also reduces the degree of competition, making investments in strategic options more affordable. These effects have little significance in an environment without strategic uncertainty. The analysis thus predicts greater consolidation in industries with more strategic uncertainty.

Is Strategic Uncertainty Special to Financial Services?

Why does this model of strategic uncertainty fit financial institutions so well? There are at least three reasons. First, deregulation in the financial services sector is opening doors to new activities at a rate that is unprecedented since the Great Depression. Second, the swirling tides of technological and regulatory changes are generating a level of uncertainty about the skills needed to operate successfully in the future that is perhaps greater in the financial services sector than in any other industry. Lastly, banks and to some extent insurers have traditionally faced limited competition in their home markets. This has created "deep pockets" across the industry and serves to support the broad strategies observed particularly in banking. The combined validity of these arguments makes the model especially suited for the financial services industry.

The precise interpretation of the model of strategic uncertainty could be amended to fit financial institutions even better. In particular, one could interpret the institution's problem as not knowing what combination of activities will give it a competitive edge in the future. In this interpretation, a financial institution is not contemplating new activities but may be contemplating "old" activities from which it traditionally chose to abstain. Entering early or, better, choosing a wider set of activities would let the institution discover what activities optimally fit together.

Relevance of Strategic Options in the European Context

I now highlight a broader interpretation of the strategic option explanation in the context of the restructuring of the European financial services industry. Industry practitioners believe that a strong position in the home market is crucial for a successful expansion in foreign markets. Generally, this seems to be the case. I give a few examples in the context of banking. Belgian banks generally have weak foreign operations. One reason is that the Belgian political situation (the split between the French- and Dutch-speaking regions) does not allow for strong domestic powerhouses. Swedish and other Scandinavian banks suffered from a financial crisis in the late 1980s and early 1990s, inhibiting their foreign aspirations. Spanish banks started to consolidate "late." However, once consolidation began, multiple mergers rapidly led to two big banks, BBVA and SCH. Their foreign aspirations are largely limited to the South American market but (after running into problems in South America) also involve other Southern European countries. The Dutch, Swiss, and—to a lesser extent—French powerhouses have strong franchises in their home markets, and all have foreign aspirations.[69]

In the interpretation of the Boot, Milbourn, and Thakor analysis, strength in the home markets allows financial institutions to invest in

---

69. The German banks face difficulties in their home market. Across the channel, HSBC and Royal Bank of Scotland have strong positions in their home markets and seek focused international expansion. For a further perspective, see Walter and Smith (2000).

strategic options.[70] An important one is investment banking. While continental European banks traditionally dominated the domestic activity in investment banking, they have had a more marginal role in investment banking in foreign markets and now also face severe competition in their domestic investment bank activity. Many of them feel that a presence in investment banking might be important for their existence as powerful banks in the future. They are willing to accept—for the moment at least—relatively low returns on those activities. The potential, but uncertain, vital role of these activities in the future defines them as a strategic option.

From the point of view of maximizing shareholder value, investing in strategic options might be desirable (if, at least potentially, sufficiently lucrative). However, how can we distinguish the "strategic option" explanation from a simple managerial entrenchment explanation? That is, managers (and governments!) may just want powerful institutions for their own sake. Distinguishing between those explanations is difficult. As the experiences of the (no longer independent) French bank Credit Lyonnais teach us, banks that are not accountable and, even worse, operate as a playground for government-appointed "cronies" are unlikely to follow value-maximizing strategies. Growth then becomes a managerial entrenchment strategy.

Banks themselves are ambivalent too. The struggle of European banks in investment banking is a perfect example: while some see it as a strategic option, others (NatWest—now Royal Bank of Scotland—and Barclays) have retreated. Also the recent partial retreat of ING from investment banking is consistent, as are the problems that Dresdner Bank faces with investment banking under the umbrella of Allianz. Although investment banking might be a valuable strategic option, lack of profitability or deep pockets may dictate a retreat. Obviously, opinions may also differ on the viability and importance of investment banking as a strategic option. Just last year, many analysts argued that the lending capacity of commercial banks could give them a competitive edge in the investment banking market. More recently, particularly considering the large losses on telecommunications-related debt incurred by some of these players, this "synergy" looks much less convincing.

I see similar ambivalence vis-à-vis insurance activities. Some think

---

70. Boot, Milbourn, and Thakor (2002).

that insurance activities are perfectly complementary to commercial banking activities (for example, to economize on the distribution network) and have embraced them (see ING and Credit Suisse-Winterthur); others choose to stay out of them (for example, AEGON). Also players may differ in their assessment of the viability and importance of insurance activities as a strategic option. But here, at least in terms of distribution to targeted customer segments, some agreement exists on the complementarity and synergies between commercial banking and insurance. The strategic consideration might be a different one. For example, AEGON may envision that its "elbow room" in taking part in the ongoing consolidation in the insurance industry would be hampered by linking up to a banking institution now. After the consolidation phase is over, it may actually subscribe to the bank-insurance model. However, it may also believe that having more focus and more choices for alliances and joint ventures is superior.

Nevertheless, I do believe that scale and scope economies are present in banking. Simultaneously, however, I observe that much of the consolidation in the European financial services sector is defensive. Consolidation has increased scale and scope mainly in domestic markets and facilitated local market power. Size has reached proportions that seriously question the presence of any more benefits of scale. And is the wider scope truly sustainable? Will it not cause dilution and loss of focus? If so, it will clearly limit the desirability of investing in strategic options. Instructive in this respect is that the operations of European financial institutions in foreign markets (where they face more competition) are generally well focused.

Summary

Strategic considerations play an important role in the restructuring of the financial services industry. The arguments developed in this section help to give a prescription about where scope and (to some extent) scale become important from a strategic perspective.

What activities are most readily subjected to these considerations? The primary deciding factor is strategic uncertainty, with the degree of competitiveness as a complementary factor. In my view, the development of alternative distribution channels (for example, the Internet) is a primary source of strategic uncertainty. Also the developments in information technology have potentially substantially broadened the feasible scope of control. This has induced uncertainty about the desirable scale and scope of operations. For the moment, bigger and broader seem the safest option.

However, the arguments developed in this chapter are subtler. Also the degree of competitiveness plays an important role. "Deep pockets" are important for the broad-scope strategy. Here the competitive environment comes in. In particular, "too much" competition would dilute the "deep pockets" and prevent or limit scope expansion. Up to recently, however, the relatively protected position of institutions in their home markets has allowed institutions to choose a broad positioning. As markets become more open, both to foreign competitors and intersector entry, this choice will be reconsidered. I believe we have entered that phase. More focus becomes rapidly inevitable.

The Future: Concluding Observations

A potentially important alternative to consolidation is the concept of an alliance. This concept is poorly developed in the context of banking. This is to some extent surprising. Banks did, and still do, engage in correspondent banking, particularly in the context of cross-border payment services. But correspondent banking is losing its importance. In particular, with the advent of information technology, international payment and settlement systems have become available (for example, the emergence of TARGET and settlement systems like Cedel and Euroclear). These developments reduce the need for correspondent banking. More important, correspondent banks may have become competitors in the areas where they were cooperating before. For example, some banks seek to gain a competitive edge by offering proprietary cross-border payment facilities. This indicates an important consideration for the feasibility of correspondent banking or alliances, for that matter. It only works if the interests of the participating institutions are sufficiently aligned.[71] But why may alliances become important?

---

71. Correspondent banks could traditionally not enter each other's markets. Interests were therefore more readily aligned.

The fundamental reason is that vertical disintegration in the value chain will gain in importance.[72] This allows for greater specialization and hence focus, with potential scale economies as well. Alliances could play an important role in this process. They may introduce more durable, yet flexible, cooperative structures, facilitating interactions between the different parties in the value chain. An example is the opening up of a bank's distribution network to products from others. In that way, institutions could exploit their local presence by capitalizing on their distribution network, and simultaneously product specialists may emerge that feed products into these distribution networks.

The applicability of this idea is broader. Financial institutions rooted in strong local relationships may gain access to more "distant" asset management services that are scale intensive and globally, rather than locally, oriented. It may well be possible to offer some of these services in an alliance (that is, "to join forces") and still capitalize on customer-related synergies. Although some will argue that a merger with these institutions would allow for a smoother operation of these services, I take issue with this point of view.

First, for several reasons, cross-border mergers may not (yet) be feasible. A focused alliance would create valuable linkages between institutions with immediate synergy benefits but could also allow the possibly nationally rooted partners to "get to know" each other. In that sense, it would be an intermediate phase. As a second argument, the alliance model based on asset management or specific investment banking activities may, if properly designed, combine the benefits of an integrated universal banking structure and a stand-alone type of organization of those activities. For example, the alliance partners all have a limited exposure to these activities, which helps them to maintain focus. In particular, cultural conflicts and distractions associated with trying to build up (or buy) an investment bank while running a relationship-rooted regional bank are prevented.[73] Obviously, the alliance model does not come without cost. The important task is to define clearly a portfolio of activities that would become part of the alliance. This would not be investment banking in the

---

72. See also Berlin (2001).

73. The experience of some Western banks is that top management gets fully distracted by the investment banking activities and spends disproportionately little time on the often more profitable non–investment banking activities.

broadest sense of the word. Similarly, in the case of asset management, the alliance partners would each maintain their own proprietary access to the customers but would join forces in the asset management operations, including research and back-office activities. This would facilitate the investments in information technology that allow the partners to capitalize on scale economies. Maintaining proprietary access by the individual alliance partners would preserve customer-related scope economies.

The same arguments could be made for bank-insurance combinations. That is, rather than merge, banks could choose to engage in an alliance with an insurer. The alliance model is indeed observed (for example, Credit Suisse–Winterthur before the merger). It is possible to distribute insurance products via a bank's distribution network based on a license agreement.[74] However, at least up to recently, the perception in the market was that the integration of information technology is only ensured with an outright merger. Thus the desired synergy in distribution (and also the complementary feeding of asset management operations) would seem to favor integration.

A key question is whether this will remain so. I tend to believe that joint ventures and alliances will gain importance in the future. It will also help if the level of uncertainty in the industry subsides a little. Vertical disintegration now may create an unpredictable dependence on other parties in the value chain. Developments in information technology actually help to provide smooth transitions between the different parties in the value chain. Economies of scale and benefits from focus could be obtained in this way.

In the end, alliances seem only feasible if the activities that are part of them can be run as a more or less separate (jointly owned) business unit with considerable independence from the "mother institutions." This is, for now, probably most likely for (smaller) regionally specialized financial institutions that may want to join forces in, for example, investment banking and asset management. For bigger institutions, alliances are, for now, less prevalent, but when these institutions (finally) choose to focus, alliances will "mushroom."

---

74. Very recently, ABN AMRO announced that it would put its (limited) insurance operations in a joint venture with Delta Lloyd. It hopes that the alliance will promote a more effective cross-selling of insurance products via its own distribution networks.

Political Considerations and National Identity:
Europe Versus the United States

The more consolidated financial sector observed in Europe gives a clear hint about what can be expected in U.S. banking when regulatory constraints become less binding (as they have become in recent years). But what can be said more fundamentally about the *diverse* European experience? I discuss political considerations in the context of differences between the banking industry in Europe and the United States.

Let me first focus on the arguably superficial common European experience as it may relate to the United States. Europe and the United States share some similar dynamics. In particular, the relaxation of constraints on interstate banking in the United States is reminiscent of the European Union banking directives liberating cross-border banking. However, a fundamental difference between the United States and Europe immediately surfaces. The domestic banks in Europe were—and are—protected as domestic flagships. A fundamental belief that foreigners should not control financial institutions has (so far) almost prevented any cross-border merger.

The political dimension is at the root of this. Even in countries where governments do not interfere directly in banking operations and where banks are considered truly commercial enterprises (and have generally been successful; for example, ABN AMRO and ING in the Netherlands), the political dimension is important. Central banks, ministries of finance, and the banks operate in close concert. This is not surprising: a very homogeneous group of executives is in charge of the financial sector, central bank, and government ministries, guaranteeing a clear national identity of domestic institutions. In countries such as France and Italy that have explicit government involvement, foreign control over domestic institutions is even more unlikely unless banks become so inefficient and weak that involvement of foreigners becomes almost inevitable. To some extent, this is happening. For example, in the bidding war for the French bank CIC, ABN AMRO was favored by some because of its excellent track record vis-à-vis competing French bidders, and the U.K. bank HSBC succeeded recently in buying up Credit Commercial de France.

The primary response to the liberating European Union directives has so far been defensive: domestic mergers are generally encouraged to protect national interests. A case in point is Germany. Many have observed that banking in that country is surprisingly dispersed despite the (traditionally!) powerful images of Deutsche Bank, Commerzbank, and Dresdner Bank (now part of Allianz). Public policy definitely aims at protecting the interests of these powerful institutions, but the consolidation is played out mainly on the *Länder* level (the separate states)—indeed, precisely at the level where the political dimension is at work. This is an important explanation for the regional and *not* national consolidation in German banking.

I conclude that the national flagship dimension has been of primary importance in Europe. Cross-border expansion is rare, and consolidation is primarily observed within national borders. For the United States, this gives little direction. Interstate expansion has been a driving force behind the consolidation in U.S. banking. Politics now seems to interfere little with interstate expansion. The political dimension in the United States seems focused on the demarcations among commercial banking, investment banking, and insurance. Powerful lobbies are successful in mobilizing (local) politicians and in this way have been able to obstruct major banking reform in the U.S. Congress, at least up to the passing of the Gramm-Leach-Bliley Act of 1999.

In other words, in both the United States and Europe vested interests are at work. In Europe national authorities are preserving their national flagships; in the United States powerful lobbies are seeking to preserve traditional demarcations between financial institutions. These observations do not yet answer the question whether national (European) authorities are serving the interests of their constituencies when advocating national flagships. This is a different issue and may have to be looked at in a game-theoretic context. If *other* countries are following these policies, an individual country may be well advised to follow the same policy. However, all would possibly be better off if none would follow a "national flagship policy."

The Future

There are powerful forces behind consolidation. I believe that consolidation is only partially driven by value-maximizing behavior. As I have emphasized, the political dimension cannot be ignored. Consolidation in Europe and the United States will continue. The regional expansion that characterizes much of the U.S. wave of mergers will carry over to Europe. Cross-border acquisitions are coming, particularly with the arrival of the euro and the European Monetary Union (EMU). The euro and EMU are catalysts that will accelerate the integration of national financial markets and induce a more pan-European view on financial services.

Strategic considerations—as highlighted in this study—have created broad powerhouses. But this will change. Competitive pressures will force financial institutions to discover their true competitive advantages and to choose an optimal configuration of services and activities. The new demarcations between the financial institutions may be very different from the past. The process of restructuring will be a fascinating one. The current developments are just an interesting start.

References

Beitel, Patrick, and Dirk Schiereck. 2001. "Value Creation and the Ongoing Consolidation of the European Banking Market." Working Paper 05/01. University of Witten/Herdecke, Institute for Mergers and Acquisitions.

Berger, Allen N. 1998. "The Efficiency Effects of Bank Mergers and Acquisitions: A Preliminary Look at the 1990s Data." In Yakov Amihud and Geoffrey Miller, eds., *Bank Mergers and Acquisitions,* pp. 79–111. Boston: Kluwer Academic.

———. 2000. "Efficiency in Banking: Professional Perspectives." In Anthony Saunders, ed., *Financial Institutions Management,* pp. 300–01. McGraw-Hill.

Berger, Allen N., J. David Cummins, Mary A. Weiss, and Hongmin Zi. 2002. "Conglomeration Versus Strategic Focus: Evidence from the Insurance Industry." *Journal of Financial Intermediation* 9: 322–62.

Berger, Allen N., Rebecca S. Demsetz, and Philip E. Strahan. 1999. "The Consolidation of the Financial Services Industry: Causes, Consequences, and Implications for the Future." *Journal of Banking and Finance* 23 (February): 135–94.

Berger, Allen N., Gerald A. Hanweck, and David B. Humphrey. 1987. "Competitive Viability in Banking: Scale, Scope, and Product-Mix Economies." *Journal of Monetary Economics* 20 (3): 501–20.

Berger, Allen N., David B. Humphrey, and Lawrence B. Pulley. 1996. "Do Consumers Pay for One-Stop Banking? Evidence from an Alternative Revenue Function." *Journal of Banking and Finance* 20 (November): 1601–21.

Berger, Allen N., William C. Hunter, and Stephen G. Timme. 1993. "The Efficiency of Financial Institutions: A Review and Preview of Research Past, Present, and Future." *Journal of Banking and Finance* 17 (April): 221–49.

Berger, Allen, and Loretta Mester. 1997. "Inside the Black Box: What Explains Differences in the Efficiency of Financial Institutions?" *Journal of Banking and Finance* 21 (July): 895–947.

Berger, Philip G., and Eli Ofek. 1995. "Diversification's Effect on Firm Value." *Journal of Financial Economics* 37 (1): 39–65.

Berglof, Erik, and Ernst-Ludwig von Thadden. 1994. "Short-Term vs Long-Term Interests: Capital Structure with Multiple Investors." *Quarterly Journal of Economics* 109 (August): 1055–84.

Berlin, Mitchell. 1996. "For Better and for Worse: Three Lending Relationships." *Business Review, Federal Reserve Bank of Philadelphia* (November-December): 3–12.

———. 2001. "'We Control the Vertical': Three Theories of the Firm." *Business Review, Federal Reserve Bank of Philadelphia* (Q3): 13–22.

Berlin, Mitchell, and Loretta J. Mester. 1992. "Debt Covenants and Renegotiation." *Journal of Financial Intermediation* 2: 94–133.

———. 1998. "Deposits and Relationship Lending." *Review of Financial Studies* 12 (3): 579–608.

Bhattacharya, Sudipto, and Gabriella Chiesa. 1995. "Proprietary Information, Financial Intermediation, and Research Incentives." *Journal of Financial Intermediation* 4 (4): 328–57.

Bolton, Patrick, and David Scharfstein. 1996. "Optimal Debt Structure and the Number of Creditors." *Journal of Political Economy* 104: 1–25.

Boot, Arnoud W. A., Stuart I. Greenbaum, and Anjan V. Thakor. 1993. "Reputation and Discretion in Financial Contracting." *American Economic Review* 83 (5): 1165–83.

Boot, Arnoud W. A., Todd T. Milbourn, and Anjan V. Thakor. 2002. "Evolution of Organizational Scale and Scope: Does It Ever Pay to Get Bigger and Less Focused?" Working paper. University of Amsterdam.

Boot, Arnoud W. A., and Anjan V. Thakor. 2000. "Can Relationship Banking Survive Competition?" *Journal of Finance* 55 (2): 679–713.

Boot, Arnoud W. A., Anjan V. Thakor, and Gregory Udell. 1991. "Credible Commitments, Contract Enforcement Problems, and Banks: Intermediation as Credibility Assurance." *Journal of Banking and Finance* 15 (June): 605–32.

Boyd, John H., and Mark Gertler. 1995. "Are Banks Dead, or Are the Reports Greatly Exaggerated?" NBER Working Paper 5045. Cambridge, Mass.: National Bureau of Economic Research, February.

Calomiris, Charles W., and Jason Karceski. 2000. "Is the Bank Merger Wave of the 90's Efficient? Lessons from Nine Case Studies." In *Mergers and Productivity,* pp. 93–161. NBER Conference Report Series. University of Chicago Press.

Chan, Yuk-Shee, Stuart I. Greenbaum, and Anjan V. Thakor. 1986. "Information Reusability, Competition, and Bank Asset Quality." *Journal of Banking and Finance* 10 (June): 243–53.

Chemmanur, Thomas J., and Paolo Fulghieri. 1994. "Reputation, Renegotiation, and the Choice between Bank Loans and Publicly Traded Debt." *Review of Financial Studies* 7 (3): 475–506.

Clark, Jeffrey A. 1996. "Economic Cost, Scale Efficiency, and Competitive Viability in Banking." *Journal of Money, Credit, and Banking* 28 (3): 342–64.

Comment, Robert, and Gregg A. Jarrell. 1995. "Corporate Focus and Stock Returns." *Journal of Financial Economics* 37 (1): 67–87.

Cornett, Marcia M., and Hassan Tehranian. 1992. "Changes in Corporate Performance Associated with Bank Acquisitions." *Journal of Financial Economics* 31 (2): 211–34.

Courtney, Hugh G., Jane Kirkland, and Patrick Viguerie. 1997. "Strategy under Uncertainty." *Harvard Business Review* (November-December): 67–79.

Cybo-Ottone, Alberto, and Maurizio Murgia. 2000. "Mergers and Shareholder Wealth in European Banking." *Journal of Banking and Finance* 24 (June): 831–59.

Degryse, Hans, and Patrick Van Cayseele. 2000. "Relationship Lending in a Bank-Based System: Evidence from European Small Business Data." *Journal of Financial Intermediation* 9: 90–109.

DeLong, Gayle L. 2001. "Stockholder Gains from Focusing Versus Diversifying Bank Mergers." *Journal of Financial Economics* 59 (2): 221–52.

Dennis, Steven A., and Donald J. Mullineaux. 2000. "Syndicated Loans." *Journal of Financial Intermediation* 9: 404–26.

Dewatripont, Mathuis, and Eric Maskin. 1995. "Credit and Efficiency in Centralized and Decentralized Economies." *Review of Economic Studies* 62 (4): 541–55.

Diamond, Douglas W. 1984. "Financial Intermediation and Delegated Monitoring." *Review of Economic Studies* 51 (3): 393–414.

———. 1993. "Seniority and Maturity of Debt Contracts." *Journal of Financial Economics* 33 (3): 341–68.

Ferrier, Gary, Shawna Grosskopf, Kathy J. Hayes, and Suthathip Yaisawarng. 1993. "Economies of Diversification in the Banking Industry: A Frontier Approach." *Journal of Monetary Economics* 31 (3): 229–49.

Flannery, Mark. 1999. "Comment on Milbourn, Boot, and Thakor." *Journal of Banking and Finance* 23 (February): 215–20.

Focarelli, Dario, Fabio Panetta, and Carmello Salleo. 2002. "Why Do Banks Merge?" *Journal of Money, Credit and Banking* 34 (4): 1047–66.

Gorton, Gary, and James A. Kahn. 1993. "The Design of Bank Loan Contracts, Collateral, and Renegotiation." NBER Working Paper 4273. Cambridge, Mass.: National Bureau of Economic Research.

Gorton, Gary, and George G. Pennacchi. 1995. "Banks and Loan Sales: Marketing Nonmarketable Assets." *Journal of Monetary Economics* 35 (3): 389–411.

Greenbaum, Stuart I., and Anjan V. Thakor. 1995. *Contemporary Financial Intermediation.* Orlando, Fla.: Dryden Press.

Hamel, Gary, and C. K. Prahalad. 1990. "The Core Competence of the Corporation." *Harvard Business Review* (May-June): 79–91.

Hamoir, Olivier, Carl McCamish, Marc Niederkorn, and Christopher Thiersch. 2002. "Europe's Banks: Verging on Merging." *McKinsey Quarterly* 3.

Hellwig, Martin. 1991. "Banking, Financial Intermediation, and Corporate Finance." In Alberto Giovanni and Colin Mayer, eds., *European Financial Integration,* pp. 35–63. Cambridge University Press.

Hoshi, Takeo, Anil K. Kashyap, and David S. Scharfstein. 1993. "The Choice between Public and Private Debt: An Analysis of Post-deregulation Corporate Financing in Japan." NBER Working Paper 4421. Cambridge, Mass.: National Bureau of Economic Research, August.

Houston, Joel, and Chris James. 1995. "Bank Information Monopolies and the Mix of Private and Public Debt Claims." Working Paper. Gainesville: University of Florida.

James, Christopher. 1987. "Some Evidence on the Uniqueness of Bank Loans." *Journal of Financial Economics* 19 (2): 217–35.

John, Kose, and Eli Ofek. 1995. "Asset Sales and Increase in Focus." *Journal of Financial Economics* 37 (1): 105–26.

Kashyap, Anil K., Raghuram Rajan, and Jeremy C. Stein. 1999. "Banks as Liquidity Providers: An Explanation for the Co-existence of Lending and Deposit-Taking." NBER Working Paper 6962. Cambridge, Mass.: National Bureau of Economic Research, February.

Kroszner, Randall S., and Raghuram Rajan. 1994. "Is the Glass-Steagall Act Justified? A Study of the U.S. Experience with Universal Banking before 1933." *American Economic Review* 84 (4): 810–32.

Lummer, Scott L., and John J. McConnell. 1989. "Further Evidence on the Bank Lending Process and the Capital-Market-Response to Bank Loan Agreements." *Journal of Financial Economics* 25 (1): 99–122.

Mayer, Colin P. 1988. "New Issues in Corporate Finance." *European Economic Review* 32 (3): 1167–83.

Mester, Loretta J. 1992. "Traditional and Nontraditional Banking: An Information-Theoretic Approach." *Journal of Banking and Finance* 16 (June): 545–566.

Mitchell, Karlyn, and Nur M. Onvural. 1996. "Economies of Scale and Scope at Large Commercial Banks: Evidence from the Fourier Flexible Functional Form." *Journal of Money, Credit, and Banking* 28 (2): 178–99.

Oliver, Wyman and Company. 2002. "The Future of European Corporate and Institutional Banking." In collaboration with Morgan-Stanley, March.

Ongena, Steven, and David C. Smith. 2000. "What Determines the Number of Bank Relationships? Cross-country Evidence." *Journal of Financial Intermediation* 9 (1): 26–56.

Petersen, Mitchell A. and Raghuram G. Rajan. 1994. "The Benefits of Lending Relationships: Evidence from Small Business Data." *Journal of Finance* 49 (1): 3–37.

———. 1995. "The Effect of Credit Market Competition on Lending Relationships." *Quarterly Journal of Economics* 110 (2): 407–43.

Pulley, Lawrence B., and David B. Humphrey. 1993. "The Role of Fixed Costs and Cost Complementarities in Determining Scope Economies and the Cost of Narrow Bank Proposals." *Journal of Business* 66 (3): 437–62.

Puri, Manju. 1996. "Commercial Banks in Investment Banking: Conflict of Interest or Certification Role?" *Journal of Financial Economics* 40 (3): 373–401.

Rajan, Raghuram G. 1992. "Insiders and Outsiders: The Choice between Informed and Arm's-Length Debt." *Journal of Finance* 47 (4): 1367–400.

Ramírez, Carlos D. 2002. "Did Banks' Security Affiliates Add Value? Evidence from the Commercial Banking Industry during the 1920s." *Journal of Money, Credit, and Banking* 34 (2): 393–411.

Saunders, Anthony. 2000. *Financial Institutions Management: A Modern Perspective,* 3d ed. Burr Ridge, Ill.: Irwin.

Schmeits, A. 2002. "Discretion in Bank Contracts and the Firm's Funding Source Choice between Bank and Financial Market Financing." Working Paper. Washington University.

Shaffer, Sherrill, and Edmund David. 1991. "Economies of Superscale in Commercial Banking." *Applied Economics* 23 (2): 283–93.

Sharpe, Steven A. 1990. "Asymmetric Information, Bank Lending, and Implicit Contracts: A Stylized Model of Customer Relationships." *Journal of Finance* 45 (4): 1069–87.

Simons, Henry C. 1936. "Rules Versus Authorities in Monetary Policy." *Journal of Political Economy* 44 (February): 1–30.

Slovin, Myron B., Marie E. Sushka, and Carl D. Hudson. 1988. "External Monitoring and Its Effect on Seasoned Common Stock Issues." *Journal of Accounting and Economics* 12 (4): 397–417.

Smith, Roy C., and Ingo Walter. 1997. *Global Banking.* New York: Oxford University Press.

Stone, Charles A., and Anne Zissu. 2000. "Securitization: The Transformation of Illiquid Financial Assets into Liquid Capital Market Securities: Examples from the European Market." *Financial Markets, Institutions, and Instruments* 9 (3-4): 133–278.

Vander Vennet, R. 2002. "Cost and Profit Efficiency of Financial Conglomerates and Universal Banks in Europe." *Journal of Money, Credit, and Banking* 34 (1): 254–82.

Walter, Ingo, and Roy C. Smith. 2000. *High Finance in the Euro-Zone.* London: Financial Times and Prentice-Hall.

Benefits and Costs of Integrated Financial Services Provision in Developing Countries

STIJN CLAESSENS

MANY COUNTRIES, ESPECIALLY DEVELOPING countries, have been reforming their financial systems over the past two decades. These reforms have involved the removal of barriers to entry, the reduction of portfolio restrictions and lowering of directed lending requirements, and the general removal of many product limits. An important part of the reform efforts has been the dismantling of regulatory barriers separating banking, insurance, and securities activities. Legal and regulatory boundaries between different financial intermediaries have been rapidly disappearing in many countries, as in the repeal in 1999 of the Glass-Steagall Act in the United States. Integrated financial services provision (IFSP) is becoming the norm around the world, with many countries today having no or very few restrictions on the ability of banks to offer securities, asset management, or insurance services in addition to commercial banking services.

Market forces have in part driven the reduction in barriers between financial services. An important market incentive for banks to widen their scope has been the disintermediation of bank assets and liabilities by capital market transactions. The disintermediation has pressured

I would like to thank Frans van Loon and colleagues for their stimulating discussions and the conference participants for their useful comments. The paper draws on joint work with Daniela Klingebiel.

banks to expand their financial services to cater to a greater set of customer needs and preferences. Technological innovations have been another important driving force, as they have provided financial institutions with a greater ability to deliver multiple financial services and exploit economies of scope. Regulators have responded to these market forces with the removal of restrictions.

While in part a response to market forces, the issue of IFSP has not been without controversy. In the United States, for example, debates about universal banking go back at least to the 1930s. Experiences then showed, in the eyes of many, the weaknesses of a universal banking model. The separation of commercial and investment banking then adopted in the United States through the Glass-Steagall Act spread over time to many other countries, especially developing countries. IFSP has also been debated in emerging markets, partly in light of the financial crises they have experienced in the last decade. Some observers have attributed the crises partly to excessive deregulation, including allowing banks to enter into securities and insurance business.

This paper reviews the current knowledge on the issue of IFSP with special emphasis on developing countries.[1] It defines IFSP as the situation in which a financial institution is able to provide all types of financial services (commercial and investment banking, securities markets, asset management, and insurance services) under one roof. Models of IFSP include universal banking, *bancassurance,* and other models, such as bank holding companies engaged in multiple types of financial services. To position the analysis, and since IFSP is, to a large degree, about the scope of permissible activities of a bank, the first section starts with a short review of why the powers of deposit-taking financial institutions (banks) are being regulated in the first place. The section also reviews recent global trends in financial services provision, especially those affecting changes in the demand for and supply of different types of

---

1. The paper does not review the issues raised by IFSP in terms of financial consolidation, supervision, or the best organizational structure for supervisory agencies (for example, single or multiple supervisory authorities). See Scott (1994, 1995); Taylor and Fleming (1999); the papers by White, by van Lelyveld and Schilder, and by Kuritzkes, Schuermann, and Weiner in this volume for reviews of these issues. Clearly, there are trade-offs, including whether one can economize on supervisory skills and achieve supervisory independence, which are important issues in emerging markets. It does not review the benefits and costs of different internal organizational models for financial institutions (see appendix B for some considerations).

financial services. The second section provides background on the degree to which the current regulatory framework allows IFSP in most developed countries and major emerging markets.

The third section reviews the analytical and empirical evidence on the costs and benefits of IFSP at the level of the financial sector, firms, consumers, and the overall economy. Aspects analyzed include the performance and efficiency of the financial sector itself, the access to and the costs of financial services for firms and households, and the possible reductions or increases in risks for the economy and the financial sector. It reviews available empirical studies on financial institutions, households, and individual countries as well as cross-country studies for developing and developed countries, both before the Glass-Steagall Act in the United States and following recent changes.

The fourth section analyzes the issues of IFSP in developing countries and reviews issues of specific relevance to emerging markets. It reviews the degree to which one observes financial conglomerates in emerging markets and the problems that are more typical in these settings. The final section concludes.

Why Regulate Banks?

Before analyzing the specific regulatory arrangements for IFSP, I review the arguments for banking system regulation in general. After all, and different from nonbank institutions, regulations rather than the market are what define a bank and the type of permissible activities in which a bank can be involved. As further background, this section also reviews recent trends in financial services provision as they affect the desire of banks to enter into securities activities and other types of financial services.

Arguments for Regulation

Arguments for banking system regulation hinge on the special nature of banks, where a bank's illiquidity and its fallout for the stability of the financial sector can cause real sector consequences. Banks have traditionally been considered special because they provide liquidity services to other firms and manage the flow of payments throughout the economy.

Disruptions in the liquidity supply and a breakdown in the payments system can have large spillover effects for the rest of the economy because they reduce real output. Bank failures or losses in capital can lead to contractions in aggregate bank credit, for example, with large social costs to bank borrowers outside the banking system. Banks are also inherently fragile and susceptible to contagious runs owing to the combination of information asymmetries, intertemporal contracting, demandable par value debt, and high leverage.[2] Even small shocks to solvency may lead to costly systemic runs, where depositors overreact to information and force the closure of even solvent institutions. The importance of banks for the smooth functioning of an economy and the vulnerability of their own financial structures have led government to treat banks as "special."

It has also been argued that banks are special because only banks can provide some essential forms of credit to corporations, especially forms of short-term liquidity. Kashyap, Rajan, and Stein argue that banks can provide short-term liquidity more cheaply than other institutions because they combine committed lending (such as lines of credit) with deposit-taking services.[3] Thus banks are more cost-efficient in providing liquidity because deposits act like loan commitments, since deposits can be withdrawn at any time. As a result, banks need a buffer stock of liquid assets to support their provision of demand deposits, just as they need a buffer stock to support their loan commitments. Since banks offer lending and deposit-taking services together, they can economize on the quantity of cash and safe securities they hold, thereby maintaining a smaller buffer than would be required by two financial intermediaries offering these services separately. These savings allow banks to provide liquidity to their customers at a lower cost than other financial institutions. Diamond and Rajan argue further that the somewhat fragile capital structure of banks, which subjects them to runs, disciplines them to monitor corporations properly.[4]

While these characteristics have been recognized for some time, many countries did not treat banks as special from a government regulation point of view until the twentieth century. In most countries, banks were private, unregulated entities. Historically, clearinghouses and other pri-

---

2. Diamond and Dybvig (1983).
3. Kashyap, Rajan, and Stein (1999).
4. Diamond and Rajan (1998).

vate monitors emerged to limit the risk-taking of financial institutions and spillovers from one financial institution to others and the real economy. Private sector solutions thus arose to deal with many of these concerns. In the last century or so, however, and especially following the Great Depression, governments have take a greater role in overseeing banks, including by providing a safety net for times of liquidity problems. These measures introduced problems of their own, in particular excessive risk-taking unchecked by depositors. Prudential regulation and supervision to prevent moral hazard and to limit bank opportunities to take more risk have therefore accompanied governments' provision of a safety net. An important element of the regulatory framework put in place has been restrictions on the type of activities banks are able to undertake. The degree of success in limiting moral hazard and the degree of risk taking arising from a public safety net have varied greatly among countries. Many financial crises, especially in emerging markets, are arguably due to the poor oversight and intervention of regulators in environments with too generous safety nets.

Recent Changes in Financial Services Industries

The nature of financial services provision has been changing rapidly in the last decade, and this is affecting the desire and need of financial institutions, especially banks, to widen their scope of activities and, in turn, the costs and benefits of financial sector regulation. An important global trend in financial services industries has been the increased substitutability between various types of financial instruments. Many financial instruments are now available to households and corporations that provide similar kinds of services. Bank deposits, for example, compete in many countries with other liabilities of financial intermediaries, such as money market funds, in the provision of savings and liquidity services and often also payment services. Many insurance products have features similar to savings products. This has implied that the demarcation between different types of financial intermediaries and financial services has become increasingly blurred from both the consumer's and the producer's point of view. The demand for and supply of various financial services have been altering as well. Consumers, households, and corporations are increasingly becoming more sophisticated and asking for a full package of financial services, preferably from a single provider. And, partly due to technological progress, producers are realizing that they can use existing client relationships more profitably by offering a wider package of financial services.

These changes are affecting the economic costs of regulatory barriers between different financial products and different types of financial institutions. As these barriers have become less effective, but still impose costs on individual financial institutions, their economic cost has risen. At the same time, the changes in the financial services industries and advances in technology have also been eroding the special nature of banks. The emergence of many substitutes for bank deposit and loan products and the fact that the proprietary information that the banks have on their borrowers is now cheaper and more widely available are altering the role of banks in providing liquidity and credit services. To the extent that banks as deposit-taking and lending institutions have become less important to financial intermediation, there may be less of a need for a public safety net and associated prudential regulation, including those regulations that limit the provision of multiple types of financial products. In spite of these developments, few countries have moved to reduce the scope of their public safety nets.

The Scope of Permissible Activities in Various Countries

This section provides background on the degree to which financial institutions in various countries across the world are permitted to provide various types of financial services and analyzes recent trends in IFSP.

While the special character of banks, insurance companies, and other financial institutions may be changing, financial institutions, especially banks and insurance companies, are still heavily regulated everywhere. The regulation of banks and insurance companies takes the form of capital adequacy or equivalent requirements and other prudential regulations, such as maximum exposure limits. The scope of permissible activities of banks, insurance companies, and other financial institutions is another important aspect of regulation. Most often, regulation rather than competition determines the range of products and services a financial institution can offer, the types of assets and liabilities it can hold and issue, and the legal structure of its organization. Two models at opposite ends of the permissible scope of financial services provision can be distinguished: (a) a separate financial system, where banks are not allowed to engage in any type of securities or other noncredit financial service activity and, vice versa, insurance and securities companies are not allowed to engage in banking activities, and (b) a completely integrated system, where a financial institution can provide all types of financial services, either directly or indirectly through subsidiaries.[5]

Financial services come in many forms, although if one unbundles the services, most, if not all, key elements are very similar.[6] Nevertheless, the rules governing the provision of financial services apply to their formal forms and not their functions. With the variety in financial products, it is difficult to capture for each country the rules in a simple form, but financial services can be classified into three broad classes: banking services (credit, deposit, payments, and so forth), securities-related services (underwriting, market making, brokerage, asset management, and so forth), and insurance services.[7] Based on data on fifty-four industrial and emerging countries surveyed by the Institute of International Bankers in 2002, it becomes clear that allowing banks to provide securities services is the norm around the world (see appendix A). Out of the fifty-four countries, only China has a "pure" separate banking system—in the sense that banks are not allowed to engage in any type of securities or insurance activities.

The majority (thirty-six) of countries surveyed, including all European Union (EU) countries, allow banks to conduct both banking and securities business, including underwriting, dealing, and brokering all kinds of securities, within the same banking organization, without any restrictions.[8] In seventeen countries, financial institutions are allowed to engage—to varying degrees—in securities activities, either through a

5. This is often called "universal banking." On the one hand, universal banking is typically thought of as including only commercial and investment banking and not insurance. On the other hand, other aspects often associated with universal banking, such as the possible ownership of nonfinancial institutions, do not relate to financial services provision. The benefits and costs of ownership of nonfinancial institutions by financial institutions (the so-called "bank and commerce" links) and associated effects, including so-called crony capitalism, are not discussed here. Instead, I continue to use the term IFSP to refer to a wide scope of financial services provision within a single institution.

6. Bodie and Merton (2000) analyze the functions that financial institutions and markets provide rather than the specific products.

7. A fourth class distinguished by the Institute of International Bankers is real estate services. Since real estate services are more than financial services, I mention them only in passing.

8. This classification uses the legal restriction as the measure. If banks are allowed to conduct securities activities in the bank itself but typically conduct securities activities in a

bank parent (thirteen) or a bank holding company structure (four). In terms of insurance services, fewer countries allow banks to provide full insurance services (either as principal or agent): only six out of the fifty-four have no restrictions whatsoever. Many countries, however, allow banks to provide insurance services through subsidiaries (twenty-six) or through affiliates (eight). Only fourteen out of the fifty-four countries do not allow banks to engage in insurance activities.[9] These data thus show that most countries allow full or close to full IFSP.

Barth, Caprio, and Levine offer a broader, although slightly less recent, survey than that of the Institute of International Bankers.[10] They document for 107 countries the regulatory restrictions in place in 1999 (or around that time) on the ability of commercial banks to engage in securities and insurance services (as well as real estate activities). Table 1 provides their overview (tables B-1 and B-2 reproduce the average for the whole sample by regional and income groups, as reported in Barth, Caprio, and Levine; appendix B also provides more detail on the definitions they used).[11] It shows that about three-quarters (eighty-four) of the 107 countries surveyed either have no restrictions whatsoever on banks providing securities services (forty-three) or permit banks to do so either through a bank parent or a bank holding company structure (forty-one). Another seventeen countries allow less than a full range of securities activities to be conducted in a bank, and only six countries prohibit the provision of securities services by banks. In case of insurance services,

---

subsidiary, then securities activities are still considered to be unrestricted. The classification also does not consider as a restriction the need to obtain approval from the regulator to conduct securities activities.

9. The classification of insurance activities is even more complex than that of securities-related activities, as regulations sometimes distinguish between the selling of insurance as an agent, as a broker, or as a principal. Furthermore, regulation may vary by type of insurance product. No attempt is made to weigh the importance of the restrictions. Any rules except those requiring general permission or imposed for prudential reasons are considered to restrict a bank's insurance activities. Alternative criteria could thus only lead to more countries with no or few limitations. As a memo item, slightly less than half of the countries (twenty-one) permit banks to provide real estate services (such as real estate investment, development, and management); some twenty-seven countries limit banks to holding only their own premises or otherwise impose limits, whereas six countries allow real estate activities mainly through subsidiaries. See appendix A.

10. Barth, Caprio, and Levine (2001b).

11. Barth, Caprio, and Levine (2001b). For completeness, the table also reports the restrictions on real estate and ownership of nonbank financial institutions by banks.

Table 1. Restrictions on the Activities of Financial Institutions

Number of countries

Degree of restrictions	Type of activity			Bank ownership of nonfinancial firms
	Securities	*Insurance*	*Real estate*	
Unrestricted	43	8	16	14
Permitted	41	47	19	38
Restricted	17	18	32	48
Prohibited	6	34	40	7
Total	107	107	107	107

Source: Barth, Caprio, and Levine (2001b).

the rules are generally less liberal, as was the case for the Institute of International Bankers sample of fifty-four countries. Only about half (fifty-five) of the 107 countries either have no restrictions whatsoever on banks providing insurance services (eight) or permit them to do so with some restrictions (forty-seven). About one-third (thirty-four) of the countries prohibit the provision of insurance services.[12]

Having no or few restrictions on securities activities is thus more the norm than perhaps expected. The perception of a general prevalence of restrictions on banks' activities may have arisen in part because the United States used to have quite restrictive regulations on the types of securities businesses that could be undertaken by commercial banks—mainly only through a bank holding company structure—and even then subject to some limits.[13] Combined with the fact that the majority of academic studies have focused on the United States, this may have led to the perception of widespread restrictions around the globe. In practice, however, U.S. financial institutions have been engaged in some degree of IFSP using various exemptions for some time. And since the Gramm-Leach-Bliley Act of 1999, financial services providers in the United States are formally free to provide banking, securities, and insurance services under one roof.[14]

12. As a memo item, most countries are still more restrictive on real estate activities, with only one-third of 107 countries (thirty-five) having no restrictions whatsoever or permitting real estate activities only within some limits.

13. Under Section 20 of the U.S. Bank Holding Company Act, revenues that commercial banks derive from their securities subsidiary (underwriting and dealing activities) used to be restricted to less than 25 percent of their overall profits. Moreover, commercial banks were not allowed to hold an equity stake in nonfinancial firms (except for trading purposes). The 1999 Gramm-Leach-Bliley Act changed this dramatically.

14. See, among others, the papers in McCoy (2002) for more detail.

The Conceptual and Empirical Case for and against IFSP

The majority of countries thus allow complete or nearly complete IFSP, or at least the combination of commercial and investment banking, and clearly the recent trend is toward greater freedom in allowing financial institutions to choose their preferred set of activities. This does not mean that financial conglomerates will become the dominant model for most financial institutions or most markets. What structure individual financial institutions choose if the permissible scope is wide—specialized, universal banks, *bancassurance,* use of alliances—will still vary and be determined by market forces. These strategic choices are not analyzed here.[15] IFSP nevertheless remains a debated topic, especially, but not only, in emerging markets. This is in part because there are many aspects to consider with different scopes of financial services provision. These aspects include the efficiency of financial services provision, access to financial services, financial sector stability, and issues of concentration of economic and political power. Theory offers some advantages and disadvantages on some of these aspects, while the empirical evidence has not always been conclusive, in large part because data are limited. I review the arguments and the available empirical evidence to date.[16] I focus on the benefits and costs of integrated banking—that is, the combination of commercial and investment banking—as that has been studied most, but I also make reference to the undertaking of insurance activities by banks. I conclude with the findings of a number of recent, comprehensive studies that include many emerging markets.

Benefits of a Wide Scope of Financial Services Provision

Full IFSP offers three benefits: it increases profits through economies of scope, it reduces the variability of profits, and it allows for the use of informational advantages.

ECONOMIES OF SCOPE. Economies of scope may arise from both the production and consumption of financial services.[17] A larger-scale production of elements common to these various financial services can lead

---

15. See Boot (in this volume).
16. For other recent reviews, see Santos (1998b) and the paper by Walter (in this volume).
17. Saunders and Walter (1994).

to cost advantages through economies of scale. Several specific cost advantages have been identified: gains through concentration of risk management, administrative functions, and integrated product development; marketing economies in the common delivery of different services; better access to information and sharing of information across different product groups; the sharing of reputational and pecuniary capital across different products and services; and enhanced potential for risk management through diversification gains. On the consumption side, economies of scope may derive from the potential for lower search, information, monitoring, and transactions costs; the negotiation of better deals because of increased leverage; and lower prices for products in a more competitive environment.

There is little empirical evidence of scope economies, possibly because financial institutions cannot or do not choose their optimal institutional structure, but also because the measurement of banks' diverse set of output products and related inputs is complicated.[18] The bulk of studies for U.S. banks conclude that economies of scope in banking, if at all present, are exhausted at very low levels of output.[19] These studies may have limited relevance, however, as U.S. banks were only allowed to offer limited investment banking services and these activities had to be located in a separate subsidiary of the bank holding company.

Empirical studies on European banks, which may be more relevant as European countries generally allow more integrated banking, have been inconclusive. Lang and Welzel report the absence of scope economies in

18. There is more evidence on economies of scale. Most empirical studies find that the bulk of scale economies are captured, but not fully exhausted, by the time a bank has $2 billion to $10 billion in assets. Early studies for U.S. banks found that economies of scale were exhausted for relatively small sizes (see Clark 1988 for a review). Later studies find evidence of scale economies up to the $2 billion to $10 billion in assets (Noulas, Ray, and Miller 1990; Hunter, Timme, and Yang 1990). Other empirical evidence for U.S. banks suggests that economies of scale may start to decline for asset sizes between $10 billion to $25 billion (Berger, Hunter, and Timme 1993). More recent evidence suggests, however, higher economies of scale for banks. This may reflect the increased importance of information technology for banks. The few tests that have been conducted for other countries largely confirm these results. In a study based on data from countries other than the United States, Saunders and Walter (1994) and Vander Vennet (1994) find economies of scale in individual loans of up to $25 million. Lang and Welzel (1995) find scale economies among German universal banks up to a size of $5 billion. Evidence for emerging countries is very limited (see Laeven 2002).

19. Berger, Hanweck, and Humphrey (1987); Berger, Hunter, and Timme (1993).

German universal banks but find such economies in small cooperative banks.[20] Vander Vennet finds that European universal banks are characterized by significantly higher levels of revenue efficiency relative to specialized banks and are also more profit efficient, suggesting some gains from integrated banking.[21] He also finds superior monitoring capabilities on the part of universal banks.

These studies refer mainly to the combination of deposit-taking banking with securities and capital market activities. The more recent approach is to combine banking—that is, to combine commercial and investment banking—with insurance and asset management. Especially the combination of banking with insurance (known as *bancassurance*) is an important change and offers, in principle, large economies of scope, in terms of sales channels, product development, risk management, marketing, and so forth. The empirical evidence on the existence of economies of scope between banking and insurance services is very limited, however. One of the few studies is by Carow, who analyzes the Citicorp–Travelers Group merger that improved the prospects for new legislation removing the barriers between banking and insurance.[22] He finds that the merger resulted in a positive wealth effect for institutions most likely to gain from deregulation. Life insurance companies and large banks (other than Citicorp and Travelers Group) had significant increases in their stock price, while the returns of small banks, health insurers, and property and casualty insurers were insignificantly different from zero. His study provides evidence that investors expected large banks and insurance companies to receive significant benefits from legislation removing barriers to *bancassurance* in the United States.

INCREASED DIVERSIFICATION AND LOWER RISK. A bank engaged in IFSP may be more stable than a specialized financial institution because of diversification benefits. These benefits can arise from two sources. First, due to diversification, the total profits of an integrated financial institution will be more stable than those of a financial institution specialized in a single product. There is some evidence of these diversification benefits. Kwan and Laderman argue that since the profits from providing different financial services are not highly correlated, there are diversifi-

20. Lang and Welzel (1995).
21. Vander Vennet (2002).
22. Carow (2002).

cation benefits from allowing broader powers.[23] Eisenbeis and Wall find a negative correlation between U.S. bank earnings and securities broker-dealer earnings over the 1970 to 1980s period.[24] Although the securities subsidiaries of U.S. banking organizations tend to be more volatile (higher standard deviation of profits) than their banking affiliates, securities subsidiaries provide diversification benefits to the bank holding company.[25]

The effect on risks of allowing banks to enter into insurance industries has been less analyzed. Studying the period before the removal of entry barriers in the United States, Allen and Jagtiani find that "synthetic universal banks comprised of portfolios of banks, securities firms, and insurance companies have significant positive excess returns, with lower market and interest rate risk exposures and higher expected returns than securities firms."[26] This confirms the risk diversification benefits from IFSP, which Allen and Jagtiani attribute to the lower exposure to interest rate risk of a conglomerate that includes insurance activities. Anecdotal evidence regarding the actual financial performance of financial conglomerates, mostly from outside the United States, also suggests that the integration of banking and insurance lowers the variability of income streams.

Second, disintermediation—when firms bypass banks and raise money directly from public markets or where they obtain other types of financial products from nonbanks, including from insurance companies—will affect an integrated financial institution less because the decline in lending business can be offset by an increase in underwriting and placing business and in other noninterest (fee) business. This, in turn, may reduce a financial institution's incentives to engage in riskier lending to maintain profits when faced with disintermediation. This effect is difficult to show at the individual bank level, but there is some

---

23. Kwan and Laderman (1999).

24. Eisenbeis and Wall (1984). See further Brewer, Fortier, and Pavel (1989); Benston (1990).

25. Kwan (1997); see also Klein and Saidenberg (1998). Others, however, find, for the period before the repeal of the Glass-Steagall Act, that hypothetical mergers of U.S. banking and securities firms would not always have reduced risks. Santomero and Chung (1992), for example, find that mergers between bank holding companies and regional securities firms would reduce overall risk, but that mergers with large firms would raise the risk of failure for the new organization.

26. Allen and Jagtiani (1996, abstract).

support at the sectoral level that financial systems with fewer restrictions are more stable.[27]

Third, there may be important dynamic and broader economic impacts of IFSP on financial sector stability and efficiency, especially in emerging and developing countries more dependent on foreign capital. To achieve an efficient utilization of external capital flows and, equally important, to avoid becoming dependent on a possibly volatile flow of external capital, the importance of sequencing reforms and ensuring that the domestic financial system is sufficiently developed before giving full freedom to external capital flows is increasingly recognized. More generally, a well-balanced financial system can reduce volatility and improve resource allocation.[28] Such a domestic financial system will include not only strong banks backed up by adequate regulation and supervision but also well-developed contractual savings—insurance companies, pension funds, and various other forms of funded security systems. A wider scope of financial activities may help to develop these nonbank elements because incentives to do so are better balanced and scarce skills are used more efficiently. Again, this effect is difficult to show, but there is some empirical support that financial systems with fewer restrictions are more diversified.[29]

INFORMATIONAL ADVANTAGES. In establishing a relationship with a firm, a financial institution incurs costs in gathering information about the firm and its investment opportunity before making lending or investment decisions. The longer the expected duration of the financial institution–firm relationship, the more willing the financial institution will be to invest in gathering firm-specific information, which, in turn, can increase the financing available to the firm for valuable investment projects. Integrated financial institutions can offer a broader set of financial products than specialized financial institutions, which allows for lower information and monitoring costs. Information derived, for example, from managing a basic bank account can be used in the supply of other financial services. And when the bank also sells insurance products to a corporation or consumer, it may gain information useful for its lending activities. An integrated bank can also design financing contracts better suited to

27. Barth, Caprio, and Levine (2001a), further reviewed below.
28. Easterly, Islam, and Stiglitz (2000); World Bank (2001).
29. Barth, Caprio, and Levine (2001a).

the borrower. Finally, as a firm switches from obtaining bank financing to raising money on the capital markets and demands a wider set of financial services, it can remain a customer if the bank provides lending, securities underwriting, and insurance services.

Empirical research confirms that the close bank-firm relationship associated with integrated banking can be a source of important benefits to firms in terms of cost and availability of funding.[30] For instance, expanded banking powers during the period before Glass-Steagall in the United States are associated with a lower cost of capital and less stringent cash-flow constraints.[31] Essentially, informational advantages associated with integrated banking can turn advantages for banks into advantages for customers, who get better and cheaper services. These gains are not always obtained, however. Findings for German firms during the 1903–13 period, the formative years of universal banking, for example, suggest that relationship banking did not consistently lessen the sensitivity of a firm's liquidity.[32]

The degree to which these informational advantages can be realized and passed on to the customer depends in part on the degree of informational asymmetries: in economies where information is generally poor, close bank-firm relationships could, in principle, be very useful.[33] At the same time, a situation with weak information may mean that a close bank-firm relationship leads to poor resource allocation due to the weak monitoring of banks themselves. The balance between these two effects will, among others, depend on the degree of competition in the financial sector and the quality of banking regulation and supervision. In low competitive environments with weaker information, banks are more likely to use their market power and retain the gains rather than pass them on.

30. Berger and Udell (1996); Petersen and Rajan (1994); Vander Vennet (2002).
31. Berger and Udell (1996); De Long (1991); Ramírez (1995, 2002).
32. Fohlin (1998).
33. Rajan and Zingales (1999). The question of scope of financial services is then also related to the costs and benefits of bank-based versus capital market–based systems, which in turn may have implications for firms' access and cost of capital and economic growth. For an overview of this literature, see Stulz (2001). For a discussion of the links between the scope of banks' powers and the orientation of a country's financial system, see Allen and Gale (2000). In practice, the distinction between a bank and a market-based financial system offers little guidance, however, on the functioning of a financial system (Beck and others 2001; Beck and Levine 2002).

Potential Risks Associated with IFSP

IFSP can come with risks.[34] These include, most importantly, conflicts of interest. In addition, increased financial risks and greater difficulty in monitoring integrated financial institutions are often mentioned. Finally, IFSP can also affect competition and concentration of economic power in a country.

CONFLICTS OF INTEREST. As a start, it is important to acknowledge that conflicts of interest are plentiful even in specialized financial institutions— that is, when financial institutions are only allowed to offer certain types of financial services. For investment banks, for example, conflicts between research and underwriting activities have received much attention lately. As such, it is important to evaluate how much larger the scope for conflicts of interest is under a wider scope of activities. It is also important to realize that the presence of potential conflicts of interest among commercial banking, investment banking, and insurance activities will depend on the development of securities and insurance markets relative to traditional banking business. In many developing countries, at least until recently, securities markets and insurance markets were not that active. As a consequence, even when IFSP was allowed, the scope of conflicts was limited. Most important, markets and regulators have dealt with conflicts of interest issues within the same line of business or across businesses through reputation, voluntary codes and private standards, self-regulation, and, to some extent, government regulation and supervision.

The possibilities for conflicts of interest nevertheless increase, in principle, when financial institutions are allowed to offer a wider array of products and have a broad set of customers—as in IFSP. In the case of commercial banks' undertaking of investment banking activities, for example, conflicts of interest can arise in the bank's advisory role to potential investors, as when the bank may promote the securities of firms it is lending to even when better investments are available in the market. It can also arise because, in its role as a trust fund manager, the bank may be tempted to "dump" the unsold part of the securities it underwrites into the trust accounts it manages for bank depositors. Or a bank may encourage its insurance part to buy at inflated prices certain securities it is underwriting.

Conflicts are often identified as one of the major potential costs of

---

34. John, John, and Saunders (1994).

permitting commercial banks to conduct securities business.[35] Typically, a bank is better informed than the public investor is about a firm's soundness and prospects when it also lends to that firm. This informational advantage may, however, be a double-edged sword. On the positive side, an integrated bank might be better positioned than a specialized investment bank to certify credibly the value of a security offered by the firm. On the negative side, an integrated bank might have a greater incentive and greater ability to take advantage of uninformed investors (for example, sell low-quality securities without revealing risks it knows from its lending relationship in an attempt to safeguard its lending portfolio or simultaneously raise its lending rates to the same borrower). Similar issues can arise in the context of banking and insurance activities being provided by one single financial institution, although the literature typically has focused on the conflicts between commercial and investment bank activities.

As in general regarding any potential conflicts, the critical issue is not whether they exist, but rather whether the incentives and opportunities to exploit them exist. Market forces in general, such as competition from other financial institutions, will reduce the incentives to exploit conflicts, as will potential damage to reputation and the monitoring by creditors and "nonmarket" monitors, such as rating agencies. When these conditions prevail, conflicts of interest have not been found to be misused in a systematic way. Earlier empirical studies of the German universal banking system have not found evidence of systematic abuse of conflicts of interest.[36] Also Gorton and Schmid find that in 1974 German banks improved the performance of German firms in which they held equity.[37] They find no evidence of conflicts of interest in the use of proxy votes by German banks at that time.

More recent studies of the German universal banking system confirm these findings. Using ownership data and analysts' forecasts of earnings per share on German companies from 1994 to 1999, Lehar and Randl test for both informational advantages and possible misuse of conflicts of interest.[38] They find evidence that banks have superior knowledge on firms where they own equity stakes, but also some evidence for conflicts

---

35. Saunders (1985); Kelly (1985); Benston (1990).
36. Bueschgen (1970); Monopolkommission (1976/77).
37. Gorton and Schmid (2000).
38. Lehar and Randl (2001).

of interest. An interesting finding is that conflicts of interest are less pronounced for large equity holdings, suggesting that client pressure more than the bank's self-interest is the important driving force of overoptimistic forecasts with respect to equity valuation. As such, the conflicts do not seem to arise from the fact that German banks are universal banks—that is, they are underwriters while holding lending and sometimes equity stakes in corporations—but from their role as underwriters and analysts.

In the pre-Glass-Steagall period in the United States, it has generally also been found that broad or universal banks did not systematically abuse their powers.[39] Securities underwritten by commercial banks' affiliates, for example, had higher prices (lower yields) than comparable securities underwritten by investment banks.[40] Other evidence for the pre-Glass-Steagall period suggests to the contrary that greater banking powers involved gains for corporations. The presence of bank directors on corporate boards, for example, helped these firms to relieve their financing constraints.[41] More recent evidence on the involvement of U.S. banks in corporate governance is given in Kroszner and Strahan.[42] They report that U.S. firms are more likely to borrow from their connected banks—that is, banks that are indirectly involved in the firms' corporate governance through board linkages—but that they do so on terms similar to those of unconnected firms.

More recent evidence on the role of U.S. banks in the simultaneous lending and securities activities, although it happened in an environment with restrictions, does not question these findings. Gande, Puri, Saunders, and Walter examine the pricing of debt securities underwritten by subsidiaries of U.S. commercial bank holding companies relative to those underwritten by investment houses.[43] They find no evidence of conflicts of interest in situations like when the purpose of the bank underwriting is to repay existing bank debt. Rather, they find evidence that banks that underwrite debt securities of firms to which they also lend provide a net certification effect. They also find that banks bring a relatively larger proportion of smaller issues to the market than investment houses do, suggesting that bank underwriting is, on net, beneficial to smaller firms.

39. Ang and Richardson (1994); Kroszner and Rajan (1994).
40. Puri (1996).
41. Ramírez (1995).
42. Kroszner and Strahan (2001).
43. Gande and others (1997, 1999).

For Israeli initial public offerings (IPOs) in the 1990s, Ber, Yafeh, and Yosha find similar evidence in the case of equity underwritings.[44] Universal banks in Israel use their superior information regarding client firms to float the stock of the cherries, not the lemons, as the accounting performance after the issue is higher than average. This suggests no conflicts of interest.

Conflicts of interest of relevance to the issue of integrated banking refer only to those arising from the potential provision of banking, securities, and insurance-related services by one financial institution. As noted, conflicts of interest can also arise among similar types of services, not just between banking and securities activities. Investment banks, for example, may face a conflict between their research and underwriting activities or between their brokerage and underwriting activities. Some of the conflicts of interest that arise when commercial banks are active in the securities business thus already exist in the normal banking business, and vice versa. The conflicts within the securities business have received considerable attention recently, especially in the United States. These conflicts are not the subject of this paper. It is worth noting, however, that conflicts of interest are more important when the financial institution acts as an agent and less important when it acts on its own account. When a financial institution acts only as a broker or as an underwriter, it has, besides its reputation and any legal liability, no direct financial exposure if the security is not properly priced or if the offering contains misleading information about the firm's prospects. When the financial institution is also acting as a bank itself, however, it will remain exposed through its lending operations even if it sells all securities of the firm and the pricing is not right. As such, conflicts between banking and securities activities may be less than conflicts among securities market activities that only involve agent functions, such as underwriting.

This is not to say that there have been no cases of misuse of information that banks have collected in their lending activities for their investment banking activities. In the case of Israel, Ber, Yafeh, and Yosha find, for example, that bank-managed funds pay too much for bank-underwritten IPOs at the expense of the investors in the funds.[45] More generally, there can be conflicts of interest in the combination of bank lending, underwrit-

---

44. Ber, Yafeh, and Yosha (2001).
45. Ber, Yafeh, and Yosha (2001).

ing, and fund management. In the United States, there have been some recent suits against commercial banks not protecting the interests of firm' shareholders when underwriting new securities (for example, in the case of Enron). Although some of the cases are still in judicial process, it does not appear that there has been a systematic abuse of conflicts between commercial and investment banking activities.

Nevertheless, conflicts of interest can be misused. The ability to exploit conflicts will often be dealt with by private standards adopted voluntarily by financial institutions—such as information-sharing rules between departments of an integrated bank—or promulgated by self-regulatory associations—such as rules on the behavior of certified financial analysts. Increasingly, many financial institutions have been tightening their internal procedures in these areas in response to market forces. In general, conflicts tend to be more important in countries where disclosure rules are weak, where information on banks' activities is limited, and where competition is limited and supervision is weak. In these circumstances, conflicts can be further restricted by legal constraints—such as disclosure requirements to be met in the issuance and distribution of securities or the separation of some activities in subsidiaries. Since, at the same time, IFSP can offer more gains in informationally weaker countries, the preferred best balance between self-regulation and government restrictions cannot easily be identified and will vary by institutional characteristics of the country.

SAFETY AND SOUNDNESS AND THE SAFETY NET. While the combination of insurance, securities, and commercial banking activities can increase the possibilities of risk diversification, it also increases the scope for bank managers to increase and shift risks, thereby raising the probability of bank failure.[46] While this has happened—in emerging markets as well as in developed countries (for example, Barings)—empirical evidence does not confirm as a general proposition that broad or universal banks fail more frequently than specialized banks.[47] As noted, there is actual evidence that the combination of financial activities reduces overall risks for individual financial institutions.[48]

---

46. Saunders (1994); Boyd, Chang, and Smith (1998).

47. White (1986).

48. To my knowledge, there are no major cases where risks have been transferred from insurance or pension fund businesses to banks; as such, it seems the risk may arise mainly from securities activities.

Nevertheless, as "banks" evolve into large financial conglomerates, combining deposit-taking functions with insurance, investment banking, asset and pension fund management, and other financial intermediation functions, safeguards can be (more) necessary to avoid the transfer of explicit and implicit deposit insurance subsidies from the banking part of the institution to the securities and other parts.[49] These safeguards can take the form of market value accounting, timely monitoring and disclosure, more risk-sensitive capital requirements, firewalls between different types of operations, risk-based pricing of deposit insurance, and prompt corrective actions, including the closure of insolvent banks. In many ways, these safeguards are similar to those being applied to normal banking operations, but they may need to be stricter and more closely enforced.

MONITORING AND SUPERVISION. Supervision of commercial banks, insurance companies, and securities entities involves different objectives. Supervision of commercial banks aims to protect the net worth of the entity and thus the rights of creditors, particularly depositors, as the bank is intermediating third-party money. The objective of supervision of insurance companies is similar to that of banks—that is, to protect the net worth of the entity. For securities firms, regulators' objective is mainly consumer protection—that is, to avoid misuses arising from the agent-type relationships typical in securities markets. The combination of insurance, securities, and commercial banking activities can make supervision by regulators and monitoring by the market more difficult as the insurance and securities businesses might have an impact on the banking business while the two activities cannot be easily monitored separately.

More generally, recent developments may have made it more difficult for supervisors to monitor financial services providers.[50] In this respect,

---

49. Kane (1996); Schwartz (1992).

50. Another reason to review the safeguards is the disappearing line between financial services and information services and other nonbank institutions involved in "near"-financial services. In many countries, information service providers, such as credit card companies, provide near-banking services. Also portals engaged in price comparisons provide near-financial services. Combined with the entry of nonfinancial service providers, the lines between financial and nonfinancial institutions are blurring quickly. In some countries, nonbanks are offering forms of payment services through multiple-purpose stored-value cards. Also the links between banking and commerce may be intensifying through direct investments, strategic alliances, and other forms of cooperation. Nonbank financial institutions, not just banks, have the potential to be sources of systemic risk. These devel-

IFSP can lead to more risks, particularly when supervisory agencies do not coordinate closely. At the same time, when IFSP leads to closer cooperation among regulators, including possibly the merger of supervisory activities in one single supervisory authority, gains may arise from combining financial services activities.[51]

Unrestricted financial activities may also lead to the formation of large and complex entities that are extraordinarily difficult to monitor.[52] Recent studies on the effects of consolidation among large financial conglomerates have analyzed this risk, among others.[53] The conclusions are that the potential effects of consolidation on the risk of individual institutions are mixed, the net result is impossible to generalize, and thus a case-by-case assessment is required. However, the report does find that consolidation increases the probability that a workout or wind-down of an impaired large and complex banking organization will be difficult and perhaps disorderly. This difficult workout need not be a concern in itself from a public policy perspective, except that it may lead to too much access to the safety net. Also, ever-larger institutions may become so politically and economically powerful that they become "too big to discipline" or "too big to disappear." As such, there are risks of (large) financial conglomerates.[54]

---

opments may result in a de facto extension of the public safety net to various forms of nonfinancial institutions in times of financial distress and create spillovers from nonfinancial corporations to the financial sector. This risk of an extension of the safety net may be especially important in emerging markets because there has been a tendency to define the safety net too widely in these countries. At the same time, a solution of regulating and supervising nonbank institutions is surely not feasible, implying that the solution has to lie in reducing the scope of and access to the safety net. See Claessens, Klingebiel, and Glaessner (2002).

51. See Claessens and Klingebiel (2001).

52. Indeed, the former head of the International Monetary Fund, Michel Camdessus, remarked in 1997 that we are witnessing "the development of new types of financial instruments, and the organization of banks into financial conglomerates, whose scope is often hard to grasp and whose operations may be impossible for outside observers—even bank supervisors—to monitor" (cited by Barth, Caprio, and Levine 2001a).

53. Group of Ten (2001).

54. Wilmarth (2002, abstract), for example, argues that the "major financial holding companies (in the U.S.) are largely insulated from market discipline and regulatory oversight, and they have perverse effects to take excessive risks at the expenses of the federal 'safety net' for financial institutions." While this may be a very strong view, it shows that there exist concerns of too large financial conglomerates even in countries like the United States, where there is little history of ex post bailouts of financial firms.

COMPETITION, INNOVATION, AND ECONOMIC CONCENTRATION. An IFSP-based financial system may lead to greater market concentration, in part as it raises the optimal scale of financial institutions and as it allows for greater linkages among financial and nonfinancial institutions. Moving to IFSP thus has the potential to reduce competition. As such, theoretical arguments can be made for why large financial conglomerates may reduce competition and hence the efficiency in the financial sector. There can also be dynamic effects of (lack of) separation on competition. One argument used to justify the separation of commercial from investment banking in the United States has been that it fosters competition and leads to more innovation within business lines. The separation creates a need among investment banks to develop more specialized services, whereas universal banks may be under less pressure to do so as they have more secure profits. Boot and Thakor, who analyze the relationship between financial innovation and scope, argue that specialized systems may foster more innovation.[55]

At the same time, there is little logic from a business perspective to separate the provision of financial services among different categories. Separation may stifle innovation in how to provide financial services in an integrated manner through more efficient marketing and production, which would lead to economic gains through reduced cost and greater efficiency. The combination of different financial services in one organization may also be very useful in countries undertaking financial reform, particularly with respect to insurance and pension or, more broadly, social security systems. The combination can transpose know-how from banking to insurance and investment management to find appropriate solutions for pension and social security problems. For countries building up new systems, allowing existing banks to expand into insurance and pension activities may also be a quicker way to build up these segments of financial services industries. Since, in general, government intervention in the form of forced separation of business activities is not assumed to lead to greater innovation, it is reasonable to argue that IFSP leads to as much innovation in the overall production and marketing of financial services as does separation.

Available empirical evidence on the effects of IFSP on competition has been limited largely to studying universal banking, and the evidence

---

55. Boot and Thakor (1997).

is mixed. A study of the German universal banking system in the period before World War I in comparison with its American and British counterparts finds that the combination of commercial and investment banking services did not influence the banking industry's level of concentration, level of market power, or financial performance.[56] In terms of concentration, the German banking system was very similar to the United Kingdom's specialized commercial banking sector, and neither system was extremely concentrated, suggesting that universality does not necessarily or uniquely propagate concentration. On average, the analysis finds that German universal banks behaved no less competitively than their American counterparts in the provision of loan services, and little evidence of deviation from competitive pricing is found in either country. International differences in bank returns on equity and on assets, although large in individual years, were only slight over extended periods. At the same time, universality was not associated with superior profitability, whether due to efficiency gains (economies of scope) or monopoly power. As such, universal banking was at worst neutral to competition and perhaps beneficial.

One of the few studies on the effects of greater scope of activities on competition in insurance services is Carow.[57] He finds that rulings by the U.S. Office of the Comptroller of the Currency and the Supreme Court removing barriers to entry by banks into the insurance industry reduced the market value of the insurance industry, while it did not change the value of banks. This suggests that the entry of banks increased competition in the insurance industry and made the industry more contestable. Empirical studies on the effects of an integrated or a separated financial system on innovation are rare, although casual observations suggest that a separate system can be more innovative in the design of specific financial products and an integrated system can be more innovative in the overall production and marketing of financial services.

A concern related to competition has been the concentration of economic power that may come along with financial institutions having a wide scope of activities, including the ownership of nonfinancial institutions. This has been a highly charged political economy issue, and some countries care more about "excessive" concentration than others. This

56. Fohlin (2000).
57. Carow (2001).

issue probably relates more to the concentration of economic power in general, including that of nonfinancial institutions through financial institutions, the degree of competition, as well as the difficulty of supervising large financial institutions, than to the particular model of financial services provision adopted.

In practice, the alleged concentration and abuse of power were nevertheless the most important aspects motivating the separation of banking activities in the United States during the 1930s. Recent studies reviewing this period suggest, however, that there was not much abuse and that the securities activities of commercial banks bore little responsibility for the banking problems of the Great Depression.[58] Some other studies have argued that the nature of universal banking can help overall economic development. Motivated by the experiences with nineteenth-century continental European industrialization, particularly in Belgium, Germany, and Italy, Da Rin and Hellman develop a model where banks can catalyze industrialization by acting as coordinators.[59] This requires them to be sufficiently large to be able to mobilize a critical mass of financial resources and to possess sufficient market power to make profits from coordination. Being a universal bank can help in both respects, as it increases the optimal scale of operations, allows banks to reap profits from possible equity issuance, and makes coordination generally easier. They argue that the lack of industrialization in Russia in the late 1800s, Spain, and Italy before the 1890s is consistent with this theory in the sense that the necessary conditions were not satisfied in these countries. In the case of Russia, the banking system was not very concentrated, and the state kept limiting the growth of new banks. In the case of Spain, banks were curtailed in their investment in manufacturing firms, whereas in Italy there were too many small banks.

Cross-Country Empirical Studies

Most studies referred to so far relate to micro, financial institution–specific analyses, testing specific hypotheses and mostly conducted for one or a relatively small set of countries that are most often at similar levels of development (for example, a sample of European countries or a

---

58. Kroszner and Rajan (1994, 1997); Benston (1994).
59. Da Rin and Hellman (2000).

comparison of Germany, Japan, and the United States). As such, they cannot analyze the role of country circumstances in determining the benefits and costs of different arrangements. Typically, they do not analyze the effects of different arrangements on overall financial sector development and the nonfinancial sector. As such, they do not provide a more general analysis of the costs and benefits for a broad sample of countries.

An important cross-country study addressing this deficiency is by Barth, Caprio, and Levine, who analyze empirically, among others, the costs and benefits of different allowable scopes of activities for over ninety countries.[60] For each of these countries, they document the regulatory restrictions in place in 1999 (or around that time) on the ability of commercial banks to engage in securities, insurance, and real estate activities. They then study the relationship of banking powers with the following measures: (1) the level of banking sector development, (2) net interest margins, (3) overhead costs, (4) nonperforming loans, and (5) the occurrence of a banking crisis. They find that restricting commercial bank activities is negatively associated with bank performance, measures 1 through 4, as compared to allowing banks to diversify into other financial activities, especially securities market activities. They also find that countries with greater regulatory restrictions on the securities activities of commercial banks have a substantially higher probability of suffering a major banking crisis. Their study thus suggests that lack of regulatory barriers—that is, more IFSP—can lead to financial sector stability.

These results provide a comprehensive, positive assessment of broad banking powers in terms of financial sector development, efficiency, and stability. Arguably, a generally stronger regulatory and supervisory framework in a country may justify less need for the countervailing positive effects of restricting banking sector activities. A positive relationship between regulatory restrictions and financial crises could thus be due to the fact that countries with weaker supervisory systems compensate by imposing more restrictions on bank activities. But the empirical results suggest that this is not the case, as the analysis controls for official supervisory procedures, capital regulations, regulations on competition, and the moral hazard engendered by generous deposit insurance schemes. Specifically, Barth, Caprio, and Levine "find no improvements in bank performance or stability from restrictions on bank activities in economies

---

60. Barth, Caprio, and Levine (2001a).

that offer more generous deposit insurance, have weak official supervision, ineffective incentives for private monitoring or that lack stringent capital standards."[61] Furthermore, their findings are not due to reverse causality or potential simultaneity, as when greater financial sector development or more financial stability leads countries to adopt more liberal rules.

Demirgüç-Kunt, Laeven, and Levine, who study the effect of bank concentration on the performance of individual banks, confirm the results of Barth, Caprio, and Levine on the benefits of placing fewer restrictions on banking activities for financial sector efficiency.[62] Using bank-level data for seventy-seven countries (some 1,500 banks), they find, among others, that fewer regulatory restrictions are associated with lower net interest margins. Although not a perfect measure of bank efficiency, the result nevertheless suggests that banks can produce financial services at lower costs when they are able to exploit their economies of scope more fully.

Cross-country evidence also supports the benefits of fewer restrictions for firm access. One study is by Beck, Demirgüç-Kunt, and Maksimovic.[63] Using data on the financing patterns of relatively small firms in forty-eight countries, they find that more restrictions on the scope of commercial banking activities increase the negative impact of a concentrated banking system on the financing constraints of small firms. In another study on patterns of firm financing, Beck, Demirgüç-Kunt, and Maksimovic find that in countries that restrict bank activities less, firms are more likely to issue equity.[64] To the extent that increased use of equity lowers firms' leverage and involves a wider pool of investors, broader bank powers can help to reduce firm and financial sector riskiness and, more generally, improve the allocation of resources through improved monitoring.

These cross-country results suggest that any policy of restricting bank powers does not produce positive results in particular institutional or policy environments—that is, it is not the case that restrictions compensate for some institutional weaknesses or market failures. Rather, Barth,

---

61. Barth, Caprio, and Levine (2001a, pp. 33–34).
62. Barth, Caprio, and Levine (2001a); Demirgüç-Kunt, Laeven, and Levine (2002).
63. Beck, Demirgüç-Kunt, and Maksimovic (2002a).
64. Beck, Demirgüç-Kunt, and Maksimovic (2002b).

Caprio, and Levine find that more restrictive regimes often arise due to political economy factors.[65] In their words, governments may regulate to support political constituencies, not to correct for institutional weaknesses or market failures. They find empirically that government integrity is lower (corruption is higher) in countries that restrict banks' activities more as well as where the government more generally plays a larger role in the financial sector. As such, political economy rather than economic reasons most likely cause developing countries to restrict more.

In terms of the effects of banking concentration that may arise from allowing IFSP, Cetorelli and Gambera show in a cross-country study that banking sector concentration promotes the growth of industries that depend heavily on external finance.[66] They also find, however, that it exerts a depressing effect on overall economic growth. Demirgüç-Kunt, Laeven, and Levine find that bank concentration has a negative and significant effect on the efficiency of the banking system, except in rich countries with developed financial systems and significant economic freedom.[67] Since empirically there is a negative relationship between restrictions on banking activities and banking concentration (that is, those countries that restrict less tend to have more concentrated banking systems), there might be a trade-off from allowing a wider scope of bank activities between financial stability and access, on the one hand, and growth and efficiency, on the other.

In summary, the cross-country studies find either that there is little relationship between regulatory restrictions on banking powers and overall financial development and industrial competition or that restrictions hinder banking system performance and access to financial services by firms. Cross-country studies are quite clear in identifying that restrictions increase the risk of a financial crisis. As such, the studies suggest that placing no restrictions on bank activities may be the best policy. Studies suggest some benefits of some degree of banking system concentration, but also some negative impact on bank efficiency and growth. Since fewer restrictions on bank activities can lead to more concentration, it is important to balance relaxing restrictions with lowering barriers to entry.

---

65. Barth, Caprio, and Levine (2001a).
66. Cetorelli and Gambera (2001).
67. Demirgüç-Kunt, Laeven, and Levine (2002).

The Corporate Structure of Banking Organizations

The discussion so far has not considered the organizational model permitted for universal banking. Whether the potential benefits can be realized by financial institutions and the degree to which any costs may arise, however, depend on the organizational model permitted for integrated banking. The organizational structure may matter as well for financial development and performance and bank stability. Appendix C provides some considerations for the organizational models often used.

Financial Conglomerates in Emerging Markets

The presence of financial conglomerates in emerging markets needs to be evaluated relative to the supply of various types of financial services being offered in these markets. In particular, the relative importance of banks and securities markets will affect the benefits and costs of IFSP. Furthermore, the allowable scope of financial services provision will influence the actual presence of financial conglomerates.

The Role of Banks and Securities Markets

While many of the global trends toward integrated financial services provision have also affected emerging markets, these economies still differ in many ways from the developed countries, resembling more the situation of currently developed countries a century ago. For one, the relative importance of banking, securities, and insurance markets in emerging markets still differs from that in more developed countries. As is often noted, most comprehensively in Demirgüç-Kunt and Levine, banks tend to be more important in developing countries.[68] On average, the size of the banking system in low-income countries is double that of stock markets (figure 1). There are exceptions, such as Malaysia, where both banking and securities markets are quite large, at least prior to the 1997 crisis, but in general banks tend to dominate financial intermediation in developing countries, with securities markets and insurance markets much smaller and less active.

---

68. Demirgüç-Kunt and Levine (2001).

Figure 1. Financial Structure in Low-, Middle-, and High-Income Economies, 1990[a]

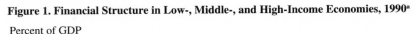

Percent of GDP

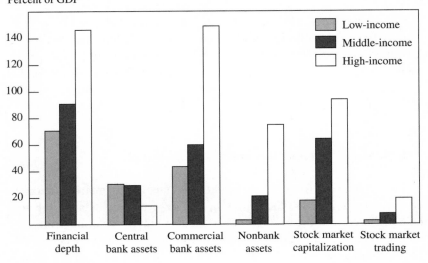

Source: Levine (1997).
a. The data are for twelve low-income countries, twenty-two middle-income countries, and fourteen high-income countries. Financial depth is measured by currency held outside financial institutions plus demand deposits and interest-bearing liabilities of banks and nonbank financial institutions (M3 money supply). Nonbank assets include insurance companies, pension funds, mutual funds, brokerage houses, and investment banks.

This relative importance reflects a commonality in the process of financial development. Low-income countries are characterized by reliance on informal finance, with lending for small investments secured through a network of social relationships and peer-group monitoring, often linked to trading and agriculture and mainly involving advances for trade from one firm to another. Foreign banks may play a large role in financing foreign trade, but a smaller role in domestic trade. As the economy develops and urbanizes, some of these networks may formalize themselves into lending associations or banks. This process of more formal financial intermediation is often accelerated when there are major new developments in the economy, for example, the opening up of new trading opportunities or new industrial discoveries, such as occurred during the industrial revolution in Europe, that generate concentrated wealth. During most of this process, however, banks dominate financial intermediation.

As countries develop, financial intermediation deepens, and banks grow relative to central banks in allocating credit. Next, nonbanks rise in importance, and insurance and pension services are introduced. Capital markets only come to play a role in the later stages of development, when legal systems and reputational capital are established and people have the trust to trade pieces of paper that represent promises to pay. While progression from one stage to another can be hastened, it is not clear that actual stages can be skipped. For example, countries have seldom—if ever—been able to develop their equity markets without having reasonably developed short-term money markets, because if the infrastructure for trading relatively low-risk instruments is lacking, riskier products, such as long-term bonds and equity, are generally absent.[69] And even among the most developed countries, capital markets are still not the most important source of financing for the corporate sector, with banks being more important in continental Europe and Japan, for example.

The Role of Financial Conglomerates

The general development process and the differences in the relative importance of bank and nonbank services—the larger role of banking services and the smaller role of insurance, pensions, and securities markets—suggest that the issue of IFSP is of less relevance for emerging markets than for developed ones. It also suggests that there are fewer reasons for having financial conglomerates in emerging markets. Yet, when defined broadly, given countries' level of general and financial sector development, "financial conglomerates" are actually quite common in emerging markets, the more so when taking into account the restrictions typically imposed on bank activities. This relatively common presence is to some extent through the direct provision of different types of financial services by a single financial institution, in spite of greater formal restrictions. More often, though, "financial conglomerates" exist indirectly through common ownership of different types of financial institutions by a single nonfinancial entity or group of individuals ("family"). Also, much of firm financing in emerging markets comes from other firms and financial institutions within the same business group—that is, groups act as (financial) conglomerates, affecting the costs and benefits of IFSP provided by financial institutions external to the group. I discuss each aspect in turn.

---

69. Although many, including international financial institutions, have actively promoted the development of stock markets, success has been limited in most emerging markets (see Claessens, Klingebiel, and Schmukler 2002).

THE ALLOWABLE SCOPE IN EMERGING MARKETS AND DIRECT IFSP. There is a clear tendency for the restrictiveness of the regime for banking activities to decline as one moves from lower-income to higher-income countries, with regimes on average less liberal in developing countries. The average restrictiveness index for securities market activities reported by Barth, Caprio, and Levine is 2.04 for developing countries compared to 1.37 for developed countries; and for insurance activities, the index is 2.90 for developing countries compared to 2.22 for developed countries.[70]

While the direct provision of multiple services in one financial institution has more formal limits in lower-income countries, the combination of commercial and investment banks is nevertheless quite common in many emerging markets. In most transition economies, except China, the universal banking model has been adopted, allowing securities market activities to be conducted directly in the bank. The average indicator of restrictiveness for securities activities for the less-developed Europe and Central Asia region (mainly transition economies) does not differ much from that for the OECD (Organization for Economic Cooperation and Development) countries. Similarly, the Middle East and North Africa region is equally as restrictive as the OECD countries are on average. The South Asia and Latin America regions are somewhat more restrictive than OECD countries are, as is Sub-Saharan Africa. The most restrictive is the East Asia and the Pacific region, with an average restrictiveness index of 2.41 (see table B-2).

Although there are somewhat more restrictions, especially in Asia and low-income countries in Africa, financial conglomerates nevertheless dominate in most emerging markets. In countries like Brazil, Mexico, Poland, and South Africa large financial conglomerates represent the bulk of the financial services industries. Banks in many Latin American countries are the most important managers and distributors of mutual funds, own large pension funds, and are becoming more involved in insurance activities. In some countries, the importance of financial con-

---

70. Barth, Caprio, and Levine (2001b). For real estate activities, the averages are 3.19 for developing countries and 2.04 for developed countries. The difference between the sample of fifty-four countries surveyed by Institute of International Bankers (2002) and the larger sample (107 countries) surveyed by Barth, Caprio, and Levine (2001b) is that the latter includes more low-income countries. The fact that the Barth, Caprio, and Levine sample shows on average more restrictions is thus another indicator that developing countries tend to have more restrictions on activities.

glomerates has been long-standing; in others, it has come about more recently. In Brazil, the links among banking, insurance, and asset management have been in place for many years, with important financial conglomerates such as Banco do Brasil, Bradesco, and Banco Itau. In other Latin American countries, the advent of financial conglomerates has been helped by the growth in (mandatory) pension funds over the past few years. In Eastern Europe, the low quality of information and the need for banks' involvement in enterprise restructuring initially made universal banking more attractive. As most countries in the region have also adopted mandatory pension systems and as the demand for nonbank services has been rising, East European banks have been widening their product offerings, including pension and insurance services. In Asia, banks have been the least active in IFSP, although in more recent years they have been widening their scope as well, in part in response to the more liberal rules, including the permission to form holding companies in Korea and the freeing of restrictions in Malaysia.

Given the small role of securities markets, nevertheless, nonbank services are still not the largest source of income for these financial conglomerates. Fee income is much less important in developing countries than in developed countries. Part of the small role of fee income relates to the more restrictive rules: the relationship between non-fee income (as a share of bank assets) and the severity of activity restrictions is then also negative (a correlation of −0.290, as reported by Demirgüç-Kunt, Laeven, and Levine).[71] Nevertheless, as a group, nontraditional banking activities are increasing as a source of income; fees accounted for 1.18 percent of banking system assets in 1999 in developing countries, up from 1 percent over the whole 1995–99 period. Still, this is much below their share in higher-income countries, and overall there are probably relatively fewer formal financial conglomerates in developing countries, especially in low-income countries, than in developed countries.[72]

INDIRECT IFSP. If I define a financial conglomerate in terms of common ownership of financial institutions, however, financial conglomerates are more important in emerging markets. As a start, it is important to

---

71. Demirgüç-Kunt, Laeven, and Levine (2002).

72. No formal statistics are available on the share of financial conglomerates even for developed countries, in part as it has been hard to come up with a common definition of a financial conglomerate.

realize that the structure of ownership of financial and nonfinancial institutions in emerging markets is quite different from that typically found in developed countries, at least different from that in the United States. A single individual or family closely controls many financial and nonfinancial corporations around the world.[73] This is through both direct and indirect ownership, including cross-ownership, pyramiding structures, dual-class voting shares, and other mechanisms separating control from ownership. Many commercial banks in emerging markets started as a family-owned business and remained closely controlled even after they have grown. Important for the analysis of financial conglomerates, in emerging markets these owners often control not only commercial banks but also other types of financial institutions. The few wealthy families controlling the commercial banks in Thailand, for example, also control some finance companies and investment banks.

As such, common control opens possibilities for some joint provision of different types of financial services by the combined entities in a group. For example, a bank borrower that accesses capital markets for the first time may receive services from an indirectly affiliated investment bank. There are substantial transaction costs and limits to these forms of IFSP, however, such as the reduced ability to share information across financial institutions. This may explain at the micro level why cross-country studies find that restrictions add to the cost of providing financial services. It may also further reduce transparency and risks to the financial system as a whole. As such, these joint ownership structures are not attractive. Nevertheless, they do constitute a form of IFSP, which may reduce the demand for formal financial conglomerates.

THE ROLE OF GROUPS. A third aspect to consider is that in general the links among financial institutions and between financial and nonfinancial corporations are much greater in emerging markets. Most of this happens through business groups with common direct and indirect ownership and, most important, common control. As documented in various studies, business groups are very common in developing countries.[74] About 60 percent of large, publicly listed firms in East Asia, for example, belong to a group. Many of these groups not only are industrial conglomerates but also have a financial institution in the group structure.

---

73. La Porta and others (1998); Claessens, Djankov, and Lang (2000).
74. Khanna and Yafeh (2001); Lins and Servaes (2002); Claessens, Djankov, Fan, and Lang (2002).

The role of the financial institution is, however, different from that found in many developed countries (except for the United States). In most developed countries when present in a group, the financial institution is most often the apex institution through which the nonfinancial corporations are controlled. In continental Europe, the financial institution is typically a bank, whereas in Japan it is typically an insurance company. In emerging markets, however, the financial institution in a group typically functions not as a vehicle to exercise control, but rather as the group bank, facilitating resource sharing. The distinguishing character of a group more generally is that the affiliated nonfinancial and financial corporations share resources to a greater extent. For the nonfinancial corporations, the resource sharing happens through intracompany loans and investments and more generally through intragroup transactions at terms more favorable than third-party transactions. As such, the commonality of group structures may mean that, for companies within the group, there is in effect IFSP, which may affect the demand for and supply of outside integrated services.

Costs and Benefits of IFSP in Emerging Markets

In spite of greater restrictions on banks' activities and less importance of securities markets, IFSP is relatively common in developing countries. Furthermore, through joint ownership and group structures, IFSP-type arrangements, including close bank-commerce links, are quite prevalent in emerging markets, perhaps more than in many developed countries. This raises a few questions: what are the specific costs and benefits of IFSP in emerging markets? Are the restrictions on activities in emerging markets more useful or more costly? And what other policy implications follow?[75]

Very few studies analyze the costs and benefits of universal banking specifically for emerging markets, and even fewer studies analyze the combination of banking and insurance or other forms of IFSP. Most relevant is the work reviewed in this paper on the role of universal banks in the late 1800s and early 1900s in Europe, Japan, and the United States, as the circumstances of those countries at that time resemble the circum-

---

75. Another set of question relates to the role of groups as conglomerates and the functioning of internal markets, which are not being addressed here.

stances of many emerging markets today. The discussion early in the process of financial sector reform in transition economies is illustrative because it was very much based on these experiences.[76] Many argued that the conditions in transition economies made the universal banking model more attractive than having separate commercial and investment banks. Allowing banks to engage in a variety of financial activities and to own shares in enterprises exploits banks' informational advantages, which were at a premium in the high-risk, limited-information environment of many transition economies. Especially early in the transition, banks also had to play a large role in enterprise restructuring, which was further facilitated by being universal banks. Combined with some need for banks to act as coordinating agencies and to concentrate scarce financial skills, and in that way facilitate the process of change, universal banking seemed to be the best model. Most transition economies opted for some type of universal banking model.

Similar arguments for IFSP apply to many other emerging markets, where information asymmetries are high, skills are limited and in need of concentration, and some coordination is still needed for large projects. This model has its risks in emerging markets, however, especially given the generally weak regulation and supervision of the financial sector. Substantial cross-holdings between banks, investment and pension funds, and enterprises in many emerging markets have led to the systematic abuse of conflicts of interest. In other countries, universal banks have misused their powers, including by allocating shares to own-managed mutual funds at too high prices. Thus exposure guidelines, which limit individual investments to a certain fraction of assets or capital, disclosure standards, and other measures aimed at addressing conflicts of interest or risk need to be strictly enforced for banks as well as financial-industrial groups, especially for lending to managers and affiliated enterprises. In addition, there may be a greater need to capitalize some activities separately in order to protect depositors. Furthermore, there may be greater risks from too much concentration in the financial sector, particularly if banking and insurance activities are allowed to combine. Together these institutions will control the bulk of savings in many emerging markets. As in the presence of economies of scope, the combination may reduce

---

76. See, for example, Brainard (1991).

potential competition, especially in small markets. The risks nevertheless mainly arise from the common ownership and control of different types of financial institutions and financial spillovers. The arguments for separating the distribution of different types of financial products in emerging markets from a risk point of view are much less strong.

Although one can try to use regulations to mitigate risks, one has to remain cognizant of the limits to supervision, especially in emerging markets. Typically, abuse arises only in part from weaknesses in regulation and more often from the very limited enforcement of supervision in these countries. Better supervision is an obvious remedy, but often not feasible in light of the shortage of human skills and low pay, which is restricted by public sector wage scales. Furthermore, greater supervisory powers can be counterproductive in the absence of checks and balances in the system.[77] Experiences suggest that risks associated with financial conglomerates usually come from two factors: (a) an excessive role of the government, including the central bank and ministries, both directly and indirectly in banks and financial groups, and (b) a lack of competition and contestability in the financial and real sectors. Financial conglomerates have been harmful mostly when the financial system has been heavily controlled, for example, through controlled interest rates or high entry barriers. Nevertheless, country circumstances could call for differentiated approaches where the scope of activities is widened as the institutional framework is strengthened and financial markets develop.

The Role of Groups

The presence of groups does affect the relative gains of moving to IFSP in emerging markets. The use of internal markets in emerging markets to allocate financial resources can add value by providing collateral across firms, overcoming information asymmetries and contracting problems, and so forth, which is particularly valuable when external financial markets are poorly developed.[78] At the same time, because of their reduced transparency and complicated structures of ownership and control, groups can have severe corporate governance problems or at least aggravate corporate governance problems that typically are already large

---

77. Barth, Caprio, and Levine (2001a).
78. Khanna and Palepu (2000).

in emerging markets.[79] Groups may also stymie the development of securities markets.

The benefits and costs from groups depend on the country's institutional context. It may be that the benefits of internal markets are the greatest in those countries in which the impact of corporate governance problems is also the most severe. That is, although the potential beneficial role of internal markets may be the greatest in countries with the least developed external financial markets, it is likely that the ability to mitigate any corporate governance problems associated with group structures is also the weakest in these countries. This suggests that reforms focusing on reducing corporate governance problems may enhance the efficiency of the use of internal markets. At the same time, such reforms will diminish the need for internal markets as they encourage the development of external financial markets. The fact that groups diminish in importance as countries develop suggests that the gains from better external markets are stronger than the benefits from internal markets. This suggests that emerging markets are better off promoting formal relationships—in the form of external financial markets, banks, and securities markets, including formal financial conglomerates—rather than relying on internal markets with many corporate governance problems. The specific reforms necessary will depend on countries' current institutional frameworks.

Conclusions

IFSP can lead to gains for the financial sector, firm, and economy in the form of a greater supply of better quality financial services, reduced financial intermediation costs, and lower risks. These gains are observed at the level of the financial institution, the firm, the household, and the whole economy. IFSP may, however, lead to risks. It can increase opportunities for conflicts of interest and risk-taking behavior by financial institutions at the ultimate cost of taxpayers through a publicly provided financial safety net. It can make financial institutions too complex to monitor by markets and supervisors. And it can reduce competition by increasing the concentration in the financial sector and making financial

---

79. Claessens, Klingebiel, and Schmukler (2002).

conglomerates politically too important to close or ignore. These possible risks associated with IFSP do impose some specific demands on financial sector regulation and supervision.

For emerging markets, the available evidence suggests that the gains from IFSP outweigh the risks, possibly even more so as human resources are scare, information asymmetries are greater, and coordination needs are still significant. Key requirements to maximize the gains are effective competition—that is, open and contestable financial systems—and strict enforcement of a number of key measures to prevent leakage from any publicly provided safety net.

APPENDIX A

Permissible Activities for Banking Organizations in Various Financial Centers

Country	Securities[a]	Insurance[b]	Real estate[c]	Bank investments in industrial firms[d]	Industrial firm investment in banks
G-10 countries plus Switzerland					
Belgium	Permitted	Permitted through subsidiaries	Generally limited to holding bank premises	Single qualifying holding may not exceed 15 percent of bank's own funds, and such holdings on an aggregate basis may not exceed 45 percent of own funds	Permitted, but subject to prior approval of authorities
Canada[e]	Permitted through subsidiaries	Permitted through subsidiaries	Permitted	Permitted up to C$250 million per entity or 10 percent of regulatory capital	Permitted, depending on size of bank, to own from 20 percent of voting shares for large banks (greater than C$5 billion in equity) to 100 percent for small banks (less than C$1 billion in equity)
France	Permitted	Permitted, usually through subsidiaries	Permitted	Permitted, but limited to 15 percent of the bank's capital; in the aggregate limited to 60 percent of the bank's capital	Not prohibited

Country					
Germany	Permitted	Permitted, but only through insurance subsidiaries	Permitted	Permitted, but limited to 15 percent of the bank's capital; in the aggregate limited to 60 percent of the bank's capital	Permitted, subject to regulatory consent based on the suitability of the shareholder
Italy	Permitted	Limited to 10 percent of own funds for each insurance company and 20 percent aggregate investment in insurance companies	Generally limited to holding bank premises	Permitted, up to 15 percent of the bank's capital, subject to approval of the Bank of Italy	Permitted, up to 5 percent of shares of the bank, subject to approval of the Bank of Italy
Japan	Some services (for example, selling of government bonds and investment trusts) permitted to banks; others permitted through subsidiaries	Some services (for example, selling insurance policies in connection with housing loans) permitted to banks; others permitted through subsidiaries	Generally limited to holding bank premises	Limited to holding 5 percent interest[f]	Permitted, provided total investment does not exceed investing firm's capital or net assets
Netherlands	Permitted	Permitted through subsidiaries	Permitted	Subject to regulatory approval for voting shares in excess of 10 percent	Subject to regulatory approval for voting shares in excess of 5 percent
Sweden	Permitted	Permitted	Generally limited to holding bank premises	Limited	Not prohibited, but such investments are generally not made
Switzerland	Permitted through specific license as securities dealer	Permitted through subsidiaries	Permitted	Permitted	Not prohibited

continued on next page

Appendix A. Permissible Activities for Banking Organizations in Various Financial Centers (continued)

Country	Securities[a]	Insurance[b]	Real estate[c]	Bank investments in industrial firms[d]	Industrial firm investment in banks
United Kingdom	Permitted; usually conducted through subsidiaries	Permitted through subsidiaries	Permitted	Permitted, subject to supervisory consultations	No statutory prohibition
United States	Permitted, but under-writing and dealing in corporate securities activities must be done through (1) a nonbank subsidiary of a bank holding company (subject to limits on revenue), (2) a nonbank subsidiary of a financial holding company (no revenue constraints), or (3) a financial subsidi-ary of a national bank (no revenues limits)	Insurance underwriting and sales are permissi-ble for nonbank subsidiaries of financial holding companies; national banks and their subsidiaries are generally restricted to agency sales activities	Generally limited to holding bank premises	Permitted to hold up to 5 percent of voting shares through a bank holding company, but a bank holding company that is designated as a financial holding company and has a securities affiliate may exercise merchant banking powers to make controlling investments, subject to certain regulatory restrictions	Permitted to make non-controlling investments up to 25 percent of the voting shares
Emerging markets					
Argentina	Permitted	Permitted, but only with regard to pension fund affiliates	Limited; based on bank capital and investment	Limited	Permitted, but subject to prior approval of authorities
Brazil	Permitted through subsidiaries	Permitted through subsidiaries	Generally limited to bank holding companies	Limited to suppliers to the bank	Permitted

Chile	Permitted	Insurance brokerage permitted	Not permitted	Not permitted	Permitted, but only up to 10 percent of a bank's shares, after which the superintendent's prior approval is required
China	Not permitted	Not permitted	Not permitted	Not permitted	Not permitted
Hong Kong	Permitted, subject to limits based on the capital of the bank	Permitted, subject to limits based on the capital of the bank	Permitted, subject to capital and other regulatory limits	Permitted, subject to limits based on the capital of the bank	Permitted, subject to regulatory consent based on suitability of the shareholder
India	Underwriting permitted; trading activities through subsidiaries	Not permitted	Generally limited to bank holding companies	Limited to 30 percent of the capital funds of the bank	Permitted up to 30 percent of the capital and reserve of the investing company subject to approval of Reserve Bank of India of the transfer of 1 percent or more of the bank's capital
Indonesia	Permitted through subsidiaries	Permitted through subsidiaries	Not permitted	Not permitted	Permitted
South Korea	Permitted through affiliates	Permitted through affiliates	Generally limited to holding bank premises and to 60 percent of bank capital	Subject to prior approval for investments in excess of 15 percent	Permitted, up to 10 percent of the bank's capital, but subject to prior approval based on suitability of the shareholder

continued on next page

Appendix A. **Permissible Activities for Banking Organizations in Various Financial Centers** (continued)

Country	Securities[a]	Insurance[b]	Real estate[c]	Bank investments in industrial firms[d]	Industrial firm investment in banks
Mexico	Permitted through affiliates	Permitted through affiliates	Generally limited to holding bank premises	Not permitted	Permitted up to 20 percent of the shares with approval
Singapore	Banks may hold equity participation in stock-brokering firms with Monetary Authority of Singapore approval	Locally incorporated banks may own insurance companies with Monetary Authority of Singapore approval	Limited in the aggregate to 20 percent of bank's capital	Interests in the excess of 10 percent, or that give the bank significant influence over the management of a company, require regulatory approval. In addition, a bank may not invest more than 2 percent of its capital funds in any individual firm	Acquisitions of 5 percent, 12 percent, and 20 percent or more each require regulatory approval
South Africa	Generally permitted, but subject to financial reporting requirements	Banks may not hold more than 49 percent of a registered insurer	Bank may not hold more than 10 percent of their total liabilities in fixed assets, loans and advances to certain subsidiaries, and investments in and loans and advances to certain associates	Banks require prior permission from the registrar to establish subsidiaries within South Africa or to acquire an interest in companies outside of South Africa	Permission is required from the registrar for holdings in excess of 15 percent and from the minister of finance for holdings in excess of 49 percent

| Philippines | Permitted; universal banks may engage in securities activities directly or through a subsidiary with limitations; regular commercial banks may engage in securities activities only through subsidiaries with limitations | Insurance companies, insurance agency, and brokerage permitted for universal banks through subsidiaries with limitations; insurance agency and brokerage permitted for regular commercial banks through subsidiaries with limitations | Permitted for universal banks through subsidiaries with limitations | Permitted for universal banks through subsidiaries with limitations | Permitted with limitations on foreign and corporate ownership |

Source: Institute of International Bankers (2002).
a. Securities activities include underwriting, dealing, and brokering all kinds of securities and all aspects of the mutual fund business.
b. Insurance activities include underwriting and selling insurance as principal and as agent.
c. Real estate activities include real estate investment, development, and management.
d. Bank investments include investments through holding company structures.
e. Updated on the basis of personal communication with Gerry Salembier, Financial Services Agency, Canada.
f. Bank holding companies and their subsidiaries are allowed to hold in the aggregate up to 15 percent of the total shares of nonfinancial companies.

APPENDIX B

Data Definitions in Barth, Caprio, and Levine

Barth, Caprio, and Levine have developed a regulatory database, which includes bank activity regulatory variables.[80] They measure the degree to which the national regulatory authorities in their sample countries allow commercial banks to engage in the following three nontraditional interest-spread-based activities:

—Securities. The ability of commercial banks to engage in the business of securities underwriting, brokering, dealing, and all aspects of the mutual fund industry.

—Insurance. The ability of banks to engage in insurance underwriting and selling.

—Real estate. The ability of banks to engage in real estate investment, development, and management.

They conducted surveys to obtain official information regarding each country's regulations concerning these activities for the year 1999. Using this information, they rate the degree of regulatory restrictiveness for each activity from 1 to 4, with larger numbers representing greater restrictiveness. The definitions of the 1 through 4 designations used are as follows:

—Unrestricted. A full range of activities in the given category can be conducted directly in the bank.

—Permitted. A full range of activities can be conducted, but all or some must be conducted in subsidiaries.

—Restricted. Less than a full range of activities can be conducted in the bank or subsidiaries.

—Prohibited. The activity cannot be conducted in either the bank or subsidiaries.

The difference between a 1 and 2 indicates only the location in which the activity is conducted, not whether the activity is restricted in any way. This type of difference, however, may matter for financial development and performance as well as for bank stability. More generally, these types of regulations determine the degree to which a bank may diversify

---

80. Barth, Caprio, and Levine (2001b).

its business operations as well as attempt to capitalize on any synergies that may arise from complementary activities.

Tables B-1 and B-2 reproduce the average for the whole sample by regional and income groups.

Table B-1. Information on Bank Regulatory, Supervisory, and Deposit Insurance Variables

Bank activity	Number of countries	Mean	Median	Standard deviation	Minimum value	Maximum value
Securities	107	1.87	2.00	0.88	1.00	4.00
Insurance	107	2.73	2.00	1.00	1.00	4.00
Real estate	107	2.90	3.00	1.07	1.00	4.00

Source: Barth, Caprio, and Levine (2001b).

Table B-2. Bank Activity Regulatory Variables, Averages by Income and Regional Groupings

Grouping	Securities	Insurance	Real estate
By income			
High income	1.43	2.32	2.38
Upper middle income	1.96	2.60	3.00
Lower middle income	2.23	2.81	3.15
Lower income	2.11	3.58	3.42
Developed countries	1.37	2.22	2.04
Developing countries or emerging markets	2.04	2.90	3.19
Offshore centers	1.88	2.75	3.00
By region			
Americas	2.18	2.59	2.82
East Asia and Pacific	2.41	2.76	3.24
Europe and Central Asia	1.51	2.27	2.27
Middle East and North Africa	1.45	3.45	3.73
South Asia	1.67	3.17	3.33
Sub-Saharan Africa	2.07	3.36	3.43
By category			
Non-OECD	2.00	2.90	3.16
OECD	1.50	2.25	2.14
Non-European Union	1.99	2.82	3.07
European Union	1.13	2.20	1.87
Non-Euroland	1.96	2.79	3.02
Euroland	1.09	2.18	1.82

Source: Barth, Caprio, and Levine (2001b).

APPENDIX C

Costs and Benefits of Different Organizational Models

Three principal organizational models can be distinguished: (a) the fully integrated banking model, (b) the bank–parent company model, and (c) the holding company model. There are two additional models. A fourth model forces complete institutional separation between commercial and investment banking—that is, the separate banking system model. A fifth model uses a narrow bank that isolates the risk of securities as well as commercial banking business from depositors. Since this model is not specific to the issue of IFSP, it is not discussed.

Integrated Banking Model

In countries where banks have full latitude, most banks locate the securities unit in a department of the bank, thereby adopting the fully integrated bank model. This way, resources can be shared among the organization's various departments with maximum flexibility, allowing the bank to fully realize informational advantages and economies of scope and scale. Moreover, it increases banks' ability to diversify its sources of revenue. At the same time, safeguards for limiting conflicts of interest and extending the safety net are limited.[81]

The Bank–Parent Company Model

In the bank-parent model, the securities business is undertaken by a subsidiary of the bank. As there is a legal separation, integration of the bank and the securities activities can only be achieved partially, and the potential for economies of scope is thus reduced. However, this model still allows for risk diversification and the potential for higher revenues through cross-selling of financial services. The bank-parent model can reduce the potential for conflicts and the extension of the safety net— provided regulations requiring firewalls between the bank and its subsidiaries and prescribing arm's-length transactions are in place.

81. Santos (1998a, 1999); Saunders (1994).

The Holding Company Model

In this model, a holding company owns both the bank and the securities subsidiary, with legal separation between the two and separately capitalized and incorporated units that offer different products and have their own management team, accounting records, and capital. This generally limits the exchange of information, personnel, or other inputs among the various units, thus reducing economies of scale and scope and the bank's ability to exploit informational advantages and synergies. The holding company structure can limit risk diversification potential as revenues generated by securities activities accrue first to that unit and then to the holding company. At the same time, the holding company can act as a source of financial strength to the bank subsidiary. Advantages of the bank holding company structure are that the potential for conflicts is reduced and that the extension of the safety net may be limited.[82]

---

82. For additional detail, see Santos (1998a).

References

Allen, Franklin, and Douglas Gale. 2000. *Comparing Financial Systems.* MIT Press.

Allen, Linda, and Julapa Jagtiani. 1996. "Risk and Market Segmentation in Financial Intermediaries' Return." Working Paper 96-36. Federal Reserve Bank of Kansas City.

Ang, James S., and Terry Richardson. 1994. "The Underpricing Experience of Commercial Bank Affiliates prior to the Glass-Steagall Act: A Re-examination of Evidence for Passage of the Act." *Journal of Banking and Finance* 18 (March): 351–95.

Barth, James R., Gerard Caprio, and Ross Levine. 2001a. "Banking System around the Globe: Do Regulation and Ownership Affect Performance and Stability?" In Frederic S. Mishkin, ed., *Prudential Supervision: What Works and Want Doesn't.* University of Chicago Press.

———. 2001b. "The Regulation and Supervision of Banks around the World: A New Database." In Robert E. Litan and Richard Herring, eds., *Brookings-Wharton Papers on Financial Services 2001.* Brookings.

Beck, Thorsten, Aslı Demirgüç-Kunt, Ross Levine, and Vojislav Maksimovic. 2001. "Financial Structure and Economic Development: Firm, Industry, and Country Evidence." In Aslı Demirgüç-Kunt and Ross Levine, eds., *Financial Structure and Economic Growth: A Cross-Country Comparison of Banks, Markets, and Development,* pp. 189–242. MIT Press.

Beck, Thorsten, Aslı Demirgüç-Kunt, and Vojislav Maksimovic. 2002a. "Bank Competition, Financing Constraints, and Access to Credit Firm." Unpublished manuscript. Washington: World Bank.

———. 2002b. "Financing Patterns around the World: The Role of Institutions." Unpublished manuscript. Washington: World Bank.

Beck, Thorsten, and Ross Levine. 2002. "Industry Growth and Capital Allocation: Does Having a Market- or Bank-Based System Matter?" *Journal of Financial Economics, Netherlands* 64 (2, May): 147–80.

Benston, G. J. 1990. *The Separation of Commercial and Investing Banking: The Glass-Steagall Act Revisited and Reconsidered.* New York: Oxford University Press.

———. 1994. "Universal Banking." *Journal of Economic Perspectives* 8 (Summer): 121–43.

Ber, Hedva, Yishay Yafeh, and Oved Yosha. 2001. "Conflict of Interest in Universal Banking: Bank Lending, Stock Underwriting, and Fund Management." *Journal of Monetary Economics* 47 (1, February): 189–218.

Berger, Allen N., G. A. Hanweck, and D. B. Humphrey. 1987. "Competitive Viability in Banking: Scale, Scope, and Product Mix Economies." *Journal of Monetary Economics* 20 (3, December): 501–20.

Berger, Allen N., W. C. Hunter, and S. G. Timme. 1993. "The Efficiency of Financial Institutions: A Review and Preview of Research Past, Present and Future." *Journal of Banking and Finance* 17 (April): 221–49.

Berger, Allen N., and G. F. Udell. 1996. "Universal Banking and the Future of Small Business Lending." In Ingo Walter and Anthony Saunders, eds., *Universal Banking: Financial System Design Reconsidered*, pp. 559–627. Chicago: Irwin.

Bodie, Zvi, and R. C. Merton. 2000. *Finance*. Prentice-Hall.

Boot, Arnoud, and Anjan V. Thakor. 1997. "Banking Scope and Financial Innovation." *Review of Financial Studies* 10 (4): 1099–131.

Boyd, John H., Chun Chang, and Bruce D. Smith. 1998. "Moral Hazard under Commercial and Universal Banking." *Journal of Money, Credit, and Banking* 30 (3, August): 426–71.

Brainard, Lawrence J. 1991. "Eastern Europe: Creating a Capital Market." In Richard O'Brien and Sarah Hewin, eds., *Finance and the International Economy*. AMEX Bank Review Prize Essays 4. AMEX Bank.

Brewer, Edijah III, D. Fortier, and C. Pavel. 1989. "Bank Risk from Nonbank Activities." *Journal of International Securities Markets* 3: 199–210.

Bueschgen, Hans E. 1970. *Universalbanken oder Spezialbanken als ordnungspolitische Alternative fuer das Bankgewerbe der Bundesrepublik Deutschland unter besonderer Beruecksichtigung der Sammlung und Verwendung von Kapital, Gutachten*. Köln: Universität zu Köln.

Carow, Kenneth A. 2001. "The Wealth Effects of Allowing Bank Entry in the Insurance Industry." *Journal of Risk and Insurance* 68 (1, March): 129–50.

———. 2001. "Citicorp–Travelers Group Merger: Challenging Barriers between Banking and Insurance." *Journal of Banking and Finance* 25 (August): 1553–71.

Cetorelli, Nicola, and Michele Gambera. 2001. "Banking Market Structure, Financial Dependence, and Growth: International Evidence from Industry Data." *Journal of Finance* 56: 617–48.

Claessens, Stijn, Simeon Djankov, J. P. H. Fan, and Larry H. P. Lang. 2002. "Disentangling the Incentive and Entrenchment Effects of Large Shareholdings." *Journal of Finance* 57: 2741–71.

Claessens, Stijn, Simeon Djankov, and Larry Lang. 2000. "The Separation of Ownership and Control in East Asian Corporations." *Journal of Financial Economics* 58 (1-2, October): 81–112.

Claessens, Stijn, and Daniela Klingebiel. 2001. "Competition and Scope for Financial Services." *World Bank Research Observer* 16 (1, Spring): 18–40.

Claessens, Stijn, Daniela Klingebiel, and Thomas Glaessner. 2002. "Electronic Finance: Reshaping the Financial Landscape around the World." *Journal of Financial Services Research* 22 (1-2): 29–61.

Claessens, Stijn, Daniela Klingebiel, and Sergio Schmukler. 2002. "The Future of Stock Exchanges in Emerging Markets: Evolution and Prospects." In Robert E. Litan and Richard Herring, eds., *Brookings-Wharton Papers on Financial Services 2002*, pp. 167–212. Brookings.

Clark, Jeffrey A. 1988. "Economies of Scale and Scope at Depository Financial Institutions: Review of the Literature." *Economic Review of the Federal Reserve Bank of Kansas City* (September-October): 16–33.

Da Rin, Marco, and Thomas Hellman. 2000. *Banks as Catalysts for Industrialization.* LSE Financial Markets Research Centre Discussion Paper 343. London School of Economics and Political Science.

De Long, Bradford. 1991. "Did J. P. Morgan Men Add Value? An Economist's Perspective on Financial Capitalism." In Peter Temin, ed., *Inside the Business Enterprise: Historical Perspectives on the Use of Information.* University of Chicago Press.

Demirgüç-Kunt, Aslı, Luc Laeven, and Ross Levine. 2002. "The Impact of Bank Concentration and Regulations on Bank Efficiency." Unpublished manuscript. Washington: World Bank. Available at www.worldbank.org/research/interest/confs/bank_concentration.htm.

Demirgüç-Kunt, Aslı, and Ross Levine, eds. 2001. *Financial Structure and Economic Growth: A Cross-Country Comparison of Banks, Markets, and Development.* MIT Press.

Diamond, Douglas W., and Philip H. Dybvig. 1983. "Bank Runs, Deposit Insurance, and Liquidity." *Journal of Political Economy* 91 (3): 401–19.

Diamond, Douglas W., and Raghuram G. Rajan. 1998. "Liquidity Risk, Liquidity Creation, and Financial Fragility: A Theory of Banking." *Journal of Political Economy* 109 (2, April): 287–327.

Easterly, William, Roumeen Islam, and Joseph E. Stiglitz. 2000. "Shaken and Stirred: Explaining Growth Volatility." *Annual World Bank Conference on Development Economics,* pp. 191–211.Washington: World Bank.

Eisenbeis, Robert, and Larry D. Wall. 1984. "Risk Considerations in Deregulating Bank Activities." *Economic Review Federal Reserve Bank of Atlanta* 69 (special issue, May): 6–19.

Fohlin, Caroline. 1998. "Relationship Banking, Liquidity, and Investment in German Industrialization." *Journal of Finance* 53: 1737–58.

———. 2000. "Banking Structure, Competition, and Performance: Does Universality Matter?" Unpublished manuscript. Pasadena: California Institute of Technology, October.

Gande, Amar, Manju Puri, Anthony Sanders, and Ingo Walter. 1997. "Banking Underwriting of Debt Securities: Modern Evidence." *Review of Financial Studies* 10 (4, Winter): 1175–202.

———. 1999. "Bank Entry, Competition, and the Markets for Corporate Securities Underwriting." *Journal of Financial Economics* 54 (2, October): 165–95.

Gorton, Gary, and Frank A. Schmid. 2000. "Universal Banking and the Performance of German Firms." *Journal of Financial Economics* 58 (1-2, October-November): 29–80.

Group of Ten. 2001. *Report on Consolidation in the Financial Sector [Ferguson Report].* Basel: Bank for International Settlements. Available at www.bis.org/publ/gten05wp.pdf.

Hunter, W. C., S. G. Timme, and W. K. Yang. 1990. "Examination of Cost Subadditivity and Multiproduct Production in Large U.S. Banks." *Journal of Money, Credit, and Banking* 22 (November): 504–25.

Institute of International Bankers. 2002. *Global Survey.* Washington. Available at www.iib.org.

John, Kose, Teresa A. John, and Anthony Saunders. 1994. "Universal Banking and Firm Risk-Taking." *Journal of Banking and Finance* 18 (December): 307–23.

Kane, Edward. J. 1996. "The Increasing Futility of Restricting Bank Participation in Insurance Activities." In Ingo Walter and Anthony Saunders, eds., *Universal Banking: Financial System Design Reconsidered*, pp. 338–417. Chicago: Irwin.

Kashyap, Anil K., Raghuram Rajan, and Jeremy Stein. 1999. "Banks as Liquidity Providers: An Explanation for the Co-Existence of Lending and Deposit-Taking." Unpublished paper. University of Chicago, January.

Kelly, E. J. 1985. "Conflicts of Interest: A Legal View." In Ingo Walter, ed., *Deregulating Wall Street: Commercial Bank Penetration of the Corporate Securities Market*, pp. 231–54. John Wiley and Sons.

Khanna, Tarun, and Krishna Palepu. 2000. "Is Group Affiliation Profitable in Emerging Markets? An Analysis of Diversified Indian Business Groups." *Journal of Finance* 55 (2): 867–91.

Khanna, Tarun, and Yishay Yafeh. 2001. "Business Groups and Risk Sharing around the World." Working Paper. University of Pennsylvania, Wharton School, and Harvard Business School.

Klein, Peter, and Marc R. Saidenberg. 1998. "Diversification, Organization, and Efficiency: Evidence from Bank Holding Companies." Unpublished manuscript. University of Georgia and Federal Reserve Bank of New York, May.

Kroszner, Randall S., and Raghuram G. Rajan. 1994. "Is the Glass-Steagall Act Justified? A Study of the U.S. Experience with Universal Banking before 1933." *American Economic Review* 84: 810–32.

———. 1997. "Organization Structure and Credibility: Evidence from Commercial Bank Securities Activities before the Glass-Steagall Act." *Journal of Monetary Economics* (August): 475–516.

Kroszner, Randall S., and Philip E. Strahan. 2001. "Throwing Good Money after Bad? Board Connections and Conflicts in Bank Lending." NBER Working Paper 8694. Cambridge, Mass.: National Bureau of Economic Research.

Kwan, Simon H. 1997. "Securities Activities by Commercial Banking Firms' Section 20 Subsidiaries Risk, Return, and Diversification Benefits." Federal Reserve Bank of San Francisco, October.

Kwan, Simon H., and Elizabeth Laderman. 1999. "On the Portfolio Effects of Financial Convergence: A Review of the Literature." *FRBSF Economic Review* 99 (2): 18–31.

Laeven, Luc. 2002. "Bank Risk and Deposit Insurance." *World Bank Economic Review* 16 (1): 109–37.

Lang, G., and P. Welzel. 1995. *Technology and Cost Efficiency in Banking: A Thick Frontier Analysis of the German Banking Industry*. Discussion Paper 130. University of Augsburg.

La Porta, Rafael, Florencio Lopez-de-Silanes, Andrei Shleifer, and Robert W. Vishny. 1998. "Law and Finance." *Journal of Political Economy* 106: 1113–55.

Lehar, Alfred, and Otto Randl. 2001. "Chinese Walls in German Banks." Unpublished manuscript. University of Vienna.

Levine, Ross. 1997. "Financial Development and Growth." *Journal of Economic Literature* 35: 688–726.

Lins, Karl, and Henri Servaes. 2002. "Is Corporate Diversification Beneficial in Emerging Markets?" *Financial Management* 31 (2, Summer): 5–32.

McCoy, Patricia C., ed. 2002. *Financial Modernization after Gramm-Leach-Bliley.* Newark, N.J.: Lexis Publishing.

Monopolkommission. 1976/1977. *Zweites Hauptgutachten.* Bonn: Bundesministerium der Finanzen.

Noulas, A. G., S. C. Ray, and S. M. Miller. 1990. "Returns to Scale and Input Substitution for Large U.S. Banks." *Journal of Money, Credit, and Banking* (February): 94–108.

Petersen, Mitchell A., and Raghuram G. Rajan. 1994. "Benefits of Lending Relationships: Evidence from Small Business Data." *Journal of Finance* 49 (March): 3–37.

Puri, Manju. 1996. "Commercial Banks in Investment Banking: Conflict of Interest or Certification Role?" *Journal of Financial Economics* 40: 373–401.

Rajan, Raghuram G., and Luigi Zingales. 1999. "Which Capitalism? Lessons from the East Asian Crisis." *Journal of Applied Corporate Finance* 11 (3, Fall): 40–48.

Ramírez, Carlos. 1995. "Did J. P. Morgan Men Add Liquidity? Corporate Investment, Cash Flow, and Financial Structure at the Turn of the Century." *Journal of Finance* 50: 661–78.

———. 2002. "Did Bank Security Affiliates Add Value? Evidence from the Commercial Banking Industry during the 1902s." *Journal of Money, Credit, and Banking* 34 (2, May): 393–411.

Santomero, Anthony, and Eek-June Chung. 1992. "Evidence in Support of Broader Bank Powers." *Financial Markets, Institutions, and Instruments* 1 (1): 1–69.

Santos, João A. C. 1998a. "Commercial Banks in the Securities Business: A Review." *Journal of Financial Services Research* 14 (1): 35–60.

———. 1998b. "Securities Activities in Banking Conglomerates: Should Their Location Be Regulated?" *Cato Journal* 18 (Spring-Summer): 93–117.

———. 1999. "Bank Capital and Equity Investment Regulations." *Journal of Banking and Finance* 23 (July): 1095–120.

Saunders, Anthony. 1985. "Conflicts of Interest: An Economic View." In Ingo Walter, ed., *Deregulating Wall Street: Commercial Bank Penetration of the Corporate Securities Market*, pp. 207–30. John Wiley and Sons.

———. 1994. "Banking and Commerce: An Overview of the Public Policy Issues." *Journal of Banking and Finance* 18 (March): 231–54.

Saunders, Anthony, and Ingo Walter. 1994. *Universal Banking in the United States.* New York: Oxford University Press.

Schwartz, Amy J. 1992. "Misuse of the Fed's Discount Window." *Review Federal Reserve Bank of St. Louis* 74 (September-October): 58–69.

Scott, David. 1994. "The Regulation and Supervision of Domestic Financial Conglomerates." Policy Research Paper 1329. Washington: World Bank.

————. 1995. "Regulation and Supervision of Financial Conglomerates: The New Groupwide Approach and What It Means for World Bank Operations." Financial Sector Development Department (FPD) Note 36. Washington: World Bank, March.

Stulz, René. 2001. "Does Financial Structure Matter for Economic Growth? A Corporate Finance Perspective." In Aslı Demirgüç-Kunt and Ross Levine, eds., *Financial Structure and Economic Growth: A Cross-Country Comparison of Banks, Markets, and Development*, pp. 143–88. MIT Press.

Taylor, Michael, and Alex Fleming. 1999. "Integrated Financial Supervision: Lessons of Northern European Experience." Research Paper 2223. World Bank, November.

Vander Vennet, Rudi. 1994. "Economies of Scale and Scope in EC Credit Institutions." *Cahiers Economiques de Bruxelles* 144: 507–48.

————. 2002. "Cost and Profit Efficiency of Financial Conglomerates and Universal Banks in Europe." *Journal of Money, Credit, and Banking* 34 (1): 254–82.

White, Eugene. 1986. "Before the Glass-Steagall Act: An Analysis of the Investment Banking Activities of National Banks." *Explorations in Economic History* 23 (January): 33–55.

Wilmarth, Arthur E. Jr. 2002. "The Transformation of the U.S. Financial Services Industry, 1975–2000: Competition, Consolidation, and Increased Risks." *University of Illinois Law Review* (2): 215–472.

World Bank. 2001. *Finance for Growth: Policy Choices in a Volatile World.* Washington.

Risk Measurement, Risk Management, and Capital Adequacy in Financial Conglomerates

ANDREW KURITZKES,
TIL SCHUERMANN, AND
SCOTT M. WEINER

Is THERE SOMETHING SPECIAL, with respect to risk and capital, about a financial conglomerate that combines banking, insurance, and potentially other financial and nonfinancial activities? To what degree is the risk of the whole less than the sum of its parts? This paper seeks to address these questions by evaluating the risk profile of a typical banking-insurance conglomerate and highlighting some of the key analytical issues relating to risk aggregation. We provide a framework of analysis that builds up this risk profile and allows for coherent dissection of a financial conglomerate's diverse set of risks. We then use the analytical results to frame a policy debate for regulating the solvency of a multi-line financial conglomerate.

Increasing industry consolidation, financial deregulation, and globalization are fueling rapid growth in the scope of large, multi-line financial

This paper represents a significant revision of an earlier report (Kuritzkes, Schuermann, and Weiner 2001). We would like to thank the following people for sharing their insights with us: Luc Henrard, Andy Hickman, Beverly Hirtle, Hendrick Korthorst, Ugur Koyluoglu, Rick Mishkin, Rein Pijpers, Ruud Pijpers, and Ivo van Es. We would also like to thank the organizers of the Netherlands-U.S. Roundtable on Financial Conglomerates for their hospitality. Any views expressed represent those of the authors only and not necessarily those of the Federal Reserve Bank of New York, the Federal Reserve System, or Alliance Capital Management, L.P.

141

conglomerates. The Joint Forum of the Bank for International Settlements (BIS) defines a financial conglomerate as "any group of companies under common control whose exclusive or predominant activities consist of providing significant services in at least two different financial sectors (banking, securities, insurance)."[1] In fact, it is fair to say that virtually all of the large, multinational financial institutions operating around the world today are, to some degree, financial conglomerates by either the strict "three of three" or the weaker "two of three" definitions.

Yet despite the increasing importance of financial conglomerates, the regulatory structure in most jurisdictions is still based largely on single business lines, on the notion that financial institutions, or their business lines, can be classified as banks or insurance companies or securities firms.[2] This is particularly true of the regulatory approach to capital adequacy, which historically has treated different regulated businesses as independent "silos" in setting capital requirements.

Analytically, the special problem of capital management in a conglomerate stems from the need to aggregate risks across diverse business lines, such as banking and insurance. Our suggested method for constructing a composite picture of risk is to follow a "building block" approach that aggregates risk at three successive levels in an organization (corresponding to the levels at which risk is typically managed):

—*Level I.* The first level aggregates the stand-alone risks within a single risk factor (for example, credit risk in a commercial loan portfolio).

—*Level II.* The second level aggregates risk across different risk factors within a single business line (for example, combining the asset, liability, and operating risks in property and casualty or life insurance).

—*Level III.* The third level aggregates risk across different business lines (for example, banking and insurance).

Our analysis adopts this building block approach because it isolates the incremental effects of cross-business diversification that are unique to a conglomerate.

Empirically, our findings show that diversification effects are greatest within a single risk factor (level I), decrease at the level of a business line (level II), and are smallest across business lines (level III). According to

1. Joint Forum (2001b, p. 5).
2. For the purposes of this paper, securities and asset management activities for third parties are deemed part of the bank or insurance group. These activities are, therefore, not explicitly and separately dealt with in this paper.

our estimates, the *incremental* diversification benefits achievable at level III by combining a bank with an insurance company are on the order of a 5–10 percent reduction in capital requirements, depending on the business mix.

In such a building block approach, the result of adding risks at the level of the holding company can be no more accurate than the stand-alone capital measures for individual risk factors (level I) and for risks within a single business line (level II). This has important implications for capital regulation. The existing regulatory capital measures at levels I and II are inherently limited and, in particular, fail to reflect significant diversification effects at those levels.

Because of the limitations of existing capital measures, we argue that a well-constructed economic risk and capital management framework offers the best chance of overcoming the problems of the silo approach to capital regulation. Specifically, such a framework can have the potential to address—in a flexible way that is sensitive to business mix—both the stand-alone distributions and correlation structures of different risk factors, leading to a composite picture of the "aggregate" risk of the organization. Finally, by defining economic capital as a "common currency" for risk, the framework has the potential to overcome inconsistent measurement of risks based on where a transaction is booked.

We suggest that supervisors respond to industry developments in risk measurement and management by supplementing existing supervision of regulated subsidiaries with oversight at the holding company level of a conglomerate's internal risk and capital management framework. This oversight should seek to validate—and to leverage—internal economic capital models, harnessing their power to frame the right questions for each institution. Ultimately, rather than focusing just on the numbers, supervision of the holding company should focus on the effectiveness of the capital decisionmaking process.[3]

The structure of the paper is as follows. We begin by placing our analysis of the risk and capital profile of banking-insurance conglomerates in the context of previous studies. Second, we discuss the limitations of a silo-based approach to regulation and describe how these limitations give rise to the key questions posed in our paper. Third, we describe an analytical framework for assessing the risk profile of a typical banking-

---

3. Estrella (1995) was one of the first to highlight the importance of this issue.

insurance conglomerate and examine the scale and scope of aggregation effects. Fourth, we highlight industry practices for measuring and managing risk and capital in a financial conglomerate. We conclude with a brief policy discussion.

Literature Review

The merits and sins of specialization versus conglomeration, small versus big, have been debated at length in the economic literature. With respect to financial institutions, much of that debate has been conducted using data and experience from the U.S. banking industry.[4] There is some evidence suggesting that economies of scale exist in banking.[5] However, to achieve those gains from strict cost efficiency has proven to be difficult.[6] Are bigger banks less risky? Demsetz and Strahan show that while large U.S. bank holding companies are better diversified than small ones, this diversification does not translate into lower risk.[7] Effectively they "spend" their diversification benefits through larger commercial and industrial (C&I) portfolios.

Economies of scope have also been used to explain the existence (or creation) of financial conglomerates. These economies of scope can take different forms: lower joint production costs, consumers who desire (and are willing to pay for) one-stop shopping, and more efficient internal capital markets.[8] Putting these firms together might achieve economies of scale and scope to lower monitoring costs, perhaps by using very large customer databases to cross-sell retail financial products and services.[9] Using the U.S. insurance industry as their laboratory, Berger, Cummins, Weiss, and Zi try to explain the coexistence of, in their terminology, the "conglomeration hypothesis"—diversified insurers—with the "strategic focus hypothesis"—pure life or property and casualty (P&C) insurers.[10]

---

4. For a review of the literature, see Berger, Demsetz, and Strahan (1999).

5. Berger, Hancock, and Humphrey (1993); Hughes and Mester (1998).

6. Berger (1998); Pilloff and Santomero (1998).

7. Demsetz and Strahan (1997).

8. On the reduction of joint production costs, see Berger, Hunter, and Timme (1993); on the desire for one-stop shopping, see Herring and Santomero (1990); on the improved efficiency of internal capital markets, see Gertner, Scharfstein, and Stein (1994).

9. On economies of scale and scope, see Mester, Nakamura, and Renault (2002).

10. Berger and others (2000).

They do so using a concept of "profit scope economies, which measures the relative efficiency of joint versus specialized production, taking both costs and revenues into account."[11] They find, "The conglomeration hypothesis tends to apply more to insurers that are large, emphasize personal lines of business, [and] use vertically integrated distribution systems . . . while the strategic focus hypothesis tends to apply more to insurers that are small, emphasize commercial lines, [and] use nonintegrated distribution systems."[12]

But are conglomerates more or less risky?[13] A stylized story promises reduction in earnings volatility as the business activities generating those earnings become more diverse. Stiroh debunks this story for the case of banking by showing that the U.S. banking industry did not achieve any obvious diversification benefits, in the form of stable profits or revenue, through an ongoing shift away from traditional interest income during the last twenty years.[14] Studies by Flannery, by Santomero and Eckles, and by Wilmarth all argue that correlation will likely go up once business and product silos are placed under one roof.[15] Moreover, risk may actually increase because monitoring declines through either the bank monitoring its counterparties or the bank being monitored less by others such as rating agencies.[16] Cumming and Hirtle argue that the risk of the whole may be greater than that of the sum of its parts, largely due to spillover effects from reputational risk.[17] Moreover, they point out that the practicalities of achieving integrated risk management are daunting and "appear to have discouraged firms from adopting consolidated risk management." Once those systems are in place, however, firms should expect to reap economies of scale in risk management.[18]

---

11. Berger and others (2000, pp. 325–26).

12. Berger and others (2000, p. 358). Berger, Demsetz, and Strahan (1999) report that consolidation appears to have increased profit efficiency in banking.

13. The idea of risk mitigation as a motivation in mergers is not new. There is a rich literature on co-insurance following the seminal paper by Lewellen (1971), which discusses the impact of mergers on debt holders (and, indirectly, shareholders).

14. Stiroh (2002). In his literature review, Stiroh points to eighteen studies collected in Saunders and Walter (1994) that examine whether nonbank activities broadly are risk reducing; nine conclude yes, six conclude no, and three have mixed results.

15. Flannery (1999); Santomero and Eckles (2000); Wilmarth (2001).

16. Winton (1999); Wilmarth (2001).

17. Cummings and Hirtle (2001); the quote in the following sentence is found on page 1. See also note 42.

18. Flannery (1999).

We examine the risk reduction, in terms of economic capital, that might be experienced by possible banking and insurance conglomerate profiles. Others have also considered different marriages between sectors. Lown, Osler, Strahan, and Sufi, using pro forma analysis of potential combinations of banks with securities firms, life insurers, or P&C insurers, find that the merger of a bank with a life insurer results in the best risk-return benefit, largely because of enhanced revenue opportunities (economies of scope) and anticipated risk reduction, rather than anticipated cost savings or manufacturing scale (economies of scale).[19] Estrella, using a different approach based on options pricing and the arbitrage pricing theory, finds potential diversification gains from virtually all combinations of banking and insurance (both life and P&C) arising from revenue gains and the already well-diversified nature of an insurance portfolio.[20] Although these results are in harmony with ours, and we use some of Estrella's correlation estimates as a robustness check on our analysis later, we are less bullish about the degree of diversification that is actually realizable.

Finally, several authors have raised concerns regarding systemic risk, either because the conglomerates are larger and might be considered too big to fail (TBTF) or because even if they are not "too big" they may become too complex to fail (TCTF).[21] Moreover, one might be concerned that bank supervisors, in order to help prevent failure of a nonbank affiliate, might be tempted to extend the safety net beyond just the bank. This would inhibit market discipline by reducing the incentive to monitor the financial institution and increase the risk of contagion across the pieces of the holding company.[22]

Against this backdrop, our study turns to a question that has not been examined previously in the literature: What does the risk structure of a financial conglomerate imply for capital adequacy, particularly at the level of the holding company? In fact, where are the major sources of risk, and, of equal importance, where are the diversification benefits within a financial conglomerate? We do not speculate on possible revenue synergies or management span-of-control issues but rather focus on

---

19. Lown and others (2000).
20. Estrella (2001).
21. On too big to fail, see Santomero and Eckles (2000); de Nicolo and Kwast (2001); Wilmarth (2001). On too complex to fail, see Herring (2002).
22. Flannery (1999); Santomero and Eckles (2000).

the size and composition of the risk pie (for example, how big is market risk in banking versus insurance) and the implications for different financial conglomerates (for example, a large universal bank merging with a small P&C insurer) from the perspective of capital adequacy.

Current Silo-Based Approach to Regulation

Despite the increasing significance of financial conglomerates, the existing regulatory structure in most jurisdictions is still based largely on single business lines, on the notion that financial institutions, or their business lines, can be classified as banks or insurance companies or securities firms.[23] This is particularly true in the regulatory approach to capital adequacy.[24] The current Basel committee (BIS I) rules for the banking industry, for example, limit capital requirements to the credit and trading activities of licensed banks. Life insurance capital regulation similarly focuses on reserve requirements for authorized underwriting activities. Capital requirements for securities firms, meanwhile, vary by jurisdiction. In countries with a universal banking heritage, such as Germany and the Netherlands, the requirements for securities firms fall under bank capital guidelines. In other countries, such as the United States, the requirements for securities firms fall under different rules set by a separate authority.[25] In Japan and the United Kingdom, through their Financial Services Authorities (FSA), regulation of all three sectors has been placed under one roof, although without a harmonized approach to capital adequacy.[26]

Limitations of the Silo Approach

The approaches to capital regulation for banks, insurance companies, and securities firms have evolved from very different starting points,

---

23. See, for instance, Herring (2002).

24. See Joint Forum (2001a, sec. III).

25. Haberman (1987); Dimson and Marsh (1995); Ball and Stoll (1998); Kupiec, Nickerson, and Golding (2001); Herring and Schuermann (2003).

26. Gramm-Leach-Bliley, with the Financial Holding Company (FHC), makes this now possible in the United States as well. An interesting recent proposal from the United Kingdom's FSA is in the form of CP136, which seeks to draft a framework for capital adequacy standards for each financial sector (FSA 2002).

Table 1. A-Rated Credit Risk

Banking regulation (BIS I)	EU credit insurance regulations	EU life insurance regulations
Treat as commercial loan	Treat as credit insurance paying credit insurance premium of 1 percent a year	Treat as an investment
Tier 1 capital = 4 percent of outstandings	Solvency capital = 16 percent of premiums ⇒ 0.16 percent of outstandings	Implicit asset risk charge = 3 percent of outstandings

under different statutory regimes, accounting conventions, time horizons, intervention triggers, and policy objectives. This approach to capital adequacy raises a number of issues.

First, the silo approach is inconsistent: it may lead to different treatment of similar types of risk depending on where the risk is booked. As an example, consider a credit exposure to an A-rated counterparty (see table 1). If the exposure were booked in a bank as a loan, it would, under current (BIS I) capital rules, require Tier I capital of 4 percent of outstandings.[27] If it were booked as a credit insurance transaction in a P&C insurance company, the same economic exposure would, under European Union (EU) regulation, require capital of only 0.16 percent of outstandings—or twenty-five times less capital than a bank loan.[28] By comparison, if the credit exposure were held as a bond in the investment portfolio of a life insurance company, it would, under EU regulation, require an (implicit) asset risk charge of 3 percent of outstandings.[29] Inconsistent treatment creates the potential for regulatory arbitrage: It may encourage institutions to book business in those subsidiaries or shell companies that face the lightest regulation, irrespective of their ability to manage or sustain the level of risk.

Second, the silo approach ignores aggregation because it fails to take account of risk concentrations or diversification across different operating subsidiaries. It is possible that an acceptable level of credit risk to a given counterparty in a firm's banking book may become an unintended concentration if it is added to exposures to the same counterparty in the

27. Basel Committee on Banking Supervision (1988).
28. Article 16a of Directive 73/239/EC, as inserted by Directive 2002/13/EC (EU non-life insurance solvency directive).
29. EU Directive 2002/12/EC (EU life assurance solvency directive).

Table 2. Limitations of the Silo Approach

Inconsistent treatment	Aggregation	Incompleteness
Capital requirements dependent on where risk is booked	Concentration of risks across legal boundaries companies	Capital requirements of unlicensed operating
Boundaries breaking down due to product innovation	Diversification across risk classes within a legal entity company	Capital requirements or funding structure of holding
Increased demand or potential for regulatory arbitrage	Diversification of risks across business activities and operating companies	"Strategic" investments in nonfinancial companies

firm's trading book or insurance investment portfolios.[30] For example, if a bank has extended a credit facility to the same business to which the insurance company has issued a catastrophic (CAT) risk insurance policy, the concentration of risks will be lost in the silo approach. More fundamentally, many of the major risk factors within an operating subsidiary will tend to be mitigated by offsetting and diversifying exposures in other businesses.

Third, the silo approach is incomplete because it ignores the capital requirements of unlicensed subsidiaries, including a top holding company. Unlicensed subsidiaries that are engaged in commercial activities impose incremental risk, even if limited to nonfinancial factors (such as business and operational risk), which suggests a need for additional capital. At the same time, it is at the holding company level that the benefits of diversification across business lines are ultimately realized. These diversification benefits, however, need to be evaluated in the context of a holding company's funding practices and capital structure, taking into account such factors as the potential for double leverage. We summarize the problems of inconsistency, aggregation, and incompleteness in table 2.

The limitations of the current silo approach will continue to be exacerbated by industry consolidation and product innovation, which will further blur the boundaries between traditional business lines and risk classifications. If the regulatory structure fails to keep pace with these developments, the whole purpose of rule-based capital requirements may

---

30. In the European Union, banking and trading book exposures within one firm (and group) are together subject to the large exposure rule.

prove to be self-defeating. There is a danger that institutions will increasingly view risk and capital reporting as a game to be arbitraged rather than as an opportunity to communicate their financial strength to the outside world.

Although there are no simple answers to these challenges, the development of integrated risk and capital frameworks for evaluating capital adequacy in a conglomerate context is progressing. These developments are being driven by a number of factors, including:[31]

—The introduction of risk measurement methodologies and analytical tools for risk and capital management as well as performance measurement,

—The evolution of enterprise risk management as a key function of the corporate center,

—The blurring of product boundaries through financial innovation and the potential for regulatory capital arbitrage,

—The increased reliance by rating agencies on enterprise-wide capital models for evaluating the ratings of financial conglomerates, and

—The pressure from some regulators for a consolidated view of risk and capital at the holding company level.

These advances in internal risk and capital management practices offer the potential for innovative and more effective regulatory approaches.

Recent Regulatory Debate

The debate in the regulatory arena around these issues has intensified in the last three to four years. Notably, the new Basel Accord, sometimes called BIS (or Basel) II, proposes to "include, on a fully consolidated basis, holding companies that are parents of banking groups to ensure that it captures risks within the whole banking group."[32] This includes especially securities and even insurance subsidiaries.[33] More recently, in September 2002, the EU Council of Ministers approved an EU directive on the supervision of financial conglomerates.[34] This directive had four

31. See also Kaufman (2000).

32. Basel Committee on Banking Supervision (2001, p. 1).

33. In Basel Committee on Banking Supervision (2001, sec. C.9, p. 2), "A bank that owns an insurance subsidiary bears full entrepreneurial risks of the subsidiary and should recognise on a group-wide basis the risks included in the whole group."

34. EU Directive on Supervision of Financial Conglomerates, Commission to the European Communities, SEC (2002) 995 Final.

main objectives: (a) to ensure that the conglomerate is adequately capitalized, with particular attention focused on preventing "multiple gearing"; (b) to introduce methods for calculating a financial conglomerate's overall solvency position; (c) to deal with issues of intragroup transactions, group-level risk exposure, and internal risk management and control processes; and (d) to adopt a provision for lead supervisor by the member states for each financial conglomerate. The EU directive represents the first effort to extend some form of solvency regulation to unlicensed holding companies of major banking-insurance groups (and other financial conglomerates) in Europe. It was preceded in 1999 in the United States by Gramm-Leach-Bliley, which subjected financial holding companies to limited forms of consolidated supervision by the Federal Reserve.

The Joint Forum has also tackled the issue of risk measurement and management in a financial conglomerate head-on.[35] This Joint Forum grew out of a tripartite group formed in 1993. The purpose of the group was to identify and provide solutions for problems that financial conglomerates pose for supervisors. It was the first time these three sets of supervisors worked together. In 1995 the group submitted the Tripartite Report, which, although not officially endorsed by the Basel Committee for Banking Supervision, the International Organization of Securities Commissions, and the International Association of Insurance Supervisors, served as the launching point for the Joint Forum consisting of these three regulatory bodies.[36] Fundamentally, the tripartite group agreed that supervision of financial conglomerates cannot be effective if individual components of a group are supervised on a purely solo basis. The solo supervision of individual subsidiaries continues to be of primary importance, but it needs to be complemented by an assessment from a group-wide perspective. The 1995 report laid out simple policy alternatives and proposed some accounting and managerial guidelines but did not provide any answers to the questions of risk diversification or concentration.

The 1999 report of the Joint Forum was meant to take forward the work completed by the 1995 report just described. The 1999 report is a set of five papers around capital adequacy, supervisory principles, and

---

35. Joint Forum (2001a). This report, in turn, builds on their earlier work (Joint Forum 1995, 2001b).
36. Joint Forum (1995).

information sharing and coordination.[37] Although the first paper on capital adequacy made significant progress on the 1995 effort, it focused less on diversification and concentration effects and more on issues such as double (or multiple) leverage and regulatory arbitrage (across distinct bodies) and provided a very simple, banking-focused approach to risk aggregation.[38]

The most recent report explicitly compares approaches to risk management and capital regulation across the three sectors of banking, securities, and insurance.[39] It not only gives the comparative regulatory view but also summarizes many of the different approaches employed by financial firms across the three sectors, including, of course, practices by financial conglomerates.

Risk Profile of a Financial Conglomerate: Measurement and Management

The special problem of capital management in a conglomerate stems from the need to aggregate risks across a diverse set of businesses.[40] This section seeks to determine the magnitude of aggregation effects by examining the risk profile of a banking-insurance conglomerate. In effect, it asks just how big a problem risk aggregation actually is. Are aggregation effects so severe that a typical conglomerate is overcapitalized to the point of inefficiency (in particular to shareholders) or undercapitalized to the point of causing undue risk of insolvency to debt holders and policyholders?

Capital Management of a Financial Conglomerate

A financial conglomerate is, by definition, a combination of diverse businesses operating under a common ownership structure. As shown in figure 1, the organization can be broken down into major business lines,

---

37. Joint Forum (2001b).

38. The 2002 EU directive on the supervision of financial conglomerates adopted the 1999 Joint Forum recommendations. See also note 34.

39. Joint Forum (2001a).

40. Given the myriad ways in which a financial conglomerate can be structured, the only valid method for aggregating risks is one that is based on underlying risk fundamentals and is independent of legal structure.

Figure 1. Illustrative Financial Conglomerate Risk Profile

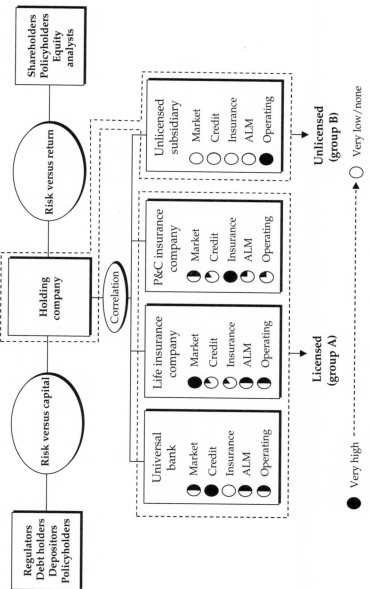

each of which has a distinct risk profile. For example, the universal banking activities—consisting of retail, corporate, and investment banking—are dominated by credit risk. Life insurance activities are dominated by market (investment) risk, and P&C activities are dominated by insurance (catastrophic) risk. In addition, unlicensed subsidiaries may be part of the conglomerate structure. Although the common ownership structure is typically a holding company, it need not be. The analysis and results in this section are independent of the specific legal structure of the conglomerate.

The capital management problem for a conglomerate is to determine—both within and across businesses—how much capital is required to support the level of risk-taking. The problem is of concern to different constituencies. On the one hand, debt holders, policyholders, regulators, and rating agencies are concerned primarily with the *solvency* of the institution. For them, the key issue is whether the institution holds sufficient capital to absorb risk—or the potential for loss—under all but the most extreme loss scenarios. Put another way, they are seeking capital to backstop the organization's risk-taking at a high degree of confidence.[41]

On the other hand, shareholders, participating policyholders, and investment analysts are concerned primarily with the *profitability* of the institution. For them, the key issue is whether the institution is earning a sufficient return (at or above the hurdle rate) on the capital invested to support risk-taking. While capital is the common denominator that links the debt holders and shareholders, their interests pull in different directions. Lower capital for a given degree of risk-taking will make an institution less solvent, but more profitable, and vice versa.

A conglomerate poses special challenges for capital management: internally, for managers charged with balancing the risk, capital, and return equation, and externally, for regulators concerned with the safety and soundness of the institution. The first challenge is to determine the stand-alone risk of an activity within a business line, such as the credit risk in a portfolio of commercial loans or the catastrophe risk in a P&C insurer's portfolio of homeowner loans. A number of techniques have been developed within banks and insurance companies to assess risk at this level.

---

41. See also Berger, Herring, and Szegö (1995) on the role of capital in financial institutions.

The next challenge is to combine the different risk factors within a business line or licensed subsidiary, such as banks, insurance companies, and securities firms that are subject to specific capital requirements. Because risks are less than perfectly correlated, they cannot be strictly added together. The potential for diversification suggests that the whole will be less than the sum of the parts.

A further challenge for a conglomerate results from the presence of unlicensed subsidiaries. They generally fall into two categories: financial subsidiaries that engage in financial businesses, such as financing, insuring, and brokering outside of a licensed banking group, insurance company, or securities firm, and commercial subsidiaries that are engaged principally in nonfinancial activities. In both cases, unlicensed subsidiaries impose an incremental need for capital, at a minimum to cover the incremental operating risks (including both business and event risk) inherent in the business. For an unlicensed financial subsidiary—such as a consumer finance or leasing company—the need for capital will be similar to that for other regulated activities. For an unlicensed commercial subsidiary, the incremental capital will be analogous to that held by a nonfinancial firm and will be needed to cover operating risks, including business and event risk.

At the same time, the top holding company within a conglomerate structure may itself be an unlicensed entity. Because of the scope of activity, the holding company raises unique issues of aggregation.

Economic Capital as a Common Currency for Risk

In order to assess capital requirements in a diverse conglomerate, there needs to be a "common currency" for risk that can equate risk-taking in one activity or business line with that in another. Economic capital is often used as that common currency for risk measurement, irrespective of where the risk is incurred. Under the economic capital approach, the risks of a conglomerate—or of the individual businesses within it—can be classified into primary components of asset risk, liability risk, and operating risk. As shown in figure 2, these risks can be decomposed further. Asset risk is typically broken down into credit risk and market-ALM (asset-liability mismatch or management) risk. Insurance liability risks can be separated into P&C catastrophe risks, P&C

Figure 2. Distributions of Risk Types

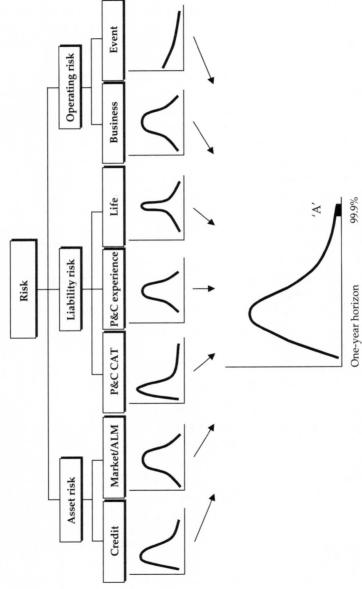

Source: Kuritzkes, Schuermann, and Weiner (2001).

experience-based risks, and life risks. Operating risks can be split into business risks and event risks.[42]

Although each of these risks has distinct statistical properties—as reflected in the stylized risk distributions shown for them—economic capital sets a common standard for measuring the degree of risk-taking. The standard is defined in terms of a confidence interval in the cumulative loss distribution, assessed over a common time horizon.[43] By setting capital for different risks at the same confidence interval, the economic capital requirements for different risk factors and types of activities can be directly compared. Only by having such a common standard can one meaningfully assess the risks for a complex conglomerate with a diversity of business activities across the financial spectrum.

A typical approach is to tie the degree of capital protection to the target debt rating of the institution. One convention is to adopt a one-year time horizon.[44] In figure 2, the economic capital requirement is set to protect against losses over one year at the 99.9 percent level—roughly equivalent to the default risk of an A-rated corporate bond. Put another way, a business that holds capital to protect against one-year losses at the 99.9 percent confidence interval would have a default risk consistent

---

42. This framework does not explicitly address what is sometimes referred to as "reputational risk." Reputational risk has two separate connotations: the first is the spillover risk to one business resulting from the insolvency of an affiliated entity. This effect is not incorporated in an economic capital framework because it is not a result of risk-taking per se. Rather, it is a result of the failure to hold sufficient capital to prevent the insolvency of the affiliate and of the legal or market conventions that transfer some or all of the resulting loss to the surviving business. This "risk" can be mitigated by setting high solvency standards for all entities within a conglomerate. Equally, if risks are correctly aggregated, then the total amount of economic capital at the top of the organization will determine the amount of financial resources (capital) necessary to support all of the organization's risk-taking at the desired confidence level, inclusive of any spillover effects. Another meaning of reputational risk refers to franchise risk associated with a major fiasco, such as the damage to a financial institution that could result from a large internal fraud or involvement in illegal money laundering. In principle, any direct losses stemming from such occurrences should be captured as an "event" risk within an economic capital framework. The more diffuse harm to franchise value is not something that capital resources are effective at alleviating. See also Santomero and Eckles (2000); Flannery (1999); Wilmarth (2001); Kuritzkes (2002).

43. The different risks have traditionally been measured at often rather different time horizons.

44. The one-year horizon is indeed typical for banking. In insurance, longer time horizons are considered.

Table 3. Types of Risk and Modeling Approaches

Type of risk	Description	Measurement and modeling approaches
Market-ALM	The risk of adverse movements in market factors, such as asset prices, foreign exchange rates, and interest rates	Value-at-Risk, scenario analysis
Credit	The risk of loss resulting from failure of obligors to honor their payments	Expected loss, unexpected loss
Life	The risk of loss due to unforeseen increase in life claims	Surplus testing
Catastrophe	The risk of loss due to catastrophe, such as hurricanes or earthquakes	Simulation, exceedence probability curves
Non-catastrophe P&C	The risk of loss due to an unforeseen increase in non-catastrophe claims, such as car accidents and fires	Frequency severity modeling, payout pattern analysis using loss triangles
Business	The risk of loss due to adverse conditions in revenue or exposure, such as decreased demand and competitive pressure	Historical earnings volatility, analogues
Event	The risk of loss due to fraud, natural disaster, and litigation	Extreme value theory

with an A debt rating. Setting capital for the individual risks within a conglomerate at this confidence interval ensures that each of them, on a stand-alone basis, is protected to a level consistent with the target rating.

Economic capital models are typically built up from the specific analytical approaches for individual risk factors. Table 3 lists common modeling approaches for the main types of risk. While the specific tools for risk factors such as credit, CAT, P&C experience, and market risks differ, the common denominator in an economic capital framework is the attempt to describe the risk distribution in probabilistic terms and to set capital at a common confidence interval.

Risk Aggregation: The Building Block Approach

Just as risks can be decomposed into individual factors, they can also be reaggregated. The distribution drawn at the bottom of table 2 shows conceptually how the various risk distributions of a financial conglomerate can be combined to yield a single, cumulative loss distribution—and economic capital requirement—for the institution.

In practice, aggregating the various risk distributions in a complex financial organization is a challenging task and somewhat arbitrary. Ultimately, the total amount of economic risk at the top of an organization is independent of how risks are aggregated within it. One proposed method for constructing a composite picture of risk is to follow a building block approach that aggregates risk at successive levels in an organization. There are three key levels, corresponding to the levels at which risks are typically managed:

—*Level I.* The first level aggregates the stand-alone risks within a single risk factor in an individual business line. Examples include aggregating the credit risks in a commercial loan portfolio, the equity risks in a life insurance investment portfolio, and the catastrophe risks in a P&C underwriting business.

—*Level II.* The second level aggregates risk across different risk factors within a single business line. Examples include aggregating the credit, market-ALM, and operating risks in a bank or combining the asset, liability, and operating risks in P&C or life insurance.

—*Level III.* The third level aggregates risk across different business lines, such as banking and insurance subsidiaries. This leads to the composite picture—or cumulative loss distribution—at the top (holding company) level.

Our analysis adopts the building block approach because it allows the risk profiles of each of the businesses within a conglomerate to be considered separately, *before introducing the cross-business aggregation effects that are unique to a conglomerate.* Put another way, level I and level II aggregation effects are already present within regulated banks and insurance companies. The unique problems of a conglomerate are associated with level III.

Differences in corporate structure, business line definitions, legal requirements, or risk management philosophy may lead some organizations to follow hierarchies in aggregating risks other than the three-level building block approach. Although this should ultimately produce the same amount of overall risk at the top of the organization, alternative approaches to risk aggregation will yield different results at lower levels.

Estimating Aggregation Effects: General Principles

The starting point for risk aggregation is to begin with stand-alone estimates of the economic capital required for individual risk factors.

Figure 3. Diversification within a Risk Factor

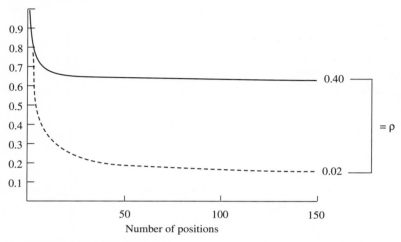

Diversification ratio

Source: Kuritzkes, Schuermann, and Weiner (2001).

Although the general concept of economic capital is explained above, the specific techniques for calculating risk at this level are beyond the scope of this paper.

Given estimates of stand-alone economic capital, one can aggregate risks—to a first-order approximation—based on the relative amounts of economic capital and then consider correlations between risk factors. As discussed in appendix A, the diversification benefits that accrue from aggregation are driven by three main factors:

—The number of risk positions (N),

—The concentration of those risk positions or their relative weights in a portfolio,

—The correlation between the positions.

In general, the diversification benefit increases with the number of positions, decreases with greater concentration, and decreases with greater correlation. These properties are depicted in figure 3, which shows the diversification benefits for a portfolio of equally weighted assets or liabilities for two different levels of correlation.

As the number of positions increases for a given level of correlation, the diversification ratio decreases—that is, there is an increase in the diversification benefit. For a given number of positions, as the correlation decreases, the diversification benefit increases.[45] For a correlation level typically experienced in market risk—around 40 percent—the full diversification benefit amounts to about one-third; this is achieved fairly rapidly, after about thirty positions. For the much lower correlations typical of a credit portfolio—around 2 percent—the diversification benefit is significantly greater—around 75 percent. However, it takes longer to get there; this limit is achieved after around 100 positions.[46]

Although the figure deals with equally weighted positions, as concentration increases the diversification benefit decreases. This is most easily seen at the extreme. The diversification benefit obtained by one risk factor that is nine times the size of another will be very small, even if the two risks are completely uncorrelated (independent). At zero correlation, the largest diversification benefit possible cannot exceed 10 percent.[47]

There is a related point, which can be illustrated using figure 3. The capital asset pricing model (CAPM) breaks total risk into specific (or idiosyncratic) and systematic risk. While the two curves represented in the graph show the systematic risk associated with average correlations of 40 and 2 percent, respectively, it is possible to conceive of different systematic risk curves for a given risk factor, reflecting different average levels of correlation. For example, a systematic risk curve for a domestic equities portfolio will have a higher level of average correlation—and lower diversification benefit—than a systematic risk curve for a globally diversified equities portfolio. Similarly, the systematic risk curve for a regionally concentrated credit portfolio will have a higher level of average correlation than a systematic risk curve for a globally diversified credit portfolio. Thus the diversification benefit obtainable within a given risk factor will vary with the scope of activity.

With these principles in mind, the general characteristics of the three levels of aggregation can be stated as follows:

---

45. The term "positions" is used to highlight the fact that this holds universally for assets, liabilities, number of risk factors, and so forth.

46. Some credit portfolios with considerably more than 100 loans do not converge on the systematic risk limit, because the loans are not equally weighted. Often, a few individual loans can each account for as much as 2–3 percent of the portfolio, which limits diversification because of concentration effects.

47. This result follows from equations A-1 and A-2 in the appendix: if $EC_1 = 9$ and $EC_2 = 1$, and $\rho = 0$, then $EC_T = \sqrt{9^2 + 1^2} > 9$ and the diversification benefit $DB < 10$ percent.

—Level I has many risk factors (individual assets or liabilities) that are neither strongly concentrated nor highly correlated. As a result, there should be a high diversification benefit at level I. The achievable diversification benefit is driven by the scope of activity.

—Level II has fewer risk factors, and they are likely to be more concentrated and more correlated. Consequently, there should be a lower diversification benefit at level II than at level I.

—Level III has only a few risk factors; some are likely to be much more highly concentrated than others, and correlations tend to be high. Level III should therefore yield the smallest diversification effects of the three levels.

These relationships are examined empirically in the following sections.

Level I Diversification

Level I diversification benefits reflect the degree of diversification achievable for a single risk factor within a given business line. At this level, the number of positions in a portfolio is quite large—typically well over 1,000 policies or loans in an insurance or loan portfolio and over 100 positions in an investment portfolio. As a result, diversification benefits will converge fairly rapidly to the systematic risk limit. Recall that for an equity portfolio, a one-third reduction is achievable due to diversification of idiosyncratic risk alone, while for credit risk the lower correlations allow for a four-fifths reduction.

Beyond the number of positions, differences in the scope of activity can have a dramatic impact on the level of systematic risk and hence on the achievable diversification benefits. As an example, figure 4 shows the increasing benefit from diversifying the credit risk of an equally weighted commercial loan portfolio internationally across geographies, essentially diversifying the portfolio with respect to the most fundamental of systematic risks: the (national) business cycle.[48] We present results using correlations based on changes in real gross domestic product from 1991 to 2000.[49]

In this example, the economic capital requirement for a U.S.-only

48. A discussion of the methodology is presented in the appendix.
49. Global is represented here by Australia, Brazil, European Union, Indonesia, Japan, and South Africa (IMF 2001).

Figure 4. Impact of Level I Diversification

Economic capital index percent

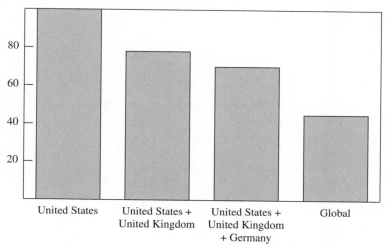

Source: Authors' calculations.

portfolio is indexed to 1.0. If that portfolio were combined with an equiv-
alent-size portfolio of U.K. commercial loans of similar ratings, the capital requirement (as a percentage of exposure) would be reduced by about
one-fifth. Adding a German portfolio of equal size would increase the
diversification benefit to 30 percent, while a fully diversified global
credit portfolio would require slightly less than half as much capital, per
unit of exposure, as the regionally concentrated U.S. portfolio. Not surprisingly, diversification is a major rationale for financial institutions to
internationalize portfolios. For a given amount of expected loss, the same
notional exposure leads to less loss volatility and lower capital requirements. This result is not unique to credit risk; rather it can be generalized
beyond just banking to insurance as well as nonfinancial activities.

The same principles apply to equity portfolios, where international
diversification is the only means of lowering the systematic risk in any
one market. And equally, in P&C insurance, diversifying CAT risk
across product lines and geographies produces a similar effect. Since
CAT risk for hurricanes and earthquakes is not correlated, a U.S. insurer
exposed to hurricanes in Florida can lower systematic CAT risk by
underwriting earthquake policies in Tokyo. This explains one of the key

benefits of internationalization for insurance companies, particularly P&C and reinsurance. As in the credit example, the diversification benefits for a single risk factor can be on the order of 50 percent or more.

Significantly, existing capital requirements typically ignore differences in level I diversification by assuming some "average" level of correlation and hence systematic risk. As an example, current (BIS I) rules for bank credit risk set a 4 percent Tier I capital requirement for all commercial lending—irrespective of the degree of diversification in the portfolio. This would continue to be true under the internal ratings–based capital reforms proposed in BIS II.[50]

Level II Diversification

Level II diversification depends on the correlation of risks within a business line. The magnitude of level II effects will differ systematically for banks, life insurers, and P&C insurers.

For banks, the dominant risk, as reflected in BIS capital rules, is credit risk.[51] This is corroborated by two benchmarking studies conducted in 2000. One was conducted by Oliver, Wyman and Company, which surveyed the internal economic capital allocations of ten large international banks in Europe and North America.[52] Capital Market Risk Advisors conducted its own survey of thirty-eight banks, six of which were classified as "large, global."[53] The results presented in figure 5 are quite similar. The stand-alone economic capital requirements for the banks—as determined by their internal models—were broken down into three major risk factors: credit risk, market-ALM risk, and operating and other risks. On average, credit risk accounted for about half of the total economic capital requirement, market-ALM risk accounted for one-fifth, and operating and other risks accounted for one-quarter to one-third of the total economic capital.

Given the relative weights of the stand-alone economic capital for the risk factors, the level II diversification benefits can be estimated from the risk factor correlations. In practice, there are a number of approaches for

---

50. The same applies to insurance, under the guildelines of both the European Union and the National Association of Insurance Commissioners.

51. Joint Forum (2001a).

52. Kuritzkes (2002).

53. Capital Market Risk Advisors (2001).

Figure 5. Economic Risk Capital Breakdowns

Oliver, Wyman and Company Survey
economic capital breakdown

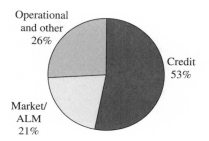

Operational
and other
26%

Credit
53%

Market/
ALM
21%

Capital Market Risk Advisors Survey
economic capital breakdown

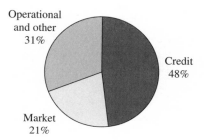

Operational
and other
31%

Credit
48%

Market
21%

calculating correlations and diversification benefits. We discuss some in the appendix and focus on the results here. Taking the economic capital breakdown of Oliver, Wyman and Company as an example, we compute the diversification benefits under three different correlation assumptions, presented in table 4. The first set is taken from Dimakos and Aas who estimate correlations for a Norwegian bank that also owns a life insurance subsidiary.[54] The second set comes from Ward and Lee who present risk aggregation results for a diversified insurer with the types of risk broken out.[55] Ward and Lee have separate correlations for market and ALM risk.[56] As we aggregate those risks here, we take the higher of the two correlations. Finally we present results based on the correlations used by Kuritzkes, Schuermann, and Weiner, which are based on interview findings and reflect the values used by Dutch and other financial conglomerates in their internal capital models.[57]

Combining the economic capital weights with the correlations, the level II diversification benefits for a "typical" bank can be estimated to be on the order of 15 to 28 percent (see figure 6). So far, this supports the propo-

54. Dimakos and Aas (2002).
55. Ward and Lee (2002).
56. We group market and ALM risk together as the interest rate risk associated with ALM is typically the dominant risk factor in market risk.
57. Kuritzkes, Schuermann, and Weiner (2001) and as cited in Joint Forum (2001a, p. 25).

Table 4. Inter-risk Correlations

Percent

	Credit	Market-ALM	Operational and other
Credit	100	30 30 80	20 44 40
Market-ALM	30 30 80	100	20 13 40
Operational and other	20 44 40	20 13 40	100

Figure 6. Diversification at Level II (Bank)

Percent

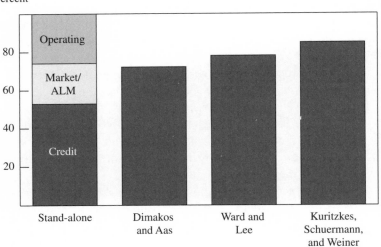

sition that as the level increases, the magnitude of the diversification benefit decreases. The explanation is straightforward: at the bank level, there are only three risk factors; they are concentrated (credit risk alone accounts for over half of total capital) and have relatively high correlations (for the more conservative Kuritzkes, Schuermann, and Weiner case, 40 percent or greater).[58] This provides a possible justification for why existing bank capital regulations ignore level II benefits: both the present and proposed BIS guidelines treat credit and market risks on a stand-alone basis and simply add together the combined requirement without any deduction for cross–risk factor diversification. Many banks do the same in their internal economic capital frameworks. This underscores the importance of level I diversification relative to level II for the banks.

The same analysis can be repeated for insurance companies. In figure 7 we show three risk profiles: a life insurer, a P&C insurer, and a diversified insurer.[59] The risk profile of the insurers differs significantly from that of a bank and also from each other. Credit risk, for example, accounts for only about 5 and 10 percent of the total economic capital of a typical P&C and life insurer, respectively, although the Ward and Lee estimate is closer to 20 percent for the diversified insurer compared to 50 percent for a bank. At the same time, market-ALM risk accounts for 50 percent of the capital requirement of a life insurer, 44 percent of risk of the diversified insurer, 37 percent of the risk of the P&C insurer, and only 21 percent of the total risk of a bank.[60]

Studies reporting correlations between risks are harder to come by for insurers than for banks. We are aware of only one, by Ward and Lee, that does so for a diversified insurer.[61] Thus we present the diversification benefit results for a life, P&C, and diversified insurer using their correlations as well as the correlations used in Kuritzkes, Schuermann, and

---

58. They may, in fact, not be all that conservative. It is well known that in times of stress, correlations often increase (see Embrechts, Klüppelberg, and Mikosch 1997; Diebold and Santomero 1999; Jorion 2000; Andersen and others 2001; Carey 2002).

59. The profile of a life insurer is from Stevens and others (2001); the profile of a P&C insurer is from Nakada and others (1999); and the profile of a diversified insurer is from Ward and Lee (2002).

60. Although grouping ALM and market risk is generically useful, life insurance has potentially distinctive ALM features stemming from the unique obligations to its policyholders. Specifically, the policyholders (that is, liabilities to the insurer) often bear some of the market risk from the asset side of the balance sheet.

61. Ward and Lee (2002).

Figure 7. Insurance Risk Profiles

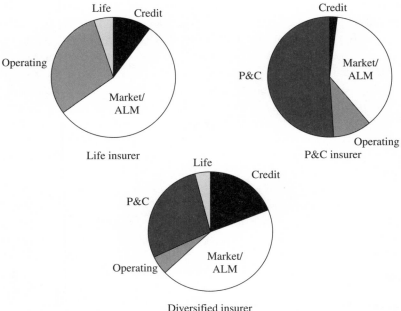

Diversified insurer

Source: Life, Stevens and others (2001); P&C, Nakada and others (1999); Diversified, Ward and Lee (2002).

Weiner.[62] With only one exception (the correlation between operating and life risk), our correlations are higher (often much higher) than those of Ward and Lee (see the appendix for details).

Figure 8 presents level II diversification benefits for a life and P&C insurer using two different correlation assumptions.[63] The lower correlations of Ward and Lee result in larger diversification benefits than do our more conservative estimates. This benefit is 46 percent for a P&C insurer and 28 percent for a life insurer, while the higher correlations result in 27 and 19 percent, respectively.

In both cases, the larger diversification benefit for the P&C insurer results from P&C risk being relatively uncorrelated with other types of risk. This lower level of correlation overcomes the high concentration that P&C risk represents in the risk profile of a P&C insurer.

62. Kuritzkes, Schuermann, and Weiner (2001).
63. The results for the diversified insurer are very similar to those of the P&C insurer.

Figure 8. Diversification at Level II (Insurance)

Percent

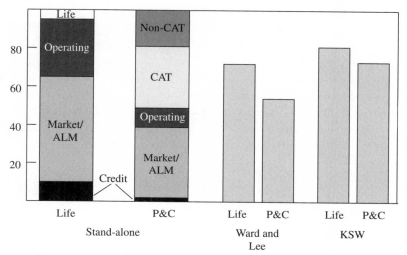

Source: Ward and Lee (2002); Kuritzkes, Schuermann, and Weiner (2001).
Note: KSW is Kuritzkes, Schuermann, and Weiner.

Despite the larger diversification benefits at level II for the insurers relative to a bank, the main hypothesis holds—namely, in moving from level I to level II, the diversification benefit decreases. While the incremental diversification benefits encountered at level II are less than at level I, they can nevertheless be economically important and often are not accounted for by regulatory capital rules.[64]

For example, the bank capital regulation (under both BIS I and BIS II) simply adds together the stand-alone requirements for credit, market, and, prospectively, operational risk without any offset for diversification. Similarly, existing European insurance capital requirements assume some "average" level of correlation within one licensed insurance entity. If several such entities form part of an insurance group, as is typically the case, any diversification effects (for example, geographic diversification) are ignored.

Considering an example from insurance, in the United States the P&C

64. Existing European insurance capital requirements assume some "average" level of correlation within one licensed entity. In case several such entities form part of an insurance group, any additional diversification effects (for example, geographic diversification) are ignored, however.

risk-based capital (RBC) formula for underwriting risk capital has two components: reserve risk and premium risk.[65] The reserve risk charge is calculated by multiplying net premiums written with a set of RBC factors. The factors are different for each line, thereby introducing some diversification benefit. This is called the loss concentration factor (LCF), which is linearly related to the ratio of the volume of the reserves for the largest line to the total reserves. Suppose that for two companies, A and B, the largest line constitutes one-fourth of total reserves—but the two lines are different. Then each line will have a different stand-alone risk and different correlations with the rest of their respective business lines. Nevertheless, the capital requirements will be the same.[66]

Level III Diversification

Having addressed the diversification benefits at level II, the incremental diversification benefits at level III can be estimated by combining banking and insurance activities in varying proportions. As discussed earlier, the three key factors in quantifying diversification benefits are the number of assets or liabilities, the concentration of risk factors, and the cross–risk factor correlations. Note, however, that in combining an insurance company with a bank, there are only two business lines, and they share many of the same risk factors (that is, exposure to a common business cycle). In addition, one of the subsidiaries may well be larger than the other one. These factors will tend to limit the possible diversification benefits.

To aid in understanding the potential diversification benefits at level III, we consider five different conglomerate profiles reflecting different possible mixes of a universal bank (bank plus securities firm), life and P&C insurers, plus, in one scenario, a small nonfinancial, commercial subsidiary (see table 5). The proportions represent the unit's level of stand-alone economic capital. These risk profiles are meant to capture a wide range of possible structures, from banking-dominated conglomerates to insurance-dominated conglomerates. For each profile, the diversification benefits are calculated by breaking down the bank, life, and P&C

---

65. Feldblum (1996).

66. The LCF formula is LCF = 0.7 + 0.3*ratio. This adjustment reduces the capital required for reserve risk. Obviously, LCF is a rough approximation for the true diversification benefit.

Table 5. Conglomerate Profiles, by Subunits[a]

Percent

Profile	Universal bank	P&C	Life	Nonfinancial
Profile 1: Bank/P&C lite	70	30	0	0
Profile 2: Bank/Life lite	70	0	30	0
Profile 3: Bank/P&C	50	50	0	0
Profile 4: Life/Bank lite	25	0	75	0
Profile: Mixed	35	30	30	5

a. We use the term "lite" to refer to the minority stake in the conglomerate. For example, the label Bank/P&C lite refers to the P&C unit as having the smaller economic capital contribution (30 percent).

businesses into their level II risk factors. The level II risks are then reaggregated based on the cross–risk factor correlations.

We then estimate diversification benefits for these profiles given the stand-alone levels of economic capital by type of risk and their correlations (see the appendix). We do so using several different sets of correlations between risks taken from different studies, including the correlations used in our original study. These correlations are presented in the appendix. In figure 9 we present the results, including an average across all four correlation specifications.

Several observations come to light. First, the overall results confirm our initial hypothesis: the benefits at level III are smaller than at level I and level II. For three of the four correlation specifications, the benefits only range from 0 to 12 percent.[67] For the specification that combines correlation estimates from Dimakos and Aas for banking and from Ward and Lee for insurance, the implied diversification is larger: 5 to 16 percent.[68] Indeed, under any of the correlation assumptions from this broad range, diversification benefits are modest. Expected benefits likely fall in the 5 to 10 percent range.[69]

Second, across the range of estimates, the largest diversification benefits stem from combining a bank with a P&C insurer. This follows

67. If a bar is missing, the diversification benefits are near zero. The results differ somewhat from those of Kuritzkes, Schuermann, and Weiner (2001) due to slight differences in stand-alone risk specification.

68. Dimakos and Aas (2002); Ward and Lee (2002).

69. There is an effect that may tend to reduce capital requirements at level III beyond the potential for diversification. Certain risks could actually be offsetting in different subsidiaries, for example, if one subsidiary is "long" the risk and the other subsidiary is "short" the risk. This could lead to a net reduction in the particular risk factor. Although

Figure 9. Conglomerate Diversification Benefits[a]

Diversification benefit, percent

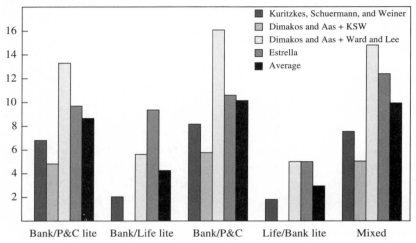

Source: Dimakos and Aas (2002); Kuritzkes, Schuermann, and Weiner (2001); Ward and Lee (2002); Estrella (2001).
a. We use the term "lite" to refer to the minority stake in the conglomerate. For example, the label Bank/P&C lite refers to the P&C unit as having the smaller economic capital contribution (30 percent).

because credit risk (the dominant risk in banking) is not correlated with catastrophe risk (the dominant risk in P&C).

Third, relative size matters. The biggest bang for the diversification buck comes from combining risks of equal size. Moving from an equally weighted bank-P&C group, for example, to a 70 percent bank–30 percent P&C combination reduces the diversification effects by about 5 percentage points on average.

The Fallacy of Composition

As noted, the diversification effects estimated through the building block approach reflect an *economic* view of risk aggregation, in which risks are first aggregated within a single risk factor, then within a business line, and then across business lines at the level of the conglomerate.

theoretically possible, the only major risk for which an offset is likely to occur is interest rate risk between banks and insurance companies. The magnitude of this effect will depend on a number of factors, including the size of the bank asset-liability mismatch gap and the insurance investment portfolio mix. For other major risk factors, banks and insurance subsidiaries are each likely to be long the risk.

Figure 10. Fallacy of Composition

Chart A. Insurance subsidiaries not aggregated into one business line

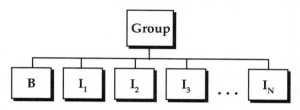

Chart B. Insurance subsidiaries aggregated into one business line

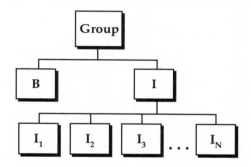

This approach to risk aggregation isolates the *incremental* effect of diversification across business lines. It also corresponds to the way risk and capital are managed at the group level in leading banking-insurance groups.

Ultimately, the total amount of economic risk at the top of an organization is independent of how risks are aggregated within it. However, to the extent that risks are added differently at each of the three levels, the magnitude of the diversification effects at those levels will also differ. This is best illustrated with an insurance example. Insurance companies tend to be broken down by geography and product line into a number of operating subsidiaries, each of which is separately capitalized under local law (chart A of figure 10). In many cases, the operating subsidiaries carry their own ratings in terms of default and policyholder protection. Historically, this has made centralized risk and capital management less pressing for insurance companies than for banks. However, the trend currently is increasingly toward centralization, especially for large, globally active insurers and more particularly for financial conglomerates, which require this centralized view of risk and capital.[70]

Figure 10 describes two possible structures for a conglomerate. They differ in the way the insurance subsidiaries are aggregated at level II. If the insurance subsidiaries are *not* aggregated into one business line at level II (chart A of figure 10), then the *perceived* aggregation benefits from level II to III could be greater than the 0–12 percent range reported above, simply because there are a greater number of small businesses at level II. [71] But this is an artifact of organizational structure; the amount of risk and the cross–business line diversification effects do not differ by moving to chart B, where the insurance subsidiaries are first aggregated into one insurance line. To be sure, there is nothing to prevent management from also splitting up the banking line into many individual subsidiaries at level II.[72] Obviously, this would not change the amount of risk or cross-business diversification effects either.

In practice, the diversification potential for insurance subsidiaries located in different geographies and hence capitalized (and regulated) separately is often not exhausted prior to level III aggregation. But the problem here is that the stand-alone insurance capital requirements fail to take account of the level of diversification already present within the insurance silo. It is not a feature of the cross–business line diversification associated with a conglomerate.

The "fallacy of composition"—or the sensitivity of perceived diversification benefits to how risk units are added within an organization—drives home a central point: Given the myriad ways in which a financial conglomerate can be structured, the only valid method for aggregating risks is one that is based on the underlying fundamentals of risk, such as the economic capital approach, and is independent of legal structure.[73]

Compounding Risk and Model Misspecification

The estimated diversification effects underscore a basic tenet of portfolio theory: the risk of the whole cannot be greater than the risk of the

70. Joint Forum (2001a); Wang (2002).
71. It is not uncommon for large insurers to have well over fifty separate subsidiaries.
72. An extreme case would be if each bank branch were a distinct subsidiary and separately capitalized.
73. Legal requirements will, however, imply restrictions on the use of capital and assets within a conglomerate.

sum of the parts.[74] *Provided stand-alone risks are correctly measured,* this means that the economic capital for a conglomerate cannot exceed the total stand-alone economic capital of the individual business units.[75] Concern that combining businesses within a single entity can somehow increase, rather than reduce, total capital is really a concern about misspecification of risks at lower levels. For example, in the case of Long-Term Capital Management, there was a compounding exposure to credit spread risk, as positions in different trading books were aggregated.[76] But the fundamental problem was that the estimates of underlying risk for individual positions were misspecified, since they failed to account for the potential for extreme credit spread movement. Ultimately, no method of risk aggregation can overcome misspecification of underlying risks. The best antidote to misspecification is to stress the model parameters and supplement traditional analysis with scenario testing across a wide range of market movements.[77]

Indeed the industry is placing greater importance on stress testing and scenario analysis to explore the edges of the risk space for the very reason that the models are almost always estimated with data dominated by "normal" times.[78] Yet risk managers care disproportionately about the "non-normal" times, that is, the tails and not the middle of the distributions. This is the risk manager's dilemma: she understands the unimportant part of the loss (or value change) distribution quite well, but not the part that really matters to her, namely the tails. With the current state of the art, this can only be characterized through stress testing and scenario analysis.[79]

Time Horizon

Another challenge of evaluating risk within a conglomerate is specifying a uniform time horizon.[80] At one end of the spectrum, market risk is

74. Cumming and Hirtle (2001) argue that the spillover effects resulting from reputational risks may result in this inequality not necessarily holding.

75. Others have also argued that the whole may actually be riskier than the sum of the parts (Santomero and Eckles 2000; Wilmarth 2001), due to reputation and spillover effects.

76. Jorion (2000); Lowenstein (2000). See also Jarrow and Turnbull (2000), for sound arguments why it is very difficult to cleanly separate market and credit risk.

77. See, for instance, Berkowitz (2000).

78. Basel Committee on the Global Financial System (2001).

79. See, for instance, the collection of papers in Embrechts (2000).

80. Joint Forum (2001a); Wilmarth (2001).

typically measured on a daily basis and scaled up to ten days for capital requirements under the Basel Accord. Credit risk is typically calibrated to a one-year horizon, as is operational risk. In banks, the convention for modeling risks and assessing capital is to adopt a one-year horizon. The logic to a one-year horizon is that it typically ties to reported business line profits and losses, corresponds to the internal capital allocation and budgeting cycle, and is a period in which an institution could access the markets for additional capital. It is also the horizon used in the new Basel Accord.[81] Alternatively, insurance companies are often capitalized for longer decision horizons.[82] This is particularly true for life insurers, where the obligation to policyholders is unique and often extends to thirty years or more.

In our approach, in order for economic capital to serve as a "common currency" for risk, a common time horizon needs to be specified. We adopt a one-year perspective rather than a longer-term view, which is the dominant practice within banking-insurance groups.[83]

Industry Practices

While the previous section provided a foundation for evaluating the risk profile and aggregation effects of a financial conglomerate, this section highlights industry practices for risk modeling and capital management within conglomerates. These trends are important for defining the "world of the possible" for policy reform.

Perhaps the most important trend, as noted by the Joint Forum, is that internationally active financial institutions are adopting economic capital as the fundamental measure of risk.[84] This is true of major banking-insurance groups, which have either implemented, or are in the process of implementing, economic capital frameworks across both banking and insurance business lines. Our earlier study confirmed that all of the major banking-insurance groups in the Netherlands are adopting economic capital as the cornerstone of an integrated risk and capital management

81. Basel Committee on Banking Supervision (2001).
82. Webb and Lilly (1994).
83. Joint Forum (2001a); Capital Market Risk Advisors (2001).
84. Joint Forum (2001a).

framework.[85] The economic capital framework allows for consistent measurement of risk factors across both banking and insurance lines. It also addresses risk aggregation at successive levels in an organization, through internal models that are sensitive to differences in risk profile and business mix.

Yet risk modeling and measurement are only relevant to the extent that they drive management decisionmaking. The corollary is that the structure of risk modeling and measurement needs to reflect both management processes and organizational structure.[86]

Financial conglomerates are building up group risk and capital management functions to oversee capital planning and decisionmaking at the level of the holding company.[87] This trend overcomes significant differences in the evolution of capital management for banks and insurance companies. Banks historically expanded through branching, which depends on a single balance sheet with centralized capital resources. When a bank entered a new market, it typically did so on the strength of the capital resources at the head office. This created a natural need for centralized risk and capital management in banking organizations.

Insurance companies, by contrast, typically expanded either by starting up or by acquiring new subsidiaries—whether in adjacent product lines or in new geographic markets. Each of the subsidiaries, in turn, was subject to separate, stand-alone capital or reserve requirements, independent of the parent. As a result, insurance companies tended to be locally capitalized—in many cases, with operating subsidiaries rated separately in terms of debt holder and policyholder protection. Historically, this made centralized risk and capital management less pressing for insurance companies than for banks.

Notwithstanding these differences, internationally active financial conglomerates—including banking-insurance groups—are putting in place centralized risk and capital management units. The dominant approach is to adopt a "hub and spoke" organizational model that corresponds to the three levels of risk modeling and measurement identified previously.

85. Kuritzkes, Schuermann, and Weiner (2001).
86. See, among others, Crouhy, Galai, and Mark (2001); Hendricks and Hirtle (1997).
87. Joint Forum (2001a).

At levels I and II are the spokes, which are responsible for risk management within business lines. Examples of activities at the spoke include the credit function within a bank or the actuarial function within an insurance subsidiary or group, each of which serves as the frontline managers for most transaction decisionmaking. Level II risk management—across risk factors within a business line—also typically takes place in the spokes, often in a finance unit that is responsible for funding and business reporting for the subsidiary.

At level III is the hub, which provides centralized oversight of risk and capital at the group level. While the hub is dependent on risk reporting from levels I and II, in many cases it is also responsible for overseeing the development of the methodology of an integrated economic capital framework that is then implemented within the spokes.[88] The specific roles of the hub vary but tend to include assuming responsibility for group-level risk reporting; participating in decisions about group capital structure, funding practices, and target debt rating; liaising with regulators and rating agencies; advising on major risk transfer transactions, such as collateralized loan obligations and securitizations; and, in some institutions, actively managing the balance sheet.

The hub and spoke system both reflects and reinforces the importance of economic capital modeling. Risk measures, as manifested by internal economic capital models, increasingly drive management decisions, not just for preventing loss but also for optimizing business through efficient capital management. The group capital structure considers disparities in the different kinds of capital: accounting capital versus economic capital versus regulatory capital versus rating agency capital. As there is no single view on the relevant measure of capital, the group's task is to balance the requirements of different constituencies (regulators, shareholders, debt holders, rating agencies) with efficient, yet prudent, capital management.[89]

The net effect is increasingly proactive management of risk, capital, and value in conglomerate companies, both within business lines and at the group level. It strongly suggests a need for regulation to keep pace with internal developments and market structure.

---

88. Joint Forum (2001a).
89. See also Berger, Herring, and Szegö (1995).

Policy Discussion

So how should one interpret our analytical results? A naive interpretation would be that, since level III diversification effects are small, silo regulation is adequate, and capital at the holding company level should simply be the sum of the parts. This would suggest that the deconsolidation approach taken in the new Basel Accord (BIS II) is essentially correct—insurance company capital should be subtracted, dollar for dollar, from holding company capital for a predominantly banking group. This is the equivalent of saying that holding company capital must equal banking capital plus insurance company capital.

A more nuanced interpretation of our results, however, is that the naive interpretation is only correct if diversification effects are already fully captured at levels I and II. But we know that is not the case with existing regulatory measures: Rules-based capital measures at both levels are based on a "lowest common denominator" approach that assumes an average level of correlation within a single risk factor and ignores cross–risk factor diversification at the business line level. As an example, consider the proposed credit risk capital rules under BIS II. The level I capital requirements for credit risk under the internal ratings–based approaches assume just a single correlation factor for all retail lending portfolios. Similarly, for the bank, the level II requirements for credit, market, and operational risk will simply be added together, with no offset for cross–risk factor diversification. A key point is that capital regulation at level III can be no more accurate than the stand-alone measures on which it is based.

Given the inherent limitations of existing regulatory measures at levels I and II, a better approach to capital regulation for conglomerates would be to adopt a more supervision-intensive approach such as that contemplated by BIS II's second pillar. Such an approach would require conglomerates to put in place their own economic capital models for assessing risk and capital at successive levels. These customized models are the only real hope of capturing the complexity of diversification at all levels within a conglomerate.

In advocating new policy, we are not starting with a clean slate. The reality is that the regulation of financial conglomerates is rooted firmly in the silo approach. Any new policy proposal focused on addressing some of the unique problems of a multiple-line financial conglomerate will

Table 6. Proposed Three-Plus-One Pillar Framework

I: Rules	*II: Supervision*	*III: Market mechanisms*	*IV: Legal firewalls*
Specific minimum capital requirements	Review of internal capital approach	Market evaluation of capital adequacy	Legal mechanism for separating risks
Lowest common denominator	Institution-specific	Aggregate judgment of multiple views	Jurisdiction- and institution-specific
Imposed by regulator	Internally driven	Externally driven	Recognized under law
Nondiscretionary, nonjudgmental	Flexible	Limited to publicly disclosed information	Both statutory and contractual

have to reflect the very different starting points and traditions of banking, insurance, and securities capital regulation. In short, the silo approach is here to stay, at least for the foreseeable future.

Estrella provides a thoughtful discussion of the difficulties and trade-offs encountered in designing regulation for financial institutions.[90] They include the different goals and objective functions of the different constituencies (see top of figure 1, for instance); the desire to achieve simplicity (emphasis on rules) and flexibility (emphasis on supervision); and the desire to allow market forces to provide a powerful monitoring and correction mechanism.[91]

The framework of the new Basel Accord is partly motivated to strike a balance among these apparently competing forces. We think the main issues surrounding risk measurement and management in a financial conglomerate can fit within that framework, perhaps with renewed emphasis on legal firewalls as a possible structural response to contagion of risks across distinct entities. This proposal is summarized in table 6 as Three-Plus-One pillars.

The Three-Plus-One pillars would combine rules-based, supervisory-based, and market-based approaches to capital regulation with legal mechanisms. The pillars are designed to be mutually reinforcing; no one pillar by itself is sufficient.

90. Estrella (2000).
91. Estrella (2000) and Santos (2001) stress that risk and capital are hard to determine in the presence of a safety net such as deposit insurance and that the two design problems (capital adequacy, deposit insurance) should be addressed simultaneously.

The first pillar would incorporate specific, rules-based minimum capital requirements for a conglomerate at the holding company level. Given the findings on the magnitude of level III aggregation effects, a simple rule-based approach to capital adequacy would be to add up the individual capital requirements for regulated subsidiaries at the parent holding company level, without any offset for diversification. Although this would tend to overcapitalize the conglomerate to some extent, the degree of overcapitalization attributable to cross–business line diversification is likely to be small—on the order of 5–10 percent.[92] The incremental capital might be justified as compensating either for the increased complexity of a multiple-line financial conglomerate or for measurement and modeling error at levels I and II; alternatively, it might be justified as imposing a somewhat higher solvency standard for a conglomerate.

The second pillar, however, should be the main load-bearing column of the regulatory framework. In the words of Estrella, this pillar would allow regulators to reap "the benefits of informed supervision. Mechanical formulas may play a role in regulation, but they are in general incapable of providing a solution to the question of how much capital a bank should have. At the margin, scarce public resources are better employed to enhance supervision than to develop new formulas whose payoff may be largely illusory."[93] Especially for a large, complex conglomerate, the supervisory review is likely to be far more important than the rules-based approach. It would enable the supervisor to evaluate the adequacy of an institution's internal risk management and capital decision processes along a number of dimensions. This pillar should be a flexible approach that allows for differences across institutions. Such differentiation is necessary to accommodate variations in business mix, risk profile, legal structure, and level of sophistication.

---

92. A 5–10 percent difference in capital is likely within the tolerance range for capital planning and is unlikely to prompt specific management action. This is especially true since regulatory capital for major financial conglomerates is a floor—and often nonbinding. The capital ratios for banks in G-10 countries, for example, currently average 11.2 percent, or 40 percent above the 8 percent (Tier I plus Tier II) regulatory requirements. The recent Joint Forum survey (2001a, p. 53) finds that banks typically operate with capital levels between 1.3 and 1.8 times required capital, securities firms from 1.2 to 1.3 times the warning level (defined as 5 percent of aggregate debit items), and insurance companies more than five times required capital.

93. Estrella (1998, p. 192).

The third pillar would leverage market judgments on capital adequacy. In the end, the market's judgment of capital for the holding company (and potentially individual subsidiaries) will be decisive, through its influence on pricing and access to funding. Although it is attractive from a theoretical standpoint to place great weight on the market's consensus, in practical terms there are too many limitations in current accounting conventions and disclosure standards for this pillar to be sufficient on its own. Similar to the sentiment expressed by the Basel Committee on Banking Supervision in BIS II, our recommendation is that regulators should encourage improved accounting rules and better disclosure of the risk and financial structure of a conglomerate to enable the market to do its job better.[94]

The fourth pillar—legal firewalls—is a possible structural response to contagion of risks. Legal firewalls might be appropriate for a "mixed conglomerate" that combines both financial and unlicensed commercial subsidiaries. In practice, a very broad range of nonfinancial subsidiaries are owned by or affiliated with financial conglomerates. Given the difficulty of evaluating the capital requirements for such a broad array of businesses, an alternative might be to segregate the risks of these activities from the financial activities in a conglomerate. They could be erected by requiring that nonfinancial subsidiaries be separately capitalized and by preventing intercompany funding of the subsidiary and cross-company guarantees. Such barriers might not fully mitigate against reputational risk, but they should go a long way toward limiting financial contagion.

The specifics around legal firewalls—What exactly are they? How will they be enforced?—are important and complex, but beyond the scope of this paper. We simply want to propose for discussion a possible solution to an obviously complex problem, namely that of assessing capital for unlicensed commercial (that is, nonfinancial) subsidiaries.

Our proposed three-plus-one framework will inevitably require more detailing—and debate—both within the regulatory community and among other constituencies. We look forward to the exchange.

---

94. To be sure, financial institutions are particularly opaque, making assessments by delegated monitors such as rating agencies and equity analysts more difficult. Indeed, Morgan (2002) measures this opacity by showing that bond raters disagree more about banks and insurance companies than about any other kind of firm.

APPENDIX A

Diversification Benefits from Aggregation

Economic Capital Calculation

One of the fundamental technical hurdles in risk measurement for a financial conglomerate—indeed for any financial firm—is the aggregation of a diverse set of risks. Just how diverse these risks can be is illustrated in figure 2. Typically, the risk manager has some knowledge of the marginal distribution of each type of risk (as is indeed illustrated in figure 2) and is interested in the joint distribution, that is, the distribution of all risks together. Aggregating these risks is technically quite challenging; a full treatment is beyond the scope of this paper. Below we give some detail of our rather simplified approach as well as provide some pointers to more sophisticated alternatives.

A Simplified Gaussian Approach

Our aggregations to overall economic capital are done using a highly simplified approach to illustrate some of the main issues. We assume that all risks are jointly normally distributed. This allows very straightforward calculation of the risks. Specifically, given the stand-alone levels of economic capital by type of risk and their correlations as described in the text, we may compute aggregate economic capital in the following way:

$$EC_T = \sqrt{\begin{pmatrix} EC_1 \\ EC_2 \\ \vdots \\ EC_N \end{pmatrix}' \begin{pmatrix} 1 & \rho_{12} & \cdots & \rho_{1N} \\ \rho_{21} & 1 & \cdots & \rho_{2N} \\ \vdots & \vdots & \ddots & \vdots \\ \rho_{N1} & \rho_{N2} & \cdots & 1 \end{pmatrix} \begin{pmatrix} EC_1 \\ EC_2 \\ \vdots \\ EC_N \end{pmatrix}} \qquad \text{(A-1)}$$

EC_T is aggregate economic capital taking diversification effects into account. At a given level of aggregation, the diversification benefit is simply 1 minus the ratio of aggregate economic capital to the sum of the stand-alone economic capital.

$$DB = 1 - \frac{EC_T}{\sum\limits_{i=1}^{N} EC_i} \qquad\qquad (A\text{-}2)$$

For each of the diversification computations, we consider N different portfolios whose stand-alone risks add up to 1. Considering the example of level I aggregation through geographic diversification (figure 4), we consider four different portfolios whose stand-alone risks add up to 1. That is, on a nondiversified basis, each geographic piece has a given amount of risk, and the sum of those risks is the nondiversified risk. We normalize to 1, so that in the U.S.-only case, the U.S. portfolio has 1.0 unit of risk, in the U.S.-U.K. portfolio, each has 0.5 unit of risk, and so forth. We then allow for the correlation across these risks to yield a diversified measure of risk relative to the nondiversified unit portfolio. For level III we follow the same logic (figure 9) by allowing each conglomerate profile to consist of a unit amount of nondiversified risk across the possible business units within the profile. We then allow for correlations across the various business activities within these business units to diversify some of the risk away. The result is the decrease in risk relative to the stand-alone risk in each individual profile.

More Advanced Approaches

The insurance literature and the finance literature have developed risk measurement methods in parallel fashion, and these lines of research have only recently crossed. One method in particular holds great promise: the computation of the joint distribution using copulas. A copula is a function that links the marginals to the joint distribution. Beyond allowing for the aggregation of diverse marginal distributions that capture some of the essential features found in risk management—like fat tails, for example—copulas also allow for richer dependence structure than allowed for by simple models like the multivariate normal.[95] Embrechts, McNeil, and Straumann were among the first to introduce this toolkit to the finance literature.[96] Li provides an application to credit

---

95. For a review of the theory, see Nelsen (1998).
96. Embrechts, McNeil, and Straumann (1999, 2002).

risk and credit derivatives.[97] Wang proposes an application to insurance with particular emphasis on enterprise-wide risk management.[98] Ward and Lee, for example, use a Gaussian copula to aggregate a diverse set of risks to arrive at the joint distribution for a diversified insurer.[99] These methods are now being put to the test, and we eagerly anticipate their reported performance.

Level III Calculations

For computing diversification benefits at level III, combining a universal bank and insurance company, we use correlations from different sources.[100] The basic idea is to produce a set of diversification benefit scenarios using correlations from different studies to help us understand the possible range of outcomes. Correlations for the first three are reproduced in tables A-1 through A-3.[101]

The correlation matrix has a block structure, with the major blocks being (universal) banking, comprising commercial banking and a securities firm, and insurance. In addition there may be an entity labeled "other," which may be thought of as a commercial subsidiary. This comes into play in only one scenario (see table 5). When the between-sector (banking-insurance) correlations between risk types are not available, we simply reduce the within-sector risk type correlations by 10 percent. One may view this "haircut" to be conservative, but, not knowing otherwise, we think it reasonable to be prudent. Moreover, the correlations from the different studies do have a wide range, from the very low correlations found in Ward and Lee to the higher ones found in Kuritzkes, Schuermann, and Weiner.[102]

97. Li (2000).

98. Wang (1998, 2002).

99. Ward and Lee (2002).

100. Kuritzkes, Schuermann, and Weiner (2001); Dimakos and Aas (2002); Ward and Lee (2002); Estrella (2001).

101. The Estrella scenario simply used his correlations as reported in Estrella (2001, table 9).

102. Ward and Lee (2002); Kuritzkes, Schuermann, and Weiner (2001).

Table A-1. Level III Correlations

Percent

	Banking					Insurance							Other
	Credit	Market	ALM	Business	Event	Credit	Market	ALM	Business	Event	P&C	Life and health	Business
Banking													
Credit	100	80	80	70	10	90	80	80	70	10	20	10	10
Market	80	100	80	70	10	80	90	80	70	10	20	10	10
ALM	80	80	100	70	10	80	80	90	70	10	20	10	10
Business	70	70	70	100	10	70	70	70	80	10	20	10	10
Event	10	10	10	10	100	10	10	10	10	40	10	10	10
Insurance													
Credit	90	80	80	70	10	100	80	80	70	10	20	10	10
Market	80	90	80	70	10	80	100	80	70	10	20	10	10
ALM	80	80	90	70	10	80	80	100	70	10	20	10	10
Business	70	70	70	80	10	70	70	70	100	10	20	10	10
Event	10	10	10	10	40	10	10	10	10	100	10	10	10
P&C	20	20	20	20	10	20	20	20	20	10	100	10	10
Life and health	10	10	10	10	10	10	10	10	10	10	10	100	10
Other													
Business	10	10	10	10	10	10	10	10	10	10	10	10	100

Source: Kuritzkes, Schuermann, and Weiner (2001). Cross-sectoral correlation submatrix is indicated with a dashed border.

Table A-2. Level III Correlations

Percent

	Banking					Insurance							Other
	Credit	Market	ALM	Business	Event	Credit	Market	ALM	Business	Event	P&C	Life and health	Business
Banking													
Credit	100	30	30	44	44	90	80	80	70	10	20	10	10
Market	30	100	80	13	13	80	90	80	70	10	20	10	10
ALM	30	80	100	13	13	80	80	90	70	10	20	10	10
Business	44	13	13	100	10	70	70	70	80	10	20	10	10
Event	44	13	13	10	100	10	10	10	10	40	10	10	10
Insurance													
Credit	90	80	80	70	10	100	80	80	70	10	20	10	10
Market	80	90	80	70	10	80	100	80	70	10	20	10	10
ALM	80	80	90	70	10	80	80	100	70	10	20	10	10
Business	70	70	70	80	10	70	70	70	100	10	20	10	10
Event	10	10	10	10	40	10	10	10	10	100	10	10	10
P&C	20	20	20	20	10	20	20	20	10	10	100	10	10
Life and health	10	10	10	10	10	10	10	10	10	10	10	100	10
Other													
Business	10	10	10	10	10	10	10	10	10	10	10	10	100

Source: Dimakos and Aas (2002); Kuritzkes, Schuermann, and Weiner (2001). Shaded cells in the banking submatrix are from Dimakos and Aas; all other cells are from Kuritzkes, Schuermann, and Weiner. Cross-sectoral correlation submatrix is indicated with a dotted border.

Table A-3. Level III Correlations

Percent

	Banking					Insurance							Other
	Credit	Market	ALM	Business	Event	Credit	Market	ALM	Business	Event	P&C	Life and health	Business
Banking													
Credit	100	30	30	44	44	90	27	27	40	40	0	0	10
Market	30	100	80	13	13	27	90	72	12	12	0	0	10
ALM	30	80	100	13	13	27	72	90	12	12	18	0	10
Business	44	13	13	100	10	40	12	12	90	9	18	9	10
Event	44	13	13	10	100	40	12	12	9	90	9	9	10
Insurance													
Credit	90	27	27	40	40	100	20	30	20	10	0	0	10
Market	27	90	72	12	12	20	100	20	20	10	0	0	10
ALM	27	72	90	12	12	30	20	100	20	10	20	0	10
Business	40	12	12	90	9	20	20	20	100	10	20	20	10
Event	40	12	12	9	90	10	10	10	10	100	10	10	10
P&C	0	0	18	18	9	0	0	20	20	10	100	0	10
Life and health	0	0	0	9	9	0	0	0	20	10	0	100	10
Other													
Business	10	10	10	10	10	10	10	10	10	10	10	10	100

Source: Dimakos and Aas (2002); Ward and Lee (2002). Shaded cells in the banking submatrix are from Dimakos and Aas; cells in the insurance submatrix are from Ward and Lee. Correlations across business lines (marked by dotted line) are given a 10 percent haircut from their within-line correlations. Thus banking market risk has a 30 percent correlation with banking credit risk, but only a 27 percent correlation with insurance market risk.

References

Andersen, Torben, Tim Bollerslev, Francis X. Diebold, and Paul Labys. 2001. "The Distribution of Realized Exchange Rate Volatility." *Journal of the American Statistical Association* 96 (March): 42–55.

Ball, Clifford A., and Hans R. Stoll. 1998. "Regulatory Capital of Financial Institutions: A Comparative Analysis." *Financial Markets, Institutions, and Instruments* 7 (3, August): 1–57.

Basel Committee on Banking Supervision. 1988. *International Convergence of Capital Measurement and Capital Standards.* Basel Committee Publication 4. Basel: Bank for International Settlements, July.

———. 2001. *The New Basel Capital Accord.* Basel: Bank for International Settlements, January. Available at www.bis.org/publ/bcbsca03.pdf [March 11, 2003].

Basel Committee on the Global Financial System. 2001. *A Survey of Stress Tests and Current Practice at Major Financial Institutions.* CGFS Publication 18. Basel: Bank for International Settlements, April. Available at www.bis.org/publ/cgfs18.pdf [February 18, 2003].

Berger, Allen N. 1998. "The Efficiency Effects of Bank Mergers and Acquisitions: A Preliminary Look at the 1990s Data." In Yakov Amihud and Geoffrey Miller, eds., *Bank Mergers and Acquisitions*, pp. 79–111. Boston: Kluwer Academic Publishers.

Berger, Allen N., J. David Cummins, Mary Weiss, and Hongmin Zi. 2000. "Conglomeration vs. Strategic Focus: Evidence from the Insurance Industry." *Journal of Financial Intermediation* 9 (4): 323–62.

Berger, Allen N., Rebecca S. Demsetz, and Philip E. Strahan. 1999. "The Consolidation of the Financial Services Industry: Causes, Consequences, and Implications for the Future." *Journal of Banking and Finance* 23 (February): 135–94.

Berger, Allen N., Diana Hancock, and David B. Humphrey. 1993. "Bank Efficiency Derived from the Profit Function." *Journal of Banking and Finance* 17 (April): 317–47.

Berger, Allen N., Richard J. Herring, and Giorgio P. Szegö. 1995. "The Role of Capital in Financial Institutions." *Journal of Banking and Finance* 19 (May): 393–430.

Berger, Allen N., William C. Hunter, and Stephen G. Timme. 1993. "The Efficiency of Financial Institutions: A Review and Preview of Research Past, Present, and Future." *Journal of Banking and Finance* 17 (April): 221–49.

Berkowitz, Jeremy. 2000. "A Coherent Framework for Stress-Testing." *Journal of Risk* 2 (2): 1–11.

Capital Market Risk Advisors. 2001. "Economic Capital Survey Overview." New York, May. Available at www.cmra.com/html/ec.html [March 11, 2003].

Carey, Mark S. 2002. "A Guide to Choosing Absolute Bank Capital Requirements." *Journal of Banking and Finance* 26 (May): 929–51.

Crouhy, Michel, Dan Galai, and Robert Mark. 2001. *Risk Management.* McGraw-Hill.

Cumming, Christine M., and Beverly J. Hirtle. 2001. "The Challenges of Risk Management in Diversified Financial Companies." *Federal Reserve Bank of New York Economic Policy Review* 7 (1): 1–17.

de Nicolo, Gianni, and Myron L. Kwast. 2001. "Systemic Risk and Financial Consolidation: Are They Related?" Finance and Economics Discussion Series (FEDS) 2001-33. Available at www.federalreserve.gov/pubs/feds/2001/200133/200133pap.pdf [March 11, 2003].

Demsetz, Rebecca S., and Philip E. Strahan. 1997. "Diversification, Size, and Risk at Bank Holding Companies." *Journal of Money, Credit, and Banking* 29 (3): 300–13.

Diebold, Francis X., and Anthony M. Santomero. 1999. "Financial Risk Management in a Volatile Global Environment." *Asia Risk* (December): 35–39.

Dimakos, Xeni K., and Kjersti Aas. 2002. "Integrated Risk Modeling." Working Paper. Oslo: Norwegian Computing Center. Available at www.nr.no/documents/samba/research_areas/BFF/publikasjoner.html [March 11, 2003].

Dimson, Elroy and Paul Marsh. 1995. "Capital Requirements for Securities Firms." *Journal of Finance* 50 (3): 821–51.

Embrechts, Paul, ed. 2000. *Extremes and Integrated Risk Management.* London: Risk Books.

Embrechts, Paul, Claudia Klüppelberg, and Thomas Mikosch. 1997. *Modelling Extremal Events for Insurance and Finance.* New York: Springer Verlag.

Embrechts, Paul, Alexander J. McNeil, and Daniel Straumann. 1999. "Correlation: Pitfalls and Alternatives." *Risk* 12 (May): 69–71.

———. 2002. "Correlation and Dependency in Risk Management: Properties and Pitfalls." In M. A. H. Dempster and H. K. Moffat, eds., *Risk Management: Value at Risk and Beyond*, pp. 176–223. Cambridge University Press.

Estrella, Arturo. 1995. "A Prolegomenon to Future Capital Requirements." *Federal Reserve Bank of New York Economic Policy Review* 1 (2): 1–12.

———. 1998. "Formulas or Supervision? Remarks on the Future of Regulatory Capital." *Federal Reserve Bank of New York Economic Policy Review* 4 (3): 191–200.

———. 2000. "Regulatory Capital and the Supervision of Financial Institutions: Some Basic Distinctions and Policy Choices." In Anthony Santomero, Steffan Viotti, and Anders Vredin, eds., *Challenges for Modern Central Banking.* Stockholm: Swedish Riksbank.

———. 2001. "Mixing and Matching: Prospective Financial Sector Mergers and Market Valuation." *Journal of Banking and Finance* 25 (December): 2367–92.

Feldblum, Sholom. 1996. "NAIC Property/Casualty Insurance Company Risk-Based Capital Requirements." *Proceeding of the Casualty Actuarial Society* 83 (158-159): 297–435.

Flannery, Mark J. 1999. "Modernizing Financial Regulation: The Relation between Interbank Transactions and Supervisory Reform." *Journal of Financial Services Research* 16 (2): 101–16.

FSA (Financial Services Authority). 2002. "Individual Capital Adequacy Standards." Consultation Paper 136. London, May. Available at www.fsa.gov.uk/pubs/cp/136/ [March 11, 2003].

Gertner, Robert H., David S. Scharfstein, and Jeremy C. Stein. 1994. "Internal Versus External Capital Markets." *Quarterly Journal of Economics* 109 (4): 1211–30.

Haberman, Gary. 1987. "Capital Requirements of Commercial and Investment Banks: Contrasts in Regulation." *Federal Reserve Bank of New York Quarterly Review* 12 (3): 1–10.

Hendricks, Darryll, and Beverly Hirtle. 1997. "Bank Capital Requirements for Market Risk: The Internal Models Approach." *Federal Reserve Bank of New York Economic Policy Review* 3 (4): 1–12.

Herring, Richard J. 2002. "International Financial Conglomerates: Implications for Bank Solvency Regimes." Paper presented at the second annual international seminar on policy challenges for the financial sector in the context of globalization, World Bank, Washington, June.

Herring, Richard J., and Anthony M. Santomero. 1990. "The Corporate Structure of Financial Conglomerates." *Journal of Financial Services Research* 4 (4): 471–97.

Herring, Richard J., and Til Schuermann. 2003. "Capital Regulation for Position Risk in Banks, Securities Firms, and Insurance Companies." In H. Scott, ed., *Capital Adequacy: Law, Regulation, and Iplementation.* Oxford University Press.

Hughes, Joseph P., and Loretta J. Mester. 1998. "Bank Capitalization and Cost: Evidence of Scale Economies in Risk Management and Signalling." *Review of Economics and Statistics* 80 (2): 314–25.

IMF (International Monetary Fund). 2001. *International Financial Statistics.* Washington, September.

Jarrow, Robert A., and Stuart M. Turnbull. 2000. "The Intersection of Market and Credit Risk." *Journal of Banking and Finance* 24 (January): 271–99.

Joint Forum. 1995. *The Supervision of Financial Conglomerates.* Basel: Bank for International Settlements, July.

————2001a. *Compendium of Documents Produced by the Joint Forum.* Basel: Bank for International Settlements, July. Available at www.bis.org/publ/joint02.htm [March 11, 2003].

————. 2001b. *Risk Management Practices and Regulatory Capital, Cross-Sectoral Comparison.* Basel: Bank for International Settlements, November. Available at www.bis.org/publ/joint03.pdf [March 11, 2003].

Jorion, Philippe. 2000. "Risk Management Lessons from Long-Term Capital Management." *European Financial Management* 6 (September): 277–300.

Kaufman, George G. 2000. "Designing the New Architecture for U.S. Banking." In Benton E. Gup, ed., *The New Financial Architecture: Banking Regulation in the 21ˢᵗ Century,* ch. 3. Westport, Conn.: Quorum Books.

Kupiec, Paul, David Nickerson, and Edward Golding. 2001. "Assessing Systemic Risk Exposure under Alternative Approaches for Capital Adequacy." Paper presented at the banks and systemic risk conference, Bank of England, May.

Kuritzkes, Andrew. 2002. "Operational Risk Capital: A Problem of Definition." *Journal of Risk Finance* 4 (1): 47–56.

Kuritzkes, Andrew, Til Schuermann, and Scott M. Weiner. 2001. "Study on the Risk Profile and Capital Adequacy of Financial Conglomerates." Study commissioned by the supervisory bodies in the Netherlands together with the representative organizations of the financial sector, Oliver, Wyman and Company, February. Available at www.oliverwyman.com/docs/rpfc.pdf or at www.dnb.nl/ publicaties/pdf/study_risk_profile.pdf [March 11, 2003].

Lewellen, Wilbur G. 1971. "A Pure Financial Rationale for the Conglomerate Merger." *Journal of Finance* 26 (2): 521–37.

Li, David X. 2000. "Default Correlation: A Copula Approach." *Journal of Fixed Income* 9 (4): 43–54.

Lowenstein, Roger. 2000. *When Genius Failed: The Rise and Fall of Long-Term Capital Management.* Random House.

Lown, Cara S., Carol L. Osler, Philip E. Strahan, and Amir Sufi. 2000. "The Changing Landscape of the Financial Services Industry: What Lies Ahead?" *Federal Reserve Bank of New York Economic Policy Review* 6 (4): 39–55.

Mester, Loretta J., Leonard I. Nakamura, and Michelle Renault. 2002. "Checking Accounts and Bank Monitoring." Wharton Financial Institutions Working Paper 01-3/R. Philadelphia: Wharton School.

Morgan, Donald P. 2002. "Rating Banks: Risk and Uncertainty in an Opaque Industry." *American Economic Review* 92 (4): 874–88.

Nakada, Peter, Hermant Shah, H. Ugur Koyluoglu, and Olivier Colignon. 1999. "P&C RAROC: A Catalyst for Improved Capital Management in the Property and Casualty Insurance Industry." *Journal of Risk Finance* 1 (1): 1–18.

Nelsen, Roger B. 1998. *An Introduction to Copulas.* Lecture Notes in Statistics 139. New York: Springer Verlag.

Pilloff, Steven J., and Anthony M. Santomero. 1998. "The Value Effects of Bank Mergers and Acquisitions." In Yakov Amihud and Geoffrey Miller, eds., *Mergers of Financial Institutions.* New York: Irwin Professional Publishing.

Santomero, Anthony M., and David L. Eckles. 2000. "The Determinants of Success in the New Financial Services Environment: Now That Firms Can Do Everything, What Should They Do and Why Should Regulators Care?" *Federal Reserve Bank of New York Economic Policy Review* 6 (4): 11–23.

Santos, João A. C. 2001. "Bank Capital Regulation in Contemporary Banking Theory: A Review of the Literature." *Financial Markets, Institutions, and Instruments* 10 (2): 41–84.

Saunders, Anthony, and Ingo Walter. 1994. *Universal Banking in the United States?* New York: Oxford University Press.

Stevens, Anthony, Tim Den Dekker, Charlie Shamieh, and Ramy Tadros. 2001. "European Capital Survey: From Feast to Famine?" *Reactions* (November). Available at www.reactionsnet.com/index5.html?/EuLibrary/blank.asp?/contents/publications/reactions/magazine/2001/nov01/header.html&/contents/publications/reactions/magazine/2001/nov01/contents.html [March 11, 2003].

Stiroh, Kevin. 2002. "Diversification in Banking: Is Noninterest Income the Answer?" Staff Report. Federal Reserve Bank of New York, September.

Wang, Shaun S. 1998. "Aggregation of Correlated Risk Portfolios: Models and Algorithms." Theory of Risk Working Paper. Arlington, Va.: Casual Actuarial Society. Available at casact.org/cotor/Wang.pdf [March 11, 2003].

———. 2002. "A Set of New Methods and Tools for Enterprise Risk Capital Management and Portfolio Optimization." Paper presented at the Casual Actuarial Society Forum, Arlington, Va., Summer. Available at www.casact.org/pubs/forum/02sforum/02sf043.pdf [March 11, 2003].

Ward, Lisa S., and David H. Lee. 2002. "Practical Application of the Risk-Adjusted Return on Capital Framework." Dynamic Financial Analysis Discussion Paper, CAS Forum (Summer). Arlington, Va.: Casual Actuarial Society. Available at www.casact.org/pubs/forum/02sforum/02sf079.pdf [March 11, 2003].

Webb, Bernard L., and Claude C. Lilly. 1994. *Raising the Safety Net: Risk-Based Capital for Life Insurance Companies.* Kansas City, Mo.: NAIC Publications.

Wilmarth, Arthur E. Jr. 2001. "How Should We Respond to the Growing Risks of Financial Conglomerates?" Public Law and Legal Theory Working Paper 034. George Washington University Law School. Forthcoming in Patricia A. McCoy, ed., *Financial Modernization after Graham-Leach-Bliley.* Newark, N.J.: Lexis Publishing.

Winton, Andrew. 1999. "Don't Put all Your Eggs in One Basket? Diversification and Specialization in Lending." Working Paper. University of Minnesota, Department of Finance, September.

Risk in Financial Conglomerates: Management and Supervision

IMAN VAN LELYVELD AND
ARNOLD SCHILDER

IN THE PAST DECADE we have seen financial conglomerates gain in importance. Financial conglomerates are groups that combine banking, securities, and insurance activities within one organization.[1] Trends such as disintermediation, globalization, and deregulation have made cross-sector consolidation possible. Consolidation has been driven by the search for revenue enhancement and cost savings and has been encouraged by improvements in information technology. So far most consolidation has been within sector and country. Nevertheless, some cross-sector groups of impressive size have been formed. An example is the ING Group, whose balance sheet at the end of 2001 equaled a little more than €705 billion. Although the external risks facing financial firms have not changed in essence, combining different activities within one organization presents new challenges both for the group's management as well as for regulators. In this paper we discuss the most important issues in this area.

The authors would like to thank Jaap Bikker, Sandra Desson, Flip Klopper, Klaas Knot, Léon Spooren, and Alfred Verhoeven for helpful comments and Danny van den Kommer for research assistance. All remaining errors are ours.

1. Reflecting continental European practice, we consider financial conglomerates that combine universal banking and insurance activities and not financial conglomerates that combine only banking and securities activities, as is more common in Anglo-Saxon countries. Thus a bank, in our definition, can be involved in both securities and commercial banking.

After outlining the developments that have led to the formation of large, complex, and diversified financial firms, or in other words financial conglomerates, we discuss the reasons that have been cited, mainly in the academic literature, for regulatory intervention, covering banking, insurance, and financial conglomerates in turn. Sheer size by itself, after all, does not merit the extensive regulation to which financial firms are subject. The reasons cited for banks are the possibility of bank runs, systemic crises, and moral hazard due to a lender of last resort and concerns regarding consumer protection. For insurance firms, the main reasons are concerns regarding consumer protection and, more generally, financial stability.

Given the good reasons that exist for regulation and supervision, within what institutional framework does this take place? Consolidation in the financial sector, for instance, would require closer coordination of regulation across the banking, securities, and insurance sectors. In the fourth section of this paper, we describe the—European—framework, with special attention to the Dutch situation. Since financial conglomerates were formed relatively early in the Netherlands, the regulatory response had to be formulated ahead of the curve as well. We highlight the motivations that played a role in creating the present Dutch regulatory structure.

Regulators are not the only stakeholders interested in the risk profile of financial firms. Many firms commit sizable resources themselves to monitor and manage risk. However, received wisdom is that in the absence of market imperfections, risk management does not add any value. The reasons for managing risk are thus based on violations of the assumptions of the Modigliani-Miller irrelevance theorems. We discuss the most important digressions in turn. Given that both management and regulators are interested in the risk profile of financial firms, they have a shared interest in accurate measurement and, consecutively, management of risk. We then briefly outline measurement methods, primarily to discuss the most important hurdles that have to be taken before a firm-wide risk management system can be implemented adequately.

Finally, we discuss the interplay between the objectives of supervisors and the goals of financial conglomerates. Are these objectives in line with each other, or are there areas in which opposite interests are evident? In what way can supervisory regulation support the developments of firm-wide risk management systems, and is this beneficial to the industry? The main issue addressed is what the framework for coming to an adequate risk management process, and thus a satisfactory level of capital, should look like. The central tenet here is the supervised institution's responsibility in this area. The concluding section summarizes our findings.

The Rise of Financial Conglomerates

An obvious definition of a financial conglomerate is a group of firms that predominantly deal with finance (that is, banks). In financial regulation, however, it has acquired a slightly different meaning: a financial conglomerate has come to mean a group of firms that engage in financial activities that have been kept separate, by law and regulation, for many years in many countries. Combinations of some of these activities—banking, securities trading, and insurance—are still forbidden in many countries. The Group of Ten gives the following definition: "A financial conglomerate is a conglomerate whose primary business is financial and whose regulated entities engage to a significant extent in at least two of the banking, securities, and insurance sectors."[2] The European Commission is proposing a more precise definition, in two steps: a group only qualifies as a financial conglomerate (a) if more than 50 percent of group activities are financial, and (b) if the shares of the banking sector (including securities activities) and the insurance sector in the total of the financial activities are within the range 10–90 percent. In addition, if the minority share has a balance sheet larger than €6 billion, the group also qualifies as a financial conglomerate. If the group is headed by an unregulated entity, it is called a mixed financial holding. This definition implies a rather flexible coverage, although the previously used definition in the Netherlands was even wider: any combination of banking and insurance would qualify as a financial conglomerate.

Consolidation in the financial sector has increased significantly over the last decade.[3] Most recent mergers and acquisitions involved firms

2. Group of Ten (2001).
3. Group of Ten (2001). As noted by National Bank of Belgium (2002), the direction of conglomeration in nonfinancial firms seems to be toward more unbundling or, in other words, refocusing. Focarelli and Pozzolo (2001) argue that regulatory restrictions are still slowing cross-border and cross-sector merger activity.

Table 1. Share of Financial Conglomerates in Bank Deposits, 2000

Country	Percent	Country	Percent
Austria	6	Italy	37
Belgium	97	Netherlands	93
Denmark	19	Portugal	67
Finland	73	Spain	10
France	67	Sweden	67
Germany	10	United Kingdom	57
Ireland	45		

competing in the same industry and country. Nevertheless, a number of highly complex financial institutions that operate across many sectors and countries have been formed. Well-known examples of groups active in more than one sector are, for instance, Citigroup-Travelers, Credit Suisse–Winterthur, Dresdner-Allianz, ING Group, and Fortis.

In Europe, financial conglomerates have captured significant market share in a number of countries and markets. As an example, we show bank deposits in Table 1. Financial conglomerates' share is significant in some markets and relatively high in the Netherlands.

A primary motive for financial consolidation seems to be revenue enhancement and cost savings.[4] Consolidation has been encouraged by improvements in information technology, financial deregulation, globalization of markets, and increased shareholder pressure for financial performance.[5] Various domestic regulatory regimes and corporate and national cultural differences are, however, discouraging consolidation.

Another motive for cross-sector consolidation is that financial segments are melting into one another, as financial institutions venture into diverse product markets (banks now also sell insurance products, for example, and insurance firms sell unit-linked products) or offer innovative, mixed products (such as investment-based mortgages).[6] New distribution channels, including the provision of financial services through the

---

4. We do not discuss, from either a theoretical or an empirical angle, whether forming a conglomerate creates or destroys value. Theoretical discussion can, for instance, be found in Boot and Schmeits (2000). Empirical evidence for the alleged existence of "conglomerate discounts" can be found in Berger and Ofek (1995), Mansi and Reeb (2002), or Scharfstein and Stein (2000).

5. See, for example, van Lelyveld and Donker (2002)

6. See Allen and Santomero (2001) for a more general description of developments in banking.

Internet, reinforce this effect. Hence, financial institutions' activities are becoming more varied and generally more complex in nature. As their organizational structures are adapted to these developments, they too become more complex.

Several forces are driving these motives to be effectual. First and foremost are the technological innovations in the field of information and communication technology, which paved the way for the development of many new products and drastically lowered the operational costs per unit. Large financial institutions are generally better able to fund the extensive investment in information technology required. In addition, deregulation has opened plenty of new markets and allowed new cooperative links between, for example, banks and insurance companies. Moreover, in Europe the generation of shareholder value has become a far more significant concern to management as well. In practice, expansion and diversification are important tools in the strategic reorientation of financial institutions in response to mounting pressure, from both inside and outside the financial sector. In this process, the establishment of the European Monetary Union has acted as a catalyst, since the currency union advances the integration of financial markets and the consequent creation of a single competitive financial environment.[7]

Regulatory Concerns about the Risk Profile of a Conglomerate

Given the fact that financial conglomerates have gained in importance in recent years, the question arises, should supervisors be concerned? Below we discuss a number of reasons why supervisors would be interested in understanding and—if necessary—influencing the risk profile of any financial institution and, in particular, financial conglomerates.[8]

In the banking literature, the arguments have generally been phrased in terms of capital regulation. Thus, for instance, managers' incentives to gamble for resurrection at some point could be contained by prescribing some level of capital. Other, noncapital, instruments to control risk might, however, be just as effective. One could think of, for instance,

---

7. According to the evidence shown by Berger, Dai, Ongena, and Smith (2002), it seems that consolidation will never become total because there will always be a demand for "local" banks.

8. This section draws heavily on Bikker and Van Lelyveld (2003).

direct supervision instead. Generally, such measures can be accommodated within the existing, capital-focused literature. In the discussion, for brevity, we use "supervision" to denote both regulation and supervision.[9]

Consolidated supervision is an essential tool of (banking) supervision. In simple terms, it is a response to the fact that financial conglomerates frequently carry on part of their business—in some cases, the major part—through subsidiaries and affiliates. Moreover, a bank or insurer may belong to a group headed by a holding company, and in such cases supervisors need to take account of the activities of the holding company and fellow subsidiaries of the bank or insurer. Consolidated supervision is therefore a comprehensive approach to supervision that seeks to evaluate the strength of an entire group, taking into account all the risks that may affect an examined institution regardless of whether these risks are carried on the books of the examined institution or on those of related entities.

Motivation for Regulation of Financial Institutions

Financial institutions are regulated and supervised for many reasons. The most important are consumer protection (that is, delegated monitoring), the functioning of financial institutions and markets, the incentives for participants, market failures, and, finally, the special nature of financial products.[10] Critics of regulation argue that market failures are nonexistent or, at most, not serious.[11] Moreover, it is argued that regulation cannot prevent failures or imperfections or is too costly, whereas some forms of regulation might even generate new sources of moral hazard. Following Llewellyn, the instruments at hand are prudential regulation and conduct of business regulation.[12] The former aims to promote solvency and thus the general safety and soundness of institutions, while the latter concerns the customer-firm relationship. Conduct of business regulation is generally framed in a consumer protection framework. It should, however, be of interest to firms themselves as well and should be seen in

9. See, for example, Llewellyn (1999), who adds a further distinction between regulation (setting specific rules), monitoring (observing compliance), and supervision (observing bank behavior in general).

10. See Allen and Herring (2001, table I) for a discussion of additional motives, including corrective measures employed.

11. The fiercest opponents of government regulation can be found in the Free Banking School. See, for instance, Dowd (1994) or White (1984).

12. Llewellyn (1999).

a wider risk management setting. Witnessing the growing importance of product liability and the possibility of reputational fallout, it becomes increasingly more important for a firm to know what you sell to whom.

In the next three subsections we consider the need for regulation and supervision of banks, insurance firms, and financial conglomerates, respectively. In addition, the third subsection also seeks to establish whether the "silo" approach or the "integrated" approach is more appropriate for the supervision of financial conglomerates. In the "silo" approach, total risk is a simple sum of sectoral risks, whereas in the "integrated" approach risk reduction for diversification effects or an add-on for contagion risk is incorporated.

Reasons for Regulation of Banks

Contrary to other firms, banks may use deposits for their funding needs. Deposits differ from other types of debt in that a substantial part of deposits may be retrieved on sight. Demand deposits generate the possibility of a bank run on an individual bank that is suspected to be insolvent. The first-come-first-served (FCFS) constraint, facing demand depositors, means that there is a strong incentive for depositors to be in the front of the queue.[13] In nonfinancial near-bankruptcies, it is more difficult to jump the queue and thus evade costs.

Another typical characteristic of banks (and other financial firms) is their opacity: it is hard to assess the total risk a bank is running. In particular, the value of longer-term investments that are not publicly traded is difficult to establish, especially at any specific point in time, let alone by relative outsiders such as (unsophisticated) depositors.[14] As the banking operations of many banks are fairly similar, financial stress emerging in one bank may indicate similar difficulties in others. In many cases it is difficult to distinguish bank-specific shocks from general shocks. Therefore, a run on one bank may generate runs on other banks, causing serious financial instability.[15] Contagion may also be reinforced because banks are interwoven through heavy interbank lending and cross-participation.

13. Chen (1999).
14. For that reason, the new Basel Capital Accord introduces a set of disclosure requirements to encourage greater transparency and reduce uncertainty.
15. Seminal contributions in this area are Bryant (1980) and Diamond and Dybvig (1983).

If bank runs are not triggered by true insolvency, they are detrimental to social welfare, because in a bankruptcy contracts have to be renegotiated or traded at a discount. Hence, special measures are required to reduce welfare-impairing bank runs and their threat of financial instability.

A typical feature of banks is that the contracts on both sides of the balance sheet have different maturities: funding is of a short-term nature, whereas lending is generally long term. This creates both liquidity risk, which is often the immediate cause of a bank run, and interest rate risk, which may damage solvency. Public authorities must act to monitor these risks and safeguard the public interest. Finally, banks have a pivotal role in the clearing and settlement of transactions and—above all—in the provision of funding, in particular to small and medium-size enterprises.

These risks are addressed by constructing a "safety net," usually including prudential regulation and supervision, a lender of last resort, and deposit insurance. A well-devised financial safety net consists of a mix of all three elements. First, the causal forces for financial fragility can be addressed with regulation and supervision, lowering the probability of financial instability. Best-practice standards on reporting can, for instance, reduce the opacity of a bank. Second, implementing a deposit insurance scheme for the deposits of households removes the panic that induces the FCFS constraint.[16] Finally, appointing the central bank as the lender of last resort, which may provide funds to illiquid but solvent banks (in principle, only against collateral), can, in some cases, also be the solution for bank-run problems.

Deposit insurance and a lender of last resort cause risk shifting. In the case of deposit insurance, risk is shifted from the bank's deposit holders to the insurer, which often consists of all other banks or taxpayers. This means that the risk of deposit holders is not priced, which makes this type of funding relatively cheap.[17] Risk insensitivity of funding creates an incentive for banks to expose themselves to more risky and thus more rewarding investment. Similarly, a lender of last resort implies that risk is

16. For an overview, see Garcia (2000). In most countries, banks pay premiums to fill a fund, whereas in others, such as the Netherlands, a pay-as-you-go system covers losses. An additional motivation for deposit insurance is consumer protection. For instance, in the Netherlands, all deposits are covered; not only the deposits that are directly demandable and hence contribute to the risk of a bank run but also nondemandable liabilities such as fixed long-term time deposits. Moreover, securities in trust are also covered to some extent.

17. Unless the deposit insurance is based on risk-sensitive premiums, as is the objective in a growing number of countries (Garcia 2000), but not in the Netherlands.

shifted from all funding parties of the bank to the taxpayer, which may provoke banks to adopt more risky behavior, because an unpriced insurance covers part of the possible damage. These moral hazard problems, brought about by instruments to reduce the fragility of banks, imply an additional reason for regulation and supervision.

Reasons for Regulation of Insurance Firms

The main reason why banking markets are thought to be unstable has to do with banks' funding by deposit holders, with their special FCFS status, in combination with their long-term assets. Insurance firms, however, are not funded by deposit holders but by policyholders, without the FCFS rights attributed to deposit holders. Policyholders have the right to surrender a policy, but processing a request to surrender takes time. This allows the insurance firm to liquidate investments under normal conditions, avoiding the "fire sale" a bank faces in a bank-run situation. In the Netherlands surrendering generally takes place under a certain discount, which covers at least the costs of administration and liquidation. Often tax treatment is less favorable if the policy is surrendered before legal minimum terms are met. Thus commuting insurance policies comes with substantial costs, and individual policyholders have no need to commute earlier than others. However, the situation may be different in other countries, where other legal conditions prevail for surrendering. Especially in the United States, the discounts may be lower and not always actuarially fair, which makes surrendering more likely and thus a greater risk for the firm.

In some respects, policyholders have a position similar to that of deposit holders: banks and life insurance firms are both opaque institutions, with a degree of riskiness, which is hard for the layperson to assess. Institutions can thus, without knowledge of the policyholder, behave in a—more—risky fashion. Firms might even attempt to gain market share with policies against actuarially insufficient premiums and then proceed to gamble with the received monies. Hence, consumer protection is an important and strong argument for prudential insurance supervision, similar to the motivation for deposit insurance. For many life insurance policies, the case for consumer protection is even stronger than for deposits, as the contracts last very long. Understandably, policyholders have difficulty assessing the current riskiness of insurance firms, but even the experts cannot foresee a firm's behavior in, say, five or ten

years, let alone over forty or sixty years. The objective of consumer protection is thus a much broader concept than can be attained by market-
conduct regulation only.

Where banks and insurance firms share their opacity and the ensuing
need for consumer protection, they seem to differ with respect to the
other arguments for supervision. At first sight, insurance firms as stand-
alone institutions are not likely to constitute a major threat to financial
stability through sudden crashes. Even where—due to the opacity of
insurers—financial difficulties in one firm may contribute to doubts
regarding other insurance firms, this need not automatically lead to panic
reactions similar to bank runs, as the surrendering of policies takes time
and involves costs for the policyholders.[18] Liquidity risk is not a major
problem for insurance firms because their balance sheets generally have
a reversed duration structure[19] (life insurance firms) and claims go
through a processing cycle, preempting surprises (property and casualty
insurers). In addition, unlike banks, insurance firms do not play a role in
maintaining the payments system.

However, some financial stability arguments remain or even become of
growing importance. First, insurers have become increasingly more inter-
twined with the banking sector, taking on significant amounts of credit
risk. A failing insurer could thus suddenly shift sizable amounts of risk
back to the banking sector, possibly causing instability. Second, in particular, life and pension insurers have material equity holdings. Failure could
imply the unwinding of these positions, putting downward pressure on
equity prices. In particular, the expectation of a sell-off could have a relatively quick impact. Third, the stability of the insurance sector is crucial
for the general confidence in the financial system and thus for economic
growth. Since insurance firms supply a product with a long lifetime, dis-
turbance of this market would have pronounced external effects.[20]
Increased uncertainty could lead to reduced investment. Work by, for
instance, Brunetti, Kisunko, and Weder shows that confidence in the
"rules of the game" is an important determinant of economic growth.[21]

18. However, a certain contribution to the system risk may occur insofar as these institutions are heavily involved in credit derivatives.
19. Banks have liabilities with a short contractual duration combined with longer-
running assets. Life insurers, in contrast, have long-term liabilities, while their assets are
of a much shorter duration.
20. For example, Bencivenga and Smith (1991).
21. Brunetti, Kisunko, and Weder (1998).

Disruption of the insurance market, especially the life and pension insurance market, would certainly deal a blow to the confidence in the financial market. In conclusion, the main arguments for supervision of insurance firms are consumer protection and financial stability in general.

Reasons for Regulation of Financial Conglomerates

The current Dutch regulatory regime for a financial conglomerate is a silo plus approach. Separate requirements hold for the bank, the securities firm, and the insurance firm, as if they were independent institutions, ignoring diversification. In addition, various rules about the organizational structure apply to the financial conglomerate as a whole. In determining the total risk of the financial conglomerate, however, diversification effects should also be considered.[22] Although possible diversification effects are not a separate motive for supervision, they would influence the overall risk profiles and would therefore be relevant in supervision of a financial conglomerate.

An aspect of a financial conglomerate that could make regulatory intervention necessary is that of regulatory consistency. Regulatory inconsistency could lead to "double gearing," where the same capital, issued by the conglomerate, is being counted twice, to satisfy both banking and insurance capital requirements. Another result of inconsistency is "excessive leveraging," which can occur when the conglomerate issues debt and gives the proceeds as equity to the regulated subsidiary. Because of regulatory inconsistency, a financial conglomerate could shift activities from one of its banks to one of its insurance firms, or vice versa, if the respective capital requirements were lower.[23] Such arbitrage is particularly likely where the regulatory framework for banks and insurance firms differs in measuring risk and determining capital requirements. This may even be the case when the regulatory frameworks would be fully harmonized, as different motives for supervision may lead to dif-

22. For the moment, we ignore the fundamental measurement problems in integrating bank and insurance risk (that is, a common unit of risk and a common time horizon).

23. Evidence for such behavior has been presented recently by the International Association of Insurance Supervisors (IAIS 2002). The IAIS concludes, based on a survey, "Regulatory arbitrage is a factor in the 'underwriting' type of transactions but does not appear to be the main driver." In such "underwriting" activities, insurers are actively selling credit protection instead of taking on credit risk through direct ownership of assets with credit risk.

ferent regulatory requirements. Moreover, some activities could also be shifted to unregulated entities within the conglomerate.

A second aspect of financial conglomerates is that financial difficulties in one subsidiary in one sector could have contagion or reputational effects on another subsidiary in a different sector, especially when using the same brand name.[24] In that case, the conglomerate may be more vulnerable than its constituting subsidiaries. Similar contagion problems may also arise with unregulated entities in a financial conglomerate. If these entities can expect support when needed, a moral hazard problem arises, as they could be tempted to take on more risk than they would otherwise have done. Unregulated entities would, in a sense, lean on the deposit insurance or the ignorance of policyholders (the so-called free-rider behavior). Also banks and insurance subsidiaries themselves may expect help from the holding company in cases of financial stress and engage in more risky behavior as part of a financial conglomerate than as a stand-alone institute. These possible risks of contagion and cross-sector moral hazard form an argument for supervisory intervention at a financial conglomerate that would be stricter than the rules applying to its composing firms and that would also include supervisory requirements for unregulated entities.[25]

A third set of issues is related to the sheer size and complexity of financial conglomerates. First, there is the moral hazard associated with the "too-big-to-fail" position of many financial conglomerates. In addition, it becomes more difficult to manage and understand the operation of a firm as the organization grows. Both these issues are not unique to financial conglomerates. Nevertheless, these issues tend to come to the fore because financial conglomerates tend to be large.

Table 2 gives an overview of the various arguments for supervisory intervention that we have discussed. It is clear that combining banking and insurance within one entity poses additional challenges for supervisors. In addition to the arguments mentioned, diversification could be an important issue in the supervision of financial conglomerates.

---

24. See, for example, the outspoken comments in the *Economist* in reaction to the loss-leader pricing and reputational fallout from conflicts of interest of analysts at Citigroup. "Thanks a Bundle," *Economist,* August 24, 2002, p. 12.

25. An integrated supervisory regime for financial conglomerates would raise practical problems, as supervision of insurance firms is based on host-country control, whereas supervision of banks is based on home-country control. As capital requirements of insurance firms are not based on an international agreement (such as the Basel Accord for banks), domestic and foreign insurance divisions face different regulatory treatment.

Table 2. Arguments for Supervision of Financial Firms

Banks	*Financial conglomerates*	*Insurance firms*
Bank runs—deposit insurance (moral hazard)	Supervisory consistency	Consumer protection
Lender of last resort (moral hazard)	Contagion risk	Financial stability
Consumer protection	Size of the firms	Financial stability

Developments in Regulation

The previous section established that supervisors have a stake in the well-being of a financial conglomerate. Before we turn to the discussion of the market failures that would cause financial conglomerates themselves to be interested in managing their risk, we first discuss two relevant issues. First, we briefly discuss the institutional structure of supervision in the Netherlands. Second, we turn to the regulation aimed at achieving supervisors' objectives.

Institutional Structure of Supervision

Historically, as in most countries, supervision in the Netherlands has been organized along sectoral lines. Banking supervision resided at the central bank (de Nederlandsche Bank, DNB), the Pensions and Insurance Board (PVK) was responsible for the pension and insurance industry, and the Securities Board (STE) was responsible for the securities firms and the exchanges. As early as 1990, however, supervisors realized that the changing financial landscape necessitated closer cooperation. To this end, the pension and insurance supervisor (the PVK) and the banking supervisor (DNB) signed the so-called protocol. In this document, the supervisors agreed to coordinate the supervision of banks or insurance companies in conglomerates. The protocol contains, inter alia, the requirement for financial conglomerates to report on group solvency, risk concentration, and intragroup transactions.[26]

---

26. A related issue to those mentioned in the previous footnote is that, in insurance, the supervisor currently focuses on the legal entity, while in banking, the supervisor focuses on the whole group.

Further consolidation of financial firms and increasingly similar product lines made policymakers realize that even further coordination of regulation and supervision was necessary. The sectoral supervisors for banking, insurance, and securities formalized cooperation through the establishment, in 1999, of the Council of Financial Supervisors. In the council, the supervisors coordinate rules and policy not specific to a particular sector. Although the council has been operating satisfactorily, it recently became evident that an even closer coordination is called for. Since September 1, 2002, a new structure of financial supervision has been in place in the Netherlands, no longer primarily organized along sectoral lines, but instead organized around functions. This function-based model closely mirrors developments in some other countries, which are also moving toward a more cross-sectoral supervisory model.

The central tenet in the new Dutch model is the distinction between prudential and market-conduct supervision.[27] Prudential supervision concentrates on the financial soundness of an institution. The aim of market-conduct supervision is to promote an orderly and transparent process in the financial markets and proper relations between market participants, thereby contributing to the protection of consumers. Systemic supervision remains the responsibility of DNB. Under the old model, the nature of the financial institution determined which supervisory authority was responsible, while under the new function-based model, DNB and the PVK both have a responsibility for prudential supervision. Closer cooperation between DNB and the PVK is currently institutionally embedded by cross-representation in their highest executive and supervisory bodies. The member of the executive board of DNB responsible for supervision and the chairman of the board of the PVK each sit on the other institution's board. The same cross-sector appointment applies to the chairmen of the supervisory boards of both institutions. Moreover, closer coordination of auxiliary services and joint research projects have been initiated. A special area of cooperation is the joint supervision of financial conglomerates. Further integration of both organizations is envisaged.

The Securities Board, meanwhile, is evolving from the supervisory authority for securities activities into an integral, cross-sector authority for conduct-of-business supervision, taking on a new name: the Authority for Financial Markets (Au-FM). The Council of Financial Supervisors

27. See Dutch Central Bank (2002) for a more in-depth discussion of the new Dutch institutional setup.

will remain as a consultative platform for common concerns such as issues of integrity (for instance, customer due diligence and anti–money laundering), new developments in supervision, and the evaluation of legislation and agreement on international operations. The new supervisory model does not entail any changes in the existing relations between the supervisory authorities and the minister of finance, nor between Parliament and the minister. The concept of "supervision at a distance" remains as important as ever for the independent and expert exercise of supervision of the financial sector.

Regulatory Policies

Regulation of financial conglomerates is changing as well. In the European community, community law supersedes national law. Once a directive has been passed in the European Parliament, national authorities have to enact these European laws in national legislation. Presently, the European Commission has proposed new regulation for supervision of financial conglomerates, which will supplement regulation covering banking, securities, and insurance.[28]

Instruments that have been defined in the new legislation are group-wide solvency requirements, reporting of large counterparties and intra-group transactions, and, last but not least, standards for internal organization and control. An important function that will be created is that of a coordinator selected from the supervisors involved. Such a coordinator will, for instance, collect and distribute prudential information, assess group-wide information, and coordinate supervisory activity, especially in times of stress. As noted, the proposed definition of a financial conglomerate contains a clause stating that the conglomerate qualifies if the balance sheet of the smaller sector exceeds €6 billion. The current definition used in the Netherlands is wider: any level of cross-sector activity qualifies a conglomerate as a financial conglomerate.

Risk Management in Financial Conglomerates

Next to the reasons for supervisors to be interested in the risk profile of a financial conglomerate, the conglomerate itself might also be inter-

28. European Commission (2001).

ested in its own risk profile. In the literature, a number of reasons have been suggested why this might be the case, as discussed in the next section. Then we discuss the fact that given that a firm is interested in its risk profile, it faces a formidable task: it has to measure risk adequately across the whole conglomerate.

Why Manage Risk?

In the stylized Modigliani-Miller world of corporate finance textbooks, neither the capital structure nor corporate risk management affects the value of the firm. Investors are able to diversify their invested wealth, and a firm is not rewarded for taking on (or shedding) firm-specific risk. Only the remaining, nondiversifiable, systemic risk carries a return. There is thus no reason for a firm ever to alter its risk profile. If market inefficiencies are introduced, however, risk management and capital structure matter and (may) add value. Five major driving forces can be identified behind firm's risk management: (1) flow of information, (2) taxes, (3) bankruptcy costs, (4) distortions due to contracting problems between firms and investors, and (5) distorted incentives for management due to imperfect contracting between management and shareholders.[29] Let us discuss these driving forces in turn.

An important reason why a firm's management would like to invest in a firm-wide risk management system is the information flow that such a system can achieve.[30] This information enables management to make better-informed decisions regarding where to invest scarce capital in order to maximize profits. It might also make management aware of certain natural hedges.[31] More specifically, it makes it possible to link risk management and capital management, as highlighted by Froot and Stein.[32] In their analysis the desirability of a given investment depends on

---

29. See Ligterink (2001) or Cummins, Phillips, and Smith (1998) for a further discussion of why firms would engage in risk management. Harris and Raviv (1991) give an excellent overview of the earlier theoretical and empirical work.

30. This seems to be a quite important argument, both for practitioners and regulators; for example, "Supervisors should monitor material risk concentrations on a timely basis, as needed, through regular reporting or by other means to help form a clear understanding of the risk concentrations of the financial conglomerate (Joint Forum 1999), and they should "recognize the interdependent nature of risks" (Lam 1999).

31. See Cumming and Hirtle (2001).

32. Froot and Stein (1998).

the extent to which its nontradable risk is correlated with the nontradable risk of the institution's portfolio.

A second driving force is that if the tax system is progressive, there is an incentive to smooth earnings to minimize taxes.[33] Risk management can reduce volatility of earnings and thus reduce the overall tax burden. If firms are not allowed to carry losses backward or forward for reporting or tax purposes, the ability to smooth is even better appreciated. Reducing volatility is also likely to increase a firm's debt capacity because the likelihood of a costly bankruptcy is reduced. Debt holders thus demand a lower risk premium, increasing the ability to borrow. Since interest payments are deductible, this, in turn, increases the tax shield that holding debt supplies.

Third is the existence of bankruptcy costs: management's expectations incorporate these costs, and this is likely to lead to underinvestment.[34] Risk management reduces the volatility of earnings and hence the probability of default. This, in turn, leads to lower expected bankruptcy costs, and thus investment decisions are closer to optimum.

A fourth driving force is that information asymmetry between contracting firms and financiers can lead to distortions. These contracting problems can occur either before or after contracting. Prior to contracting, a firm generally has private information about its credit quality that the market does not have. Overcoming such informational asymmetry makes external financing expensive so that firms do not undertake all projects with a positive net present value.[35] A similar divide runs between old and new shareholders. Accurate measurement of risk and returns, with accompanying disclosure, can persuade financiers to invest in the firm.

After contracting, there is an incentive for the equity holders to change the risk profile of the firm. From their perspective, each additional "unit of risk" is typically expected to add value because of the equity holders' limited liability. Debt holders, however, are aware of these incentives and thus ask for a risk premium. Compared with optimum, this leads to underinvestment. Adherence to a strict policy to limit risks would reduce this problem (as long as such policies are credible).

---

33. Smith and Stulz (1985).
34. From management's point of view, bankruptcy poses a major cost, especially if they have invested (human) capital in the firm (Smith and Stulz 1985).
35. Myers and Majluf (1984).

A final reason why the investment decision can be distorted, and thus a firm-wide risk management system is helpful, is because of the so-called principal-agent problem: the informational asymmetry between a firm's management (the agents) and its owners (the principals), the equity holders. It is difficult for the principal to assess the ability (or effort) of management, even ex post. Accurate and transparent risk management makes it easier for the equity holders (the principals) to reveal management's role.

A conclusion that can be drawn from the presented literature is that trying to control the volatility of cash flows is worthwhile. Tax considerations, bankruptcy costs, and various forms of asymmetric information can cause hedging behavior to add value for stakeholders. Most of the literature assumes shareholders to be the only stakeholders, but this restriction can generally be eased without loss of generality.

How to Manage Risk

Risk management presupposes adequate risk measurement.[36] Risk measurement, however, still differs across banking and insurance activities within financial conglomerates, reflecting, among other things, differences in the dominant types of risk that have traditionally been faced. Banks used to focus mainly on credit risk, but more recently they have paid some attention to other risks such as market, interest rate, and operational risk. Insurance companies, however, mainly focused on insurance risks, but recently they have paid more attention to risks on their asset side. To construct a common risk language across the whole of a financial conglomerate, differences in the sector-specific frameworks should be identified, and, if possible, agreement should be found consistently covering all relevant risks.

Risk measurement typically starts bottom-up in the different business lines within a financial institution. An example is the value-at-risk (VaR) model for market risk, which is common in banking. VaR was first introduced on trading floors of investment banks but is currently widely used in other areas. A consequence of the bottom-up approach is

---

36. Risk measurement, risk assessment, and risk management are often used interchangeably. Here risk measurement refers to the quantification of risk. Risk assessment is a broader concept in the sense that it also entails interpreting qualitative pieces of information. Risk management, in turn, encompasses risk assessment as well as risk mitigation.

that each individual type of risk is identified individually, and, consequently, its effect on the financial conglomerate as a whole is modeled separately. Since measurement methods have been designed with such diverse backgrounds, coming to a common measure of risk is quite a challenge. Within the industry, however, there seems to be a convergence toward a notion of "economic capital," which could serve as a common standard of risk. Economic capital can be defined as the amount of capital that a firm itself deems necessary to support the economic risk (that is, the unexpected losses) it originates given some tolerance level for default.

Since currently most enterprise-wide risk management systems are built on modular models, it is important to have a classification that covers all risks. Consecutively, a module for each risk area can be developed.[37] Many such classifications exist, and for the present purposes the exact demarcation between the risks is not relevant as long as all risks in both the banking as well as the insurance sector are encompassed.[38] An important remark in this respect is that the modular nature of measurement makes it difficult to incorporate diversification effects in the risk measurement framework. This effect is especially important for a financial conglomerate.

Depending on the type of risk being measured, managers can use value-at-risk, earnings-at-risk, or stress tests to assess the level of risk. Moreover, correct measurement of firm-wide risk should not only capture risk but also aggregate all relevant risks across an institution. In the aggregation, diversification effects should be taken into account. Due to its complexity, we do not discuss the technical details of adequate measurement in depth. Some remarks about the most important issues in risk measurement for financial conglomerates are, however, in order.

First, to come to a valid comparison of risk, the evaluation period should be comparable across areas of risk. The horizon over which risks are assessed is generally much longer in insurance than in banking. Second, another issue is the accurate measurement of returns, which is essential for risk measurement. Many assets and liabilities do not have an

---

37. Ideally we would like to identify all risk drivers (for instance, interest rates) and then jointly model the reaction to the volatility in the discerned risk drivers.

38. See Working Group on Economic Capital Models (2003) for a comprehensive typology of applicable risks.

easily observable market price. Fair value accounting might partly solve this problem if a reasonable, approximate price can be determined for nontraded assets and liabilities. Third, what is a reasonable frequency to compute economic capital?[39] Theory tells us that, for each individual investment, a firm should compute all relevant parameters.[40] For all practical purposes, this is not feasible, and many parameters will be determined only periodically. Finally, in many areas of risk, new measurement methods are continually developing. Operational risk, for instance, has seen considerable development. Business risk, however, is generally still a residual category of risk, notionally motivated by intoning the business environment. How do we combine information deriving from systems in different states of maturity?[41]

Once management has an adequate view of the risks present, objectives can be formulated. Risk management objectives can then be achieved in three ways: a firm can (1) modify its mix of activities or processes, (2) adjust its capital structure, or (3) hedge directly (using a financial instrument or insurance contract). These actions are not mutually exclusive; rather they complement one another. Note that the choice of "production methods" could also include accounting choices. Petersen and Thiagarajan present evidence that sometimes firms use accounting choices to reduce the volatility of accounting income.[42] With regard to the capital structure, it is obvious that one way the capital structure can be adjusted is through dividend policy. Another more direct way is through placement or buy-back of either equity or debt.

Risk Management in the Supervisory Review

As is well known, the proposed capital accord for banks (Basel II) comprises three pillars.[43] The first pillar is designed to set minimum solvency requirements, possibly using banks' internal models. In the second

39. An issue here, as noted by Kritzman, Lowry, and van Royen (2001), is that risk is measured as the uncertainty surrounding returns at the end of a set period. Such a focus on the outcome ignores the effects of interim losses, no matter how severe. It thus assumes that a firm is capable of withstanding any level of interim loss.
40. Froot and Stein (1998).
41. Cumming and Hirtle (2001).
42. Petersen and Thiagarajan (2000).
43. Basel Committee on Banking Supervision (2001)

pillar, the supervisory review, the institution under supervision and the supervisor enter into a dialogue about the required level of economic capital, after jointly setting the desired level of solvency. Through disclosure of relevant information, transparency, an aspect of the third pillar, serves to enable stakeholders to take remedial action.[44] An important practical issue is, of course, the chosen supervisory model, a point we return to at the end of this section.

The second pillar constitutes a codification of the essence of prudential supervision. First, banks themselves are expected to be able to assess the amount of—economic—capital required, apart from any regulatory requirement whatsoever. This is an essential difference compared to the present approach in that the supervisor is no longer responsible for giving detailed prescriptions; rather the institution has its own responsibility. Second, supervisors, too, must be capable of forming an opinion. Such a judgment should not be confined to an evaluation of the process followed by the banks in assessing the economic capital requirement but should extend to the adequacy of the resulting level of economic capital as well.

The general spirit of the supervisory review approach could also be applied to insurance firms and hence to the whole of a financial conglomerate. The Dutch pension and insurance supervisor (PVK) has drawn up general principles that are very much in line with the Basel proposal.[45] Moreover, KPMG, in a study for the European Commission, and Oliver, Wyman and Company, in a study for Dutch regulators, echo the same sentiments.[46] The present requirements for an insurer's technical provisions, for instance, can be seen as an analog to the pillar 1 minimum capital requirements. In addition to these minimum requirements, additional capital charges are levied for risks that are not fully captured in actuarial modeling. However, given the ample margin between actual and regulatory capital, it seems that, in the industry's view, not all risks are currently captured in the regulatory assessment of capital. An example of a risk that is not captured (sufficiently) could, for instance, be concentration risk. If it is clear that this risk is present, this should give rise to additional capital charges.

44. This last pillar also increases attention for what may be defined as "rating agencies capital," that is, the amount of capital required to maintain a given rating.

45. PVK (2001, p. 9). These general principles, however, still have to be worked out in detail.

46. KPMG (2002); Oliver, Wyman and Company (2001).

In the Basel II consultative package, the supervisory review is defined as proceeding from four general principles, which can briefly be stated as follows: (1) banks themselves should assess how much capital they require, (2) supervisors must review and evaluate the process involved by the assessments performed as well as the capital adequacy determined by banks, which in practice is likely to imply that (3) the solvency requirement as assessed by the firm is expected to exceed the minimum requirement according to pillar 1, and, finally, (4) supervisors must be able to intervene at an early stage before developments have reached a critical point.

Although all four general principles merit separate attention, we only discuss the general framework with a focus on general principle 2: How would a supervisor evaluate an institution's risk assessment and capital adequacy policy? General principle 1 has already been worked out to some extent in numerous general guidelines and best-practice papers like, for example, the Federal Reserve guidelines for reviewing methods of assessing economic capital.[47] Although formulating more detailed guidance would definitely be useful, this would go beyond the purpose of the present paper.

A possible general framework in which to implement a supervisory review might follow the steps shown in figure 1. Financial conglomerates would be expected to employ an internal model to determine economic capital. Supervisors would not require a financial conglomerate to use a separate, obligatory model to determine economic capital, and adequate implementation of general principle 1 thus would suffice.[48] The supervisor's role would be to assess the adequacy of the process though which the institution determines economic capital. This assessment would be comprehensive and would include measurement and capital management policy. In addition to assessing the process, the supervisor also would assess the outcome (that is, the level of economic capital).

It is important also to bear in mind that enterprise-wide risk management is currently the preserve of the more sophisticated (that is, larger) financial conglomerates. The wide definition currently proposed by the European Commission implies, however, that most financial conglomer-

---

47. Board of Governors of the Federal Reserve System (1999).

48. See FSA (2002, p. 33), where output from banks' economic capital models "may be used as a substitute for determining capital in certain aspects."

Figure 1. Implementing a Supervisory Review

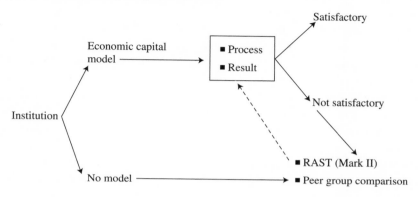

ates will not have implemented such a system. For institutions not using adequate models ("no model" in figure 1), supervisors shall need to form a judgment. This implies that supervisors must work toward a more comprehensive implementation of general principle 2. To this effect, the Dutch supervisors are still considering whether to extend the present method of risk analysis or to opt for an entirely novel method, possibly involving peer group comparison.

Internationally, supervisors use different methods for assessing an institution's degree of risk. A well-known categorization for bank risks is the one used by three major U.S. regulators: the CAMEL rating.[49] The components are Capital, Asset Quality, Management, Earnings, and Liquidity and are seen to reflect the financial performance, financial condition, operating soundness, and regulatory compliance of the banking institution. In 1996, in order to make the rating system more risk-focused, a sixth component—Sensitivity to market risk—was added to the CAMEL rating, resulting in CAMELS. Each of the component factors is rated on a scale of 1 (best) to 5 (worst), and these components are combined somewhat subjectively into a single rating, on a scale of 1 to 5. Many other systems are using categorizations that are more or less compatible.

The Dutch supervisors have taken a slightly different tack for some

49. The supervisors are the Federal Reserve, Office of the Comptroller of the Currency, and Federal Deposit Insurance Corporation.

time now.[50] DNB has a comprehensive risk analysis methodology in place, supported by a flexible Risk Analysis Software Tool (RAST). The pension and insurance supervisor, PVK, has a methodology (MARS) that is still in the development stage. Presently, the Dutch banking supervisor and the pension and insurance supervisor are merging their respective approaches. For the merged approach, the exact delineation of the risk areas differs because, contrary to the American bank-focused CAMELS, insurance risks have to be explicitly accommodated, but this is a relatively innocuous point. More important, a clear conceptual difference is drawn between risks, on the one hand, and mitigating controls, on the other. This practical distinction does not conflict with the theoretical treatment of risks in the literature. Controls can be seen as a way to avoid negative returns and can thus be seen as part of the investment decision that is central in most theoretical papers.

The present risk analysis methodology is well suited to channel supervisory attention to those areas within a financial institution that are either opaque or risky from a supervisory standpoint. To move forward to pillar 2 capital requirements, however, will be quite a challenge.[51] First, the current method of aggregating individual scores to an overall score is designed to highlight extreme valuations, especially bad evaluations. However, if, based on the score from the risk analysis, an (additional) capital requirement will be levied, a suitable aggregation algorithm should be devised. Second, once a supervisor has determined the relative riskiness of an institution, he has to take the next step and move from the risk assessment to the capital requirement. How does one translate an assessment into a capital requirement? Third, once the appropriate level of capital has been determined, the institution has to be informed whether its own assessment of capital is deemed adequate. One option is to withhold comment as long as the institution's capital ratio is above the regulatory minimum. As long as this is the case, discussing capital with the institution is relatively easy for the line supervisor. However, since the assessment is an iterative process, it is conceivable that firms will try to sound out where the regulatory minimum lies. In the end, the institu-

---

50. Both Dutch approaches are similar in spirit and akin to ARROW, the approach of the English Financial Services Authority. The Norwegian and Swedish supervisors are developing risk analysis systems along very similar lines.

51. See FSA (2002) for thoughts on how the transformation could be achieved.

tion will discover where the minimum lies at the cost of some, possibly costly, uncertainty. Other important questions that remain to be answered are whether a supervisor can use an internal economic capital model without too many modifications and whether a supervisor should be able and willing to adequately replicate an institution's model or whether this is a lost race to begin with. It is clear that many challenges remain.

The described framework will also be evolutionary. If internal developments in the supervised conglomerates warrant this, the supervisor will be able to rely more and more on the internal models of the firms. A key ingredient in this "supervision at a distance" is good corporate governance. Only if the corporate governance structure is judged sound can the results of the internal models be incorporated in the supervisory review. Another development in this area is the convergence in supervisory practices. Since financial conglomerates have numerous supervisors, the supervisory approach, as seen from the perspective of the firm, will become more consistent as supervisory practices converge. Since a clear supervisory treatment is also in the interest of the supervised institution, because it reduces uncertainty, a converged approach can also start on a voluntary basis, as is, for instance, the case for Fortis. Fortis is a party in the memorandum of understanding between the Dutch and Belgian sectoral supervisors involved in this Dutch-Belgian financial conglomerate, and it voluntarily supplies extra information to the supervisors.

Presently, the Dutch supervisors are studying a number of outstanding issues. Following the Oliver, Wyman and Company study, Freshfields, a law firm, was asked to investigate the effectiveness of legal firewalls between the legal entities constituting a financial conglomerate.[52] If such firewalls could protect some parts of the conglomerate from adverse shocks occurring in other parts of the conglomerate, then the threat of contagion could be reduced. Another initiative is the Working Group on Economic Capital. In this group, supervisors and representatives of industry, both banking and insurance, are jointly investigating "best practice" for economic capital models in the Netherlands. The first report, describing how risks are measured in financial conglomerates, has been published recently.[53] Together with future reports, the working group's

52. Oliver, Wyman and Company (2001).
53. Working Group on Economic Capital Models (2003).

work should sketch a comprehensive picture of economic capital models and their uses.

Conclusions

Financial conglomerates have become an important part of the financial landscape in a number of countries. In the United States, the restrictions on cross-sector mergers have been eased only recently. In Europe such restrictions were lifted somewhat earlier and have, in some countries, led to financial conglomerates with significant market shares and of impressive size.

Sheer size alone, however, does not warrant the wide-ranging regulation and supervision that are applied to banking and, to a lesser extent, insurance. We discussed a number of reasons that have been cited in the literature for regulating and supervising financial institutions, summarized in table 1. For banks, the arguments discussed were the possibility of bank runs, systemic crises, and moral hazard due to a lender of last resort as well as concerns about consumer protection. For insurance firms, the main argument is consumer protection. Bringing banking and insurance together in a financial conglomerate yields the risks of supervisory inconsistency and of contagion. An ameliorating factor is that the combination of diversified (that is, less than perfectly correlated) activities will result in a diversification bonus. However, other concerns are related to the size of financial conglomerates. Since many conglomerates are large, the moral hazard of too-big-to-fail attitudes arises, resulting in additional risk.

After discussing the reasons for regulation and supervision, we turned to the institutional setup of supervision in the Netherlands. It is clear that, following the trend in the Dutch banking and insurance markets, the institutional setup had to be adapted accordingly. In a number of steps, the sectoral supervisors have come to a structure based on functional activity. Two bodies are responsible for prudential regulation and supervision: the Dutch Central Bank (DNB) and the Pensions and Insurance Supervisory Authority (PVK), currently linked through executive cross-representation and a memorandum of understanding. The Netherlands Authority for Financial Markets (Au-FM) is responsible for market conduct. Such a structure should result in the efficient regulation and supervision of financial conglomerates as well as of firms operating in just a single sector.

Financial firms have their own reasons to care about their risk profile. In the classical world of a Miller and Modigliani textbook, the capital structure of a firm is irrelevant. If investors are interested in less risk, they can reduce risk by diversifying their portfolio. The firm is thus only rewarded for that part of a firm's risks that is not diversifiable (that is, systemic risk). Firms, however, do care about their risk profile because reality deviates from the perfect world assumed by Miller and Modigliani. Information flow, taxes, bankruptcy costs, and imperfect information and incentives all supply motives for managing risk.

Both supervisors and the industry are thus interested in the management of risk. The question is how to converge to a modus operandi that allows for the most efficient way to achieve the stated objectives. The supervisory review, as proposed in the new Basel Accord, suggests a framework that would seem to be fruitful. The central tenet in the supervisory review is that it is the responsibility of the supervised institution itself to have a proper measure of risk and a process for managing this risk. The role of the supervisor is thus no longer one of supplying detailed guidelines but shifts to analyzing the integrity of the risk management process as a whole, including the resulting level of capital. A necessary condition for the incorporation of internal models in the supervisory review is that the corporate governance is adequate. Only then can we rely on "supervision at a distance."

The question of how to judge a firm's economic capital model, however, raises numerous issues that still have to be addressed. Issues are, among others, the accurate measurement of returns, the evaluation period, the frequency of computation, and the different states of maturity of methods across different risk areas. Together with the industry, the Dutch supervisors hope to find solutions to these issues. These solutions will not only be useful to industry but also help the supervisors to improve their assessment of the risk management processes and the resulting capital levels.

References

Allen, Franklin, and Richard Herring. 2001. "Banking Regulation Versus Securities Market Regulation." Working Paper 01/29. Philadelphia: Wharton School.

Allen, Franklin, and Anthony M. Santomero. 2001. "What Do Financial Intermediaries Do?" *Journal of Banking and Finance* 25 (February): 271–94.

Basel Committee on Banking Supervision. 2001. "The New Basel Capital Accord, Second Consultative Document." Basel: Bank for International Settlements.

Bencivenga, Valerie, and Bruce D. Smith. 1991. "Financial Intermediation and Endogenous Gowth." *Review of Economic Studies* 58 (2, April): 195–209.

Berger, Allen N., Qinglei Dai, Steven Ongena, and D. C. Smith. 2002. "To What Extent Will the Banking Industry Be Globalized? A Study of Bank Nationality and Reach in 20 European Nations." International Finance Discussion Paper 725. Federal Reserve System Board of Governors.

Berger, Philip G., and Eli Ofek. 1995. "Diversification's Effect on Firm Value." *Journal of Financial Economics* 37 (1): 39–65.

Bikker, Jaap A., and Iman P. P. van Lelyveld. 2003. "Economic Versus Regulatory Capital for Financial Conglomerates." In Thea G. Kuppens, Henriëtte M. Prast, and Sandra A. T. Wesseling, eds., *Banking Supervision at the Crossroads*. Cheltenham, U.K.: Edward Elgar Publishing.

Board of Governors of the Federal Reserve System. 1999. "Assessing Capital Adequacy in Relation to Risk at Large Banking Organizations and Others with Complex Risk Profiles." SR Letter 99-18.

Boot, Arnoud W. A., and Anjolein Schmeits. 2000. "Market Discipline and Incentive Problems in Conglomerate Firms with Applications to Banking." *Journal of Financial Intermediation* 9 (3): 240–73.

Brunetti, Aymo, Gregory Kisunko, and Beatrice Weder. 1998. "Credibility of Rules and Economic Growth: Evidence from a Worldwide Survey of the Private Sector." *World Bank Economic Review* 12 (3): 353–84.

Bryant, John. 1980. "A Model of Reserves, Bank Runs, and Deposit Insurance." *Journal of Banking and Finance* 4 (December): 335–44.

Chen, Yehning. 1999. "Banking Panics: The Role of the First-Come, First-Served Rule and Information Externalities." *Journal of Political Economy* 107 (5): 946–68.

Cumming, Christine M., and Beverly J. Hirtle. 2001. "The Challenges of Risk Management in Diversified Financial Companies." *Federal Reserve Bank of New York Economic Policy Review* 7 (1): 1–17.

Cummins, J. David, Richard D. Phillips, and Stephen D. Smith. 1998. "The Rise of Risk Management." *Federal Reserve Bank of Atlanta Economic Review* 83 (1): 30–40.

Diamond, Douglas W., and Philip H. Dybvig. 1983. "Bank Runs, Deposit Insurance, and Liquidity." *Journal of Political Economy* 91 (3): 401–19.

Dowd, Kevin. 1994. "Competitive Banking, Bankers' Clubs, and Bank Regulation." *Journal of Money, Credit, and Banking* 26 (2): 289–308.

Dutch Central Bank. 2002. "Structure of Financial Supervision." *Quarterly Bulletin of de Nederlandsche Bank* (March): 37–42.

European Commission. 2001. "Towards an EU Directive on the Prudential Supervision of Financial Conglomerates." Brussels.

Focarelli, Dario, and Alberto Franco Pozzolo. 2001. "The Patterns of Cross-Border Bank Mergers and Shareholdings in OECD Countries." *Journal of Banking and Finance* 25 (December): 2305–37.

Froot, Kenneth A., and Jeremy C. Stein. 1998. "Risk Management, Capital Budgeting, and Capital Structure Policy for Financial Institutions: An Integrated Approach." *Journal of Financial Economics* 47 (1): 55–82.

FSA (Financial Services Authority). 2002. "Individual Capital Adequacy Standards." Consultation Paper 136. London.

Garcia, Gillian G. H. 2000. "Deposit Insurance: A Survey of Actual and Best Practices." Occasional Paper 197. Washington: International Monetary Fund.

Group of Ten. 2001. "Consolidation in the Financial Sector." Basel: Bank for International Settlements.

Harris, Milton, and Artur Raviv. 1991. "The Theory of Capital Structure." *Journal of Finance* 46 (1): 297–355.

IAIS (International Association of Insurance Supervisors). 2002. "Credit Risk Transfer between Insurance, Banking, and Other Financial Sectors." Draft issues paper. Bank for International Settlements, Basel, Switzerland.

Joint Forum. 1999. "Risk Concentration Principles." Basel: Bank for International Settlements.

KPMG. 2002. "Study into the Methodologies to Assess the Overall Financial Position of an Insurance Undertaking from the Perspective of Prudential Regulation." Brussels, May.

Kritzman, Mark, Kenneth Lowry, and Anne-Sophie van Royen. 2001. "Risk, Regimes, and Overconfidence." In Richard M. Levich and S. Figlewski, eds., *Risk Management*, pp. 129–44. Boston: Kluwer Academic Publishers.

Lam, James. 1999. "Enterprise-Wide Risk Management: Staying Ahead of the Convergence Curve." *Journal of Lending and Credit Risk Management* 81 (10): 16–19.

Ligterink, Jeroen. 2001. "Corporate Financial Risk Management." University of Amsterdam.

Llewellyn, David T. 1999. "The Economic Rationale for Financial Regulation." FSA Occasional Paper 1. London: Financial Services Authority.

Mansi, Sattar A., and David M. Reeb. 2002. "Corporate Diversification: What Gets Discounted?" *Journal of Finance* 57 (5): 2167–83.

Myers, Stewart C., and Nicholas S. Majluf. 1984. "Corporate Financing and Investment Decisions When Firms Have Information That Investors Do Not Have." *Journal of Financial Economics* 13 (2): 187–221.

National Bank of Belgium. 2002. "Financial Conglomerates." *Financial Stability Review, National Bank of Belgium* 1 (July): 61–79.

Oliver, Wyman and Company. 2001. "Study on the Risk Profile and Capital Adequacy of Financial Conglomerates." London.

Petersen, Mitchell A., and S. Ramu Thiagarajan. 2000. "Risk Measurement and Hedging: With and Without Derivatives." *Financial Management* 29 (4): 5–29.

PVK (Pensioen- & Verzekeringskamer). 2001. "De uitgangspunten voor een financieel toetsingskader." Apeldoorn.

Scharfstein, David S., and Jeremy C. Stein. 2000. "The Dark Side of Internal Capital Markets: Divisional Rent-Seeking and Inefficient Investment." *Journal of Finance* 55 (6): 2537–64.

Smith, Clifford W., and René M. Stulz. 1985. "The Determinants of Firms' Hedging Policies." *Journal of Financial and Quantitative Analysis* 20 (4): 391–405.

van Lelyveld, Iman P. P., and Marieke Donker. 2002. "Technology and the (Re)Location of Financial Activity: A European Perspective." In Morten Balling, Frank Lierman, and Andy Mullineaux, eds., *Technology and Finance: Challenges for Financial Markets, Business Strategies, and Policy Makers*, pp. 131–61. London: Routledge.

White, Lawrence H. 1984. *Free Banking in Britain: Theory, Experience, and Debate, 1800–1845*. Cambridge University Press.

Working Group on Economic Capital Models. 2003. "Risk Measurement within Financial Conglomerates: Best Practices by Risk Type." DNB Research Series Supervision 51. de Nederlandsche Bank, February.

Cross-Sector Supervision: Which Model?

JEROEN J. M. KREMERS,
DIRK SCHOENMAKER, AND
PETER J. WIERTS

THE ORGANIZATIONAL STRUCTURE of financial supervision is, or has been, under revision in many countries—including the United Kingdom, Germany, the Netherlands, the United States, and Australia—in response to market developments. Several papers have been written about the different models adopted, either promoting a single model in isolation or comparing different models and concluding that there is no uniform best model, but that each should be seen within the context of its own financial system.[1]

The purpose of this paper is to take the analysis one step further by focusing on the key question as regards the organizational structure: what are the pros and cons of combining different supervisory activities within one organization? In this context, we start by briefly describing the old and new Dutch supervisory models. The question is: how did we arrive at the new model? To answer this question, we take a closer look at financial market developments. We then compare cross-sector organizational models for financial supervision. We introduce a new framework for comparing these models and apply it to the functional model of the Netherlands and the integrated model of the United Kingdom. While confirming the familiar conclusion that there is no uniform best model,

---

1. Briault (2002); Lumpkin (2002); Taylor (1995).

Figure 1.

The Old Dutch Model

	Financial stability			Conduct of business		
		Microprudential		Non-securities		
	Macroprudential	Sectoral	Cross-sectoral	Sectoral	Cross-sectoral	Securities
Banks		DNB		DNB		
Insurance companies	DNB	PVK	RFT	PVK	RFT	STE
Securities firms		STE		STE		

DNB = De Nederlandsche Bank; PVK = Pension and Insurance Supervisor (Pensioen-en Verzekeringskamer); STE=Securities Supervisor (Stichting Toezicht Effectenverkeer); RFT= Board of Financial Supervisors (Raad van Financiële Toezichthouders)

The New Dutch Model

	Financial stability		
	Macroprudential	Microprudential	Conduct of business
Banks			
Insurance companies	DNB		AFM
Securities firms			

DNB = De Nederlandsche Bank; AFM = Authority for Financial Markets (successor to STE)

this paper also systematically investigates the trade-offs involved in different organizational structures.

A New Dutch Model

Figure 1 provides a broad overview of the old and new Dutch organizational models of supervision. The old model was sectoral, with a separate supervisor for banks, insurance companies, and securities firms. In 1999, a cross-sectoral element was added: the Board of Financial Supervisors (RFT), in which the existing supervisors share responsibility for cross-sectoral issues. The Board of Financial Supervisors developed cross-sector issues such as the supervision of financial conglomerates, the harmonization of consumer information for financial products, and the harmonization of fit and proper management principles for financial institutions. During this process it became clear that cross-sector issues dominate the policy debate, and a consensus emerged that a more fundamental reform of the organizational structure of supervision would be necessary.

The new Dutch model—the "twin peaks" model—is based on the objectives of supervision. De Nederlandsche Bank (DNB) is responsible for financial stability, while the Authority for Financial Markets (AFM) specializes in conduct-of-business supervision.[2] Financial stability is about promoting the safety and soundness of financial institutions and enhancing the stability of the financial sector as a whole. Conduct-of-business relates to promoting a fair and transparent market process and protecting the interests of investors and consumers. The underlying principle is that market developments should be accommodated as much as possible, while at the same time maintaining the effectiveness and efficiency of the objectives of financial supervision. The new Dutch model is where we are now, but how did we get here?

Market Developments

Financial systems evolve as a result of continuous pressure for efficiency. Over the past several decades, there have been striking developments in intermediation processes and institutional design.[3] Disintermediation and the disappearance of traditional sectoral boundaries between banking, securities, and insurance can be seen as particular forms of organizational evolution, just as is the unbundling of different kinds of financial activity within a group. From the perspective of regulation and supervision, it is important to create a supervisory system that accommodates market developments, and not to steer market developments in one particular direction or another. The task of the regulator and supervisor is not to predict market developments, but rather to create an infrastructure that is robust to different kinds of development, such as the bundling or

2. Currently, DNB is responsible for prudential supervision of banks and securities firms, while the Pensioen-en Verzekeringskamer (PVK) is responsible for prudential supervision of insurance companies and pension funds. DNB and PVK have integrated through cross-board appointments and joint teams. They will merge in 2004.

3. For a detailed description, see Walter (2003).

unbundling of financial activities. Regulators need to monitor and analyze market developments, and their response should be driven by the quest for efficiency and effectiveness in terms of the objectives of financial supervision. Financial institutions may be big or small, be specialized or integrated, and serve wholesale markets, retail markets, or both. It is highly relevant to have an *understanding* of what financial institutions look like in practice, but not to favor one kind of organizational form over another. For the past few years, the trend has been toward the integration and bundling of activities, although there have been signs recently that a turning point has been reached, which again would require careful monitoring.

The main argument for the supervisory reform in the Netherlands has been that, no matter where markets are heading, the sectoral boundaries of the old model are not sustainable. So, how should one regulate such a highly dynamic industry, characterized by ongoing innovation and organizational evolution? The answer has been found in a functional approach to financial market developments and supervision. Markets may be dynamic, but the functions these markets provide to savers and investors are far more stable. The primary function of any financial market is to allocate economic resources, both across borders and across time, in an uncertain world.[4] In the same vein, the objectives of financial supervision are more stable than the institutional characteristics of financial markets. Kees van Dijkhuizen, for example, compares the dynamics of financial market developments and the objectives of supervision since 1952, when the prudential supervision of banks was given its legal basis in the Netherlands.[5] The institutional characteristics of financial markets have changed dramatically (see below). By contrast, the objective of prudential supervision, which is to maintain the solvency and liquidity of financial institutions in order to protect the interests of creditors, is the same today as it was fifty years ago.

The Netherlands is not alone in this. In his summary of international trends such as the blurring of boundaries between financial products and the increase in number and importance of financial conglomerates, Clive Briault notes:

4. For an elaboration of the functional approach to the financial sector, see Merton and Bodie (1995).
5. Van Dijkhuizen (2003).

Table 1. The Dutch Financial Sector in Perspective

Indicator	Total	World ranking
Area (1,000 sq km)[a]	42	133
Population (in millions)[a]	16	60
Gross domestic product (US$ billions)[b]	375	14
Foreign financial claims (US$ billions)[c]	344	10
Claims on U.S. (US$ billions)	55	8
Claims on Brazil (US$ billions)[d]	16	3
Stock market capitalization (US$ billions)[b]	695	8
Presence of banks in top 30 (by tier one capital, in US$ billions)[e]	48	7
Equity of banks/GDP (percent)[f]	14	5

Sources:
a. CIA, *The World Factbook 2001*
b. World Development Indicators database, World Bank, August 2002
c. BIS International banking and financial market developments
d. BIS Consolidated international banking statistics for July 2002
e. *The Banker*, July 2002
f. Bank Profitability: Financial Statements of Banks, OECD, 2000

Banks, insurance companies and securities firms are now competing in the same market for the same customers, with similar and often even identical products, and via the same distribution channels . . . the functions of banking and insurance services also overlap and supplement one another in their core financial dimensions such as savings, financial procurement and risk protections . . . a similar convergence effect may be seen amongst product vendors and the distribution channels for all financial products, so that organizationally separate regulation can no longer cope.[6]

The Dutch Financial Sector in Perspective

Table 1 measures the size of the Dutch financial sector alongside other indicators such as area, population, and GDP and puts these in global perspective. When measured by area or population, the Netherlands is a small country. In terms of GDP, it is a medium-size or large country. Indicators of the size of the financial sector, however, show that the Netherlands is among the largest financial centers in the world, in terms of both stock market capitalization and the presence of large financial institutions. Table 2, which measures the size of large financial institutions as a share of GDP in the Netherlands and in the United States, shows that Dutch financial institutions are large in comparison with the economy as a whole.

6. Briault (2002, p. 7).

Table 2. Top Five Dutch and U.S. Financials

Dutch Financials	Equity (US$ billion)	Equity/ GDP	U.S. Financials	Equity (US$ billion)	Equity/ GDP
1. ING	23	6.0%	Citigroup	89	0.9%
2. Rabobank	18	4.8%	Berkshire Hathaway	58	0.6%
3. ABN Amro	16	4.2%	AIG	52	0.5%
4. Fortis (B/NL)	16	4.2%	Bank of America	49	0.5%
5. Aegon	16	4.2%	JP Morgan Chase	46	0.5%

Sources: Bankscope (except for Aegon, Berkshire Hathaway and AIG: annual report); World Development Indicators database, World Bank, August 2002.

The Emergence of Large Complex Financial Groups

Since the liberalization of structural policies in the Netherlands in 1990, permitting the combination of universal banking and insurance within a financial group, large financial groups have become the dominant players in the financial markets. The diminishing importance of stand-alone institutions in the traditional financial sectors is illustrated by the fact that financial conglomerates now account for about 90 percent of banking, 70 percent of securities, and 60 percent of insurance (measured in terms of market shares).

The use of the phrase *financial conglomerate* for a class of financial groups may suggest that these groups look similar in practice. Figure 2 shows that in fact there are huge differences between financial conglomerates.[7] It illustrates the different shapes and sizes of the five largest Dutch financial groups, with both balance sheet totals and the relative importance of their banking and investment versus insurance sectors. It shows that there are financial groups whose activities are predominantly in banking or insurance, as well as mixed financial groups, which include considerable banking (including securities) and insurance business. Compare, for example, the activities of Fortis, which include insurance (46 percent), consumer and commercial banking (33 percent), merchant

7. According to the directive for regulating financial conglomerates (Directive 2002/87/EC of the European Parliament and the Council of 16 December 2002), a group is defined as a financial conglomerate if more than 50 percent of group activities are financial and if the shares of the banking sector (including securities activities) and the insurance sector in total financial activities are within the range 10–90 percent. In addition, if the minority share has a balance sheet larger than 6 billion euros, the group qualifies as a financial conglomerate.

Figure 2. Banking versus Insurance within the Five Largest Financial Groups in the Netherlands, 1999

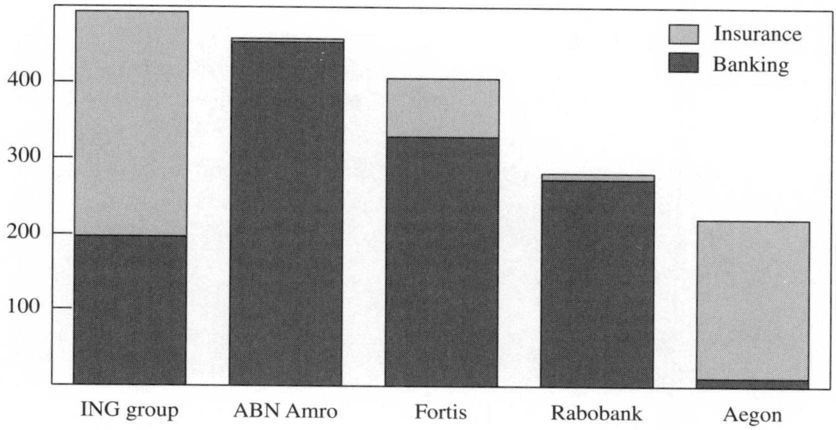

Source: De Nederlandsche Bank

banking, and private asset management; with those of Rabobank, which include retail banking (48 percent), wholesale banking (32 percent), leasing, insurance, and asset management.[8]

Conflicts of Interest?

For the past few years, the trend in financial conglomerates has been toward the integration and bundling of activities, although there have recently been signs that this is changing—especially in the United States—due to conflicts of interest between commercial and investment banking. The classical case of conflict of interest is a universal bank having an incentive to take advantage of investors by issuing overpriced securities in companies to which it has loans outstanding at times when those firms' prospects are not as positive as the public believes. The analysts at the investment bank may be involved by misleading investors on the true prospects of the firm. Another possibility may be that a bank underprices its loans to a company in return for being allowed to enter the profitable business of investment banking for that company (see Ingo

8. Figures are measured as income/operational results and originate from the annual reports (2001) of Rabobank and Fortis.

Walter's paper in this volume for a detailed analysis of potential conflicts of interest and the impact on the optimal size of conglomerates).

What is relevant for this discussion is that both recent cases and the classical case of conflict of interest, as described in the literature, relate to the combination of commercial banking and investment banking, not to the combination of banking and insurance. Perhaps, theoretically, large complex groups could use their credit lines to urge companies to buy their insurance products as well, or underprice their insurance products in order to enter the investment banking market. However, we are not aware of empirical evidence showing this potential conflict of interest to be important in practice.

The Development of Financial Conglomerates: Integration of Activities

Conglomerates have integrated activities at the commercial, organizational, and financial levels. *Commercial integration* refers to the provision of integrated products in the field of banking, insurance, and investment. The process of product development consists of several phases. During the first phase, conglomerates cross-sell their insurance products via their banking distribution channel, and vice versa. During the next phase, complex financial products are developed that contain elements of different classes of traditional sectoral products. Finally, conglomerates may present themselves as integrated financial service providers, instead of as a bank or an insurer.

Organizational integration refers to the centralization of activities that previously belonged with sectoral parts of the group. This may apply to functions such as risk management, asset management, and the group's administrative organization. Centralization implies that strategic decisionmaking is transferred from the functional or sectoral entities of the group to the level of the group as a whole (that is, the holding level). During this process, the difference between the legal structure and the operational structure of the group will increase. In consequence, it becomes harder to attribute activities to the legal entities on which the division of supervisory responsibilities is based. A large difference between legal structure and organizational structure will complicate the execution of supervision, since supervision is based on statutory power to supervise legal entities and this may not correspond to where activities actually take place.

Financial integration means that the group presents itself as a single financial institution on the capital markets. Funding, by means of equity and debt, is centralized, the top holding of the group is listed on the stock exchange, and the group publishes consolidated accounts. Intragroup exposures will increase during the process of financial integration.

The approach of the Netherlands in regulating financial conglomerates is to identify changes in the risk profile as a result of combining different activities, and then to tailor regulatory and supervisory measures accordingly (for a summary, see the appendix; see also Iman van Lelyveld and Arnold Schilder's paper in this volume on the development of integrated supervision in the Netherlands). A crucial characteristic of the Dutch approach is that it responds to the market developments of organizational integration at conglomerates. The regulatory framework will include both the holding level of conglomerates and all integrated activities that are essential to the functioning of the group as a whole. This is different from the U.S. approach, which seems to ignore the integration of activities; the Federal Reserve System concentrates on supervising the financial holding company, while the functional supervisors take a "solo" approach to different legal parts of the group.[9]

Organizational Structure of Supervision: Comparing Cross-Sectoral Models

In response to the disappearance of sectoral boundaries within the financial sector, two organizational structures for supervision have emerged: the functional model and the integrated model. In the functional model, there is a separate supervisor for each objective: systemic supervision, prudential supervision, and conduct-of-business supervision. In the integrated model, there is a single financial services regulator for prudential supervision and conduct-of-business supervision, while the central bank remains responsible for overall financial stability. It has

9. One of the reasons for establishing the Joint Forum for supervising financial conglomerates, with Tom de Swaan as the first chairman, has been the insight that it is no longer appropriate to supervise an insurance company on a solo basis if that insurer is part of a financial group. The Joint Forum was established in 1996 by three international supervisory organizations; the Basel Committee on Banking Supervision (Basel Committee), the International Organization of Securities Commissions (IOSCO), and the International Association of Insurance Supervisors (IAIS).

rightly been emphasized in many publications that there is no uniform best model, since the development of each organizational model should be seen in the context of the history of its national financial system.[10] Furthermore, different cross-sectoral models are recent and have not been tested in a crisis situation. It is too early to test the performance of different models using the objectives of supervision as a yardstick.

A Framework for Comparing Cross-Sectoral Models

The main purpose of this paper is to take the analysis of the organizational structure of supervision further by focusing on the key question: what are the pros and cons of combining different supervisory activities within a single organization? The trade-offs are made explicit by listing the synergies and conflicts of supervisory interest involved. This is similar to the approach that has been applied to financial institutions, that is, analysing synergies and conflicts of interest of combining financial activities within a financial institution.

Figure 3 summarizes the potential synergies and conflicts of supervisory interests. The first possible synergy results from combining systemic supervision (traditionally a central bank task, also referred to as macroprudential supervision) and prudential supervision of financial institutions. The link between stability issues at the microlevel (the level of the financial institution) and at the macrolevel (economywide) is especially relevant in a concentrated financial sector, with large, systemically relevant financial institutions. The synergies between both functions also refer to the possibility of acting decisively and swiftly in the event of a crisis. Crisis management usually requires key decisions to be taken within hours, rather than days. Combining both micro- and macroprudential supervision within a single institution ensures that relevant information is available at short notice and that a speedy decision to act can be taken if necessary (Charles Goodhart discusses how the collection, transmission, and interpretation of information would suffer if potentially systemic financial crises were to be handled by a committee).[11]

The second synergy in figure 3 ("one-stop supervision")—between prudential supervision and conduct-of-business supervision—relates to the fact that the organization confronts all types of financial institutions

10. See, for example, Lumpkin (2002) and Briault (2002).
11. Goodhart (2000).

Figure 3.

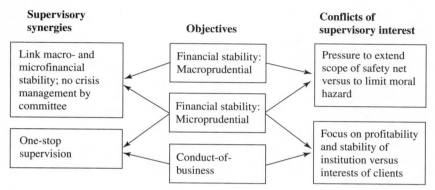

with one supervisor only. Furthermore, synergies in the execution of supervision are exploited by combining different supervisory activities within one institution. This might also generate efficiency gains by combining support services for different supervisory tasks.

Figure 3 also shows potential conflicts of interest in combining supervisory functions within a single organization. It starts by showing a possible conflict of interest between systemic supervision and prudential supervision, which relates to the possibility of lender of last resort (LOLR) operations by the central bank. The debate is about how to balance the benefits of LOLR operations (avoiding systemic risk, for example, financial panic or bank runs) against its costs (moral hazard). The answer adopted by many central banks is to prefer private sector solutions for financial institutions in trouble,[12] and to strictly limit the possibility of LOLR operations to the characteristics of banks that caused the systemic risk in the first place. In general, banks are seen as "special," since claims on banks are such important assets to a wide spectrum of economic agents, and because of the possibility of a contagion effect caused by banks in trouble.[13] However, when financial groups integrate (see the previous section of this paper on market developments) and prudential supervision can no longer be based on sectoral boundaries, it may become more difficult to separate the aspects of financial institutions that justify the possibility of LOLR operations. The question of how to limit

12. Economic and Financial Committee (2001).
13. Greenspan (2001).

the moral hazard aspects of the financial safety net remains relevant and needs to be answered by introducing institutional safeguards that limit safety net spillovers.[14]

The potential conflict of interest between prudential supervision and conduct-of-business supervision (the second conflict in figure 3) relates to the different nature of their objectives. The prudential supervisor will be interested in the soundness of financial institutions, including their profitability, while the conduct-of-business supervisor will focus on the interests of clients. Mixing up the responsibilities of financial stability and conduct of business could create incentives for the supervisor to give preference to one objective over the other. As a result, the conduct-of-business supervisor is ideally situated to supervise possible conflicts of interest between a financial institution and its clients, since it will only focus on the interests of the clients (which is exactly what a conduct-of-business supervisor is for). Furthermore, the stability objective is consistent with preserving public confidence and may require discretion and confidentiality, which could be counterproductive to the transparency objective.[15] Typically, conduct-of-business supervision is more publicly and politically visible than the financial stability objective, which relies more on confidentiality.[16] A clear dividing line between both institutions recognizes the difference in the nature of their objectives.

Applying the Framework: the Dutch and U.K. Models

Figure 3 allows comparison between the two organizational structures for cross-sectoral supervision that have emerged: the functional and the integrated models. As shown in figure 4, both the functional model of the Netherlands and the integrated model of the United Kingdom are twin peak models. In the Netherlands model, the organizational dividing line has been inserted between the objectives of financial stability (both micro and macro) and conduct of business. One institution is responsible for micro- and macroprudential supervision in the pursuit of financial

14. The U.S. solution in the Gramm-Leach-Bliley Act has been to (1) require that non-banking activities take place in legal entities separate from the bank; (2) limit the transactions that can occur between a bank and nonbank affiliates; and (3) create a system of functional regulation to limit direct contact between bank examiners and nonbanking affilitiates. See Feldman, Lyard, and Willardson (2000).

15. Padoa-Schioppa (2003).

16. Jonk, Kremers, and Schoenmaker (2001).

Figure 4. Comparing Twin Peaks Models: The Netherlands and the UK Model

The Netherlands

	Financial stability		Conduct of business
	Macroprudential	Microprudential	
Banks			
Insurance companies	DNB		AFM
Securities firms			

DNB = De Nederlandsche Bank; AFM = Authority for Financial Markets (successor to STE).

The United Kingdom

	Financial stability		Conduct of business
	Macroprudential	Microprudential	
Banks			
Insurance companies	BoE	FSA	
Securities firms			

BoE = Bank of England; FSA = Financial Services Authority

stability. The other specializes in promoting a fair and transparent market process and protecting the interests of investors and consumers. The U.K. model combines microprudential and conduct-of-business supervision within an integrated financial supervisor—the Financial Services Authority (FSA)—while the central bank remains responsible for macroprudential supervision, that is, the stability of the financial system as a whole.

THE NETHERLANDS MODEL. In line with the synergies described in figure 3, the advantages of the Dutch model relate to combining all matters of financial stability within one institution. Given the size of Dutch financial institutions (see table 2), prudential problems can become systemic, warranting both micro- and macroperspectives on financial markets developments. The advantages also became clear in the aftermath of September 11, when De Nederlandsche Bank was able to immediately combine and take action on information flows from its directorates as regards payment systems, prudential supervision (financial institutions), and monetary policy. The model also avoids possible conflicts of interest between prudential supervision and conduct-of-business supervision (figure 3). The advantages of a separate conduct-of-business supervisor can be illustrated by recent investigations into conflicts of interest between investment banking and commercial banking within financial institutions. In the United States, the Securities and Exchange Commission has the right profile for investigating such topics, since they are about conflicts of interest between the financial institution and its clients, and it is the role of the SEC to focus on the interests of the clients. Similarly, the Authority for Financial Markets investigates these issues within the Netherlands. Finally, institutional safeguards are needed in the Dutch model to limit financial safety net spillovers.

THE U.K. MODEL. The main advantage of the U.K. model is that it has an integrated supervisor for all financial institutions (see figure 3, "one-stop supervision"). As Briault notes: "In the UK, the FSA . . . has benefited from the economies of scale arising from the move to a single set of central support services . . .; a unified management structure; and a unified approach to standard-setting, authorisation, supervision, enforcement, consumer education and tackling financial crime."[17]

Figure 3 also highlights issues that may be of relevance in the U.K. model. First, it may be difficult to balance prudential and conduct-of-business concerns, especially given the potentially conflicting nature of these topics. For example, conduct-of-business concerns are more publicly and politically visible than prudential concerns and may override them, consuming the bulk of the time of the integrated supervisor's senior management. Another potential drawback of the organizational dividing line between micro- and macroprudential supervision is that it requires "crisis management by committee," which may make it more difficult to make and execute decisions rapidly.

Conclusion

The argument for reforming the Dutch supervisory system has been that the sectoral boundaries of the old model were not sustainable. The

17. Briault (2000, p. 16).

objectives of supervision are more stable than are the institutional characteristics of financial markets, so they provide a better focal point for the organizational structure of supervision. Market developments should be accommodated as much as possible, while maintaining the effectiveness and efficiency of financial supervision. The new Dutch supervisory structure adheres to these objectives by dividing supervisory tasks between the complementary objectives of financial stability and conduct-of-business supervision. In the Dutch case, with several large, systemically relevant financial groups, the balance of arguments has produced an organizational structure in which *all* financial stability matters are combined within a single institution (that is, there is no crisis management by committee) and in which a separate supervisor—with a clear profile—is responsible for conduct-of-business supervision.

APPENDIX A

The Dutch Supervisory Approach to Financial Conglomerates

The approach of the Netherlands in regulating financial conglomerates is to identify changes in the risk profile as a result of combining different activities, and then to tailor regulatory and supervisory measures accordingly. First, the combination of activities such as banking and insurance might lower the total risk profile of a conglomerate, due to diversification effects. A detailed analysis of the possibilities of risk reduction resulting from opportunities for diversification is outside the scope of the paper. The general conclusion of the Dutch supervisors has been that the available empirical evidence does not justify a change of the present rules for determining the capital adequacy of conglomerates, which is simply to add the regulatory capital of the banking part and the insurance part.[18] Second, combining activities may also increase risks, as summarized in box 1. As regards contagion, for example, a concern is whether problems in the insurance, securities, or unregulated parts of the conglomerate might spill over to the banking part of the conglomerate, and thereby raise issues of systemic stability. The most topical issues are those of conflicts of interest and reputational risks; in particular as a result of recent events as described in the text.

The legal framework for supervising financial conglomerates is under construction at both the national and the European levels. Given the dominant position of financial conglomerates within the Netherlands and the country's long experience with conglomerates, the Dutch legislation on the supervision of financial conglomerates will take the supervisory approach further than the Eureopean Commission's Financial Conglomerates Directive, which applies to the EU as a whole.[19]

The Financial Conglomerates Directive introduces the concept of supervision on a groupwide basis, to be executed by a single coordinator. To summarize, the groupwide assessment will apply to the following items:

18. For empirical estimates, see Oliver, Wyman and Company (2001) and Bikker and van Lelyveld (2002).

19. Financial Conglomerates Directive 2002/87/EC.

Box 1. Risks Posed by Financial Conglomerates

Double or multiple gearing: the risk that the equity of the group is being used as regulatory capital adequacy funds for two or more separately supervised legal entities of the group.

Risk concentration: several entities within the group might be exposed to the same risk factors. This might lead to risk concentrations at the level of the group for individual counterparties, counterparties in specific geographical locations, or industrial sectors.

Regulatory arbitrage: if the same risks within separately supervised legal entities within the group are exposed to different solvency requirements, it may be profitable for the conglomerate to move activities to the entity with the lowest requirements. This might impede the effectiveness of supervision. In the end, regulatory arbitrage is not necessarily counterproductive as it puts pressure on the supervisors to create a level playing field.

Reputational risk/contagion: the group as a whole might be affected if a separate label or entity within the group experiences reputational or financial problems.

Conflicts of interest: combining different activities within a group might increase the risk that the interests of the customers of the group will be harmed as a result of a conflict of interest between the group and its clients, the entities within the group or between the clients and different entities within the group.

Groupwide capital adequacy. The solvency requirements for each financial sector in a conglomerate shall be covered by equity in accordance with corresponding sectoral rules. The capital requirement for the group as a whole equals the sum of the requirements for the constituting parts. The capital shall be available at groupwide level. Multiple gearing, which is the multiple use of capital at the level of the conglomerate, is not allowed.

Risk management processes (including risk concentration, intragroup transactions, and internal controls). This includes supervision, at the level of the conglomerate, of risk management processes. As an example, the risk management process shall ensure a periodic review of the strategies and policies of the conglomerate with respect to all the risks they assume. Furthermore, risk monitoring systems should be well integrated in the organization and measures should be taken to measure, monitor, and control risks at the level of the conglomerate. Finally, conglomerates should report significant intragroup transactions and risk concentrations, and these will be subject to supervisory overview.

Fit and proper character of holding management. The persons who direct the business of a financial holding company should be of sufficiently good repute and have sufficient experience to perform their tasks.

The proposed changes to Dutch law will also broaden the scope of supervisory instruments to include all integrated and centralized activities that are essential for the functioning of the financial group as a whole. This is essential, given the difference between the legal and the operational structure of the conglomerate, as outlined in the text above. The approach is to supervise at the point where the business is done and not to hide behind legal entities.

References

Bikker, Jaap A., and Iman P. P. van Lelyveld. 2002. "Economic versus Regulatory Capital for Financial Conglomerates." Research Series Supervision 45. Amsterdam: De Nederlandsche Bank (April).

Briault, Clive. 2002. "Revisiting the Rationale for a Single National Financial Services Regulator." Special Paper 135. London School of Economics (February).

Dijkhuizen, C. van. 2003. "A Functional Approach to Fifty Years of Financial Supervision." In *Banking Supervision at the Crossroads,* edited by T. G. Kuppens, H. M. Prast, and A. A. T. Wesseling. Edward Elgar (forthcoming).

Economic and Financial Committee. 2001. *Report on Financial Crisis Management.* Brussels: European Council.

Feldman, Ron J., Lyon, James M., Willardson, Niel D. 2000. "Have We Only Just Begun? Challenges in Implementing the GLB Regime." *Special Issue 2000. The Region.* Federal Reserve Bank of Minneapolis.

Goodhart, Charles A. E. 2000. "The Organizational Structure of Banking Supervision." Special Paper 127. London School of Economics, Financial Markets Group.

Greenspan, Alan. 2001. "The Financial Safety Net." Remarks presented at the 37th Annual Conference on Bank Structure and Competitions of the Federal Reserve Bank of Chicago, Chicago, May 10, 2001.

Jonk, Annet, Jeroen J. M. Kremers, and Dirk Schoenmaker, "A New Dutch Model." *Financial Regulator* 6 (3): 35–38.

Lumpkin, Stephen A. 2002. "Supervision of Financial Services in the OECD Area." Financial Market Trends 81 (April). Paris: Organization for Economic Cooperation and Development.

Merton, Robert C., and Zvi Bodie. 1995. A Conceptual Framework for Analyzing the Financial Environment." In *The Global Financial System: A Functional Perspective,* edited by Dwight B. Crane and others. Harvard University Press.

Oliver, Wyman and Company. 2001. "Study on the Risk Profile and Capital Adequacy of Financial Conglomerates." London.

Padoa-Schioppa, Tommaso. 2003. "Financial Supervision: Inside or Outside Central Banks?" In *Financial Supervision in Europe,* edited by Jeroen J. M. Kremers, Dirk Schoenmaker, and Peter J. Wierts. Edward Elgar.

Taylor, Michael. 1995. "Twin Peaks: A Regulatory Structure for the New Century." London: Centre for the Study of Financial Innovation.

Walter, Ingo. 2003. "Financial Integration across Borders and across Sectors: Implications for Regulatory Structures." In *Financial Supervision in Europe,* edited by Jeroen J. M. Kremers, Dirk Schoenmaker, and Peter J. Wierts. Edward Elgar.

What Constitutes
Appropriate Disclosure for
a Financial Conglomerate?

LAWRENCE J. WHITE

T HIS IS A PROPITIOUS TIME to be discussing issues of disclosure for financial conglomerates. After two-plus decades of debating whether to end the limitations of the Glass-Steagall Act and the Bank Holding Company Act on the participation of banks in other parts of the financial services universe, Congress finally passed the Gramm-Leach-Bliley Act in 1999. Less than three years later, two large financial conglomerates—Citigroup and J. P. Morgan Chase—received stunning public rebukes for their role in the accounting and corporate governance manipulations of some of their clients. Simultaneously, the Basel Committee on Banking Supervision of the Bank for International Settlements (BIS) proposed a revision (Basel II) to its 1988 capital standards, in which market discipline—driven by public disclosure—is one of the three pillars for strengthening the safety and soundness of banks.[1]

The author would like to thank Mark Carey, Richard Herring, Anjela Kniazeva, Diana Kniazeva, Robert Litan, James Moser, and the participants at the roundtable for valuable comments on an earlier draft.

1. See Basel Committee on Banking Supervision (1998a, 2000a, 2001b, 2001c, 2001d, 2001f, 2001g). One justification often advanced for the efforts of BIS to improve the safety and soundness of banks—to reduce systemic risk internationally among banks—is weak. National bank regulators already have the tools—akin to restrictions on the size of loan that any bank can extend to a single borrower—to limit the exposure of their national banks. Instead, the Basel approach should be seen primarily as an effort to limit the com-

This paper addresses the issues of disclosure for financial conglomerates principally from the perspective of the Basel committee: that is, disclosure is important for the safety and soundness of banks. However, I reach substantially different conclusions with respect to three important issues: the role of market value accounting, the frequency of disclosures, and the role of subordinated debt.

I start by asking why any special disclosure might be required for financial conglomerates. This question immediately leads to a discussion of what is special about financial conglomerates. I also address the question, Disclosure to whom? There are at least two potential audiences for information disclosure: (a) financial regulators and (b) the public investors, creditors, and customers of a financial conglomerate. Issues related to the appropriate structure for a financial conglomerate and the revelation of information that should accompany that structure also are raised. Finally, I return to the title of this paper: What constitutes appropriate disclosure for a financial conglomerate?

Much of the discussion refers to the financial and regulatory institutions of the United States and their experiences. The insights and lessons to be drawn from the discussion, however, have wider applications.

Why Should There Be Any Special Disclosure for Financial Conglomerates?

I start with fundamentals. Why should there be any special disclosure for financial conglomerates? This, of course, naturally leads to an even more basic question: What is special about financial conglomerates that would warrant special disclosure?

The specialness of a financial conglomerate must rest with the presence of a depository or an insurance company embedded within it.[2] I start with a depository—specifically a bank.[3]

---

petitive subsidization of banking across countries. If a country permits its banks to operate at insufficient levels of capital (but everyone knows that transactors with those banks will be bailed out in the event of financial difficulties), this constitutes an implicit subsidy for those banks. See White (1996a).

2. As is argued below, some of the same issues that arise for depositories and insurance companies also arise for defined-benefit pension plans. But defined-benefit pension plans are almost always embedded in the employer that offers pensions to its employees and

Figure 1. Stylized Balance Sheet of the ABC Bank (Solvent), as of December 31, 200X

Assets	Liabilities
$100 (loans)	$92 (deposits)
	- -
	$8 (net worth, owners' equity, capital)

Why Banks Are Special

The specialness of banks is generally attributed to their generic combination of assets and liabilities: relatively illiquid assets (usually loans) and highly liquid liabilities (deposits). This combination makes them potentially vulnerable to the withdrawal of depositors' funds, known as runs.[4] In addition, banks are at the center of the payments system, so they have constant creditor-borrower relationships among themselves, leaving them exposed to potential losses (and preemptive runs) at each other's hands.

This specialness of a bank is best illustrated by a stylized balance sheet, presented in figure 1. The bank's assets are primarily the loans that it makes. Its liabilities are primarily the deposits that it has gathered (and uses to fund its assets). The difference between the value of its assets and the value of its liabilities is its net worth or owners' equity. In the financial world, this is frequently described as capital. The bank of figure 1 is

---

rarely are part of a separate financial conglomerate. Consequently, they are not relevant for the immediate issues at hand.

3. Unless otherwise indicated, the term "banks" broadly covers all depositories: financial institutions that hold financial assets as their primary assets and fund themselves with deposits that are highly liquid (that is, they can be withdrawn largely on demand at fixed nominal values).

4. See, for example, Diamond and Dybvig (1983); Postlewaite and Vives (1987); Chen (1999).

Figure 2. Stylized Balance Sheet of the ABC Bank (Insolvent), as of December 31, 200Y

Assets	Liabilities
$80 (loans)	$92 (deposits)
	−$12 (net worth, owners' equity, capital)

solvent and would be considered adequately capitalized by the standards established by the Basel committee in 1988.[5]

The bank's capital is simply the arithmetic difference between the bank's assets and its liabilities. The bank's capital has no separate existence or measurement, except as represented by this arithmetic difference.

Let us now examine a second stylized balance sheet in figure 2, where the bank has suffered a substantial reduction in the value of its assets. Instead of the positive capital of $8 in figure 1, the value of the bank's deposit liabilities in figure 2 exceeds the value of its assets by $12; its capital is −$12. It is badly insolvent.

Typically, the depositors do not have recourse against the owners of the bank to cover the shortfall—because of a legal structure of limited liability for the owners of a corporation (the bank), because of a legal structure of personal bankruptcy that accords limited liability for the owners of a bank, or both. Consequently, the depositors have to absorb and distribute the loss among themselves.

---

5. This bank has a ratio of assets to capital of 12.5 to 1. This is frequently described as a leverage ratio. The concept of leverage is readily grasped by noting that an increase in the value of the assets by $4 would also increase net worth by $4; but the former *percentage* increase would be only 4 percent, while the latter *percentage* increase would be 50 percent—a 12.5-fold multiple in the percentage increase. The same percentage multiplying effect applies to decreases in asset value.

Although the absorption of loss by liability holders is a general problem where limited liability is present,[6] it is a special problem with respect to banks, for at least three reasons. First, some bank depositors may be relatively unsophisticated, poorly informed, and in a poor position to protect themselves against the losses from a bank's insolvency;[7] also banks are more opaque (and thus more difficult to be informed about) than are other enterprises.[8]

Second, and related to the first, banks are especially vulnerable to runs by imperfectly informed depositors, who may be uncertain about the financial condition of their bank and who fear that they may have to absorb some losses. Because the bank's loan assets are generally less liquid than its deposit liabilities (it typically keeps only a little cash on hand), even a solvent bank cannot immediately satisfy the demands for withdrawals of all of its depositors—or even the demands of more than a small fraction of depositors. If forced to meet the demands of more than that small fraction, the bank must (a) borrow from somewhere,[9] (b) call in its loans or liquidate its illiquid assets at short notice and likely at less value than would occur from a more orderly and leisurely sale, or (c) shut its doors and delay paying its depositors until its loans are repaid or assets can be sold in an orderly way, thereby reneging on its liquidity commitment to its depositors.

Accordingly, a "prisoner's dilemma" may well arise. Although a bank may be solvent and informed depositors know that it is solvent, they may fear that other depositors are worried about the condition of the bank and that the latter's withdrawals would strain the bank's resources. In that case, even the knowledgeable depositors would race to the bank to withdraw their funds first. But such a general race to the bank would strain even solvent banks, thus making everyone worse off.

Third, there may be a "contagion" effect, where depositors of one bank, seeing a run on another bank, may fear for the solvency of their

---

6. And lenders (liability holders) generally try to protect themselves, through covenants and lending restrictions, against the risk-taking and other behavior of corporate owners that could cause losses for the lenders.

7. That is, they are unlikely to develop covenants and lending agreements.

8. See Morgan (2002).

9. A lender of last resort—the central bank—can provide loans to a bank and thus help it to deal with depositor withdrawals. But then the central bank is effectively a creditor to the bank and must concern itself with the bank's solvency.

bank—or may just fear that other depositors of their bank will become worried and begin to withdraw. Alternatively, because banks are at the center of the payments system and are frequently in the position of being a short-term lender or borrower vis-à-vis other banks, the insolvency of one bank may cause a cascade of insolvencies of other creditor banks (or may cause a contagion of runs by banks-as-creditors who have imperfect information and fear insolvency).

Some version of these scenarios (plus the perceived position of banks as special lenders) has caused the American polity, since the early nineteenth century, to consider banks to be special and to develop special regulatory regimes to deal with their specialness. At the center of such regimes have been efforts to maintain their solvency—to keep them "safe and sound." Since 1933 federal deposit insurance has provided an additional layer of assurance (and thus an additional damper on potential runs) by protecting depositors against regulatory failure.[10] In an important sense, with deposit insurance in place, safety-and-soundness regulations become the rules that protect the deposit insurer (as well as uninsured depositors and other creditors).

There are four major components to safety-and-soundness regulation:[11] (a) minimum capital requirements,[12] (b) limitations on activities,[13] (c) management competency requirements, and (d) in-the-field examiners and supervisors to enforce the rules. The minimum capital requirements are the direct efforts to maintain a bank's solvency. This was the primary focus of the 1988 Basel Accord and remains the first of the three pillars of Basel II. The limitations on activities can be seen as efforts to limit risk;[14] some important structural issues are related to these limitations and to the revelation of information, a subject to which I return

10. Deposit insurance provided by individual states stretches back to New York's initial efforts in 1829; the states' efforts did not have sustained success.

11. Outside of the United States, this is frequently described as prudential regulation.

12. Capital plays two important roles. First, it is a direct indicator of the extent of the bank's solvency—the buffer of protection for depositors against a fall in the value of the bank's assets. Second, since capital is the owners' equity, it provides a disincentive for the bank's owners to take risks.

13. Activities mean broadly all kinds of assets, liabilities, or ongoing business operations.

14. However, limitations on banks' activities have also taken on a heavy political overtone in the United States, as industries that have feared banks' competition have lobbied heavily to prevent banks from entering their areas.

below. Management competence is related to operational risk, which is a component of the capital requirement that is the first pillar of Basel II. And the enforcement of the rules requires in-the-field examiners and supervisors, with effective supervision serving as the second pillar of Basel II.

Limitations on Activities and the Appropriate Structure for a Bank

Let us proceed on the assumptions of the previous section: banks are special, and safety-and-soundness regulation is an appropriate means of dealing with their specialness. Placing limitations on activities has been a traditional tool of safety-and-soundness regulation. The logic for limitations can be seen from a reexamination of figures 1 and 2. If the bank is to remain solvent (that is, its capital is to remain positive) despite the uncertainties of future outcomes, then minimum capital requirements must be specified for all of the activities that could negatively affect the bank's balance sheet.

There is an immediate implication.[15] The only activities that are appropriate for a bank are those that are "examinable and supervisable" and thus can be regulated in a manner that is consistent with the safe-and-sound operation of a bank. In practice, this would mean an activity for which regulators are capable of setting suitable capital requirements and making judgments about the competence of the bank's management of the activity.[16] This examinable-and-supervisable decision ought to be a regulatory judgment, but the political appointees heading the regulatory agency should be held accountable for those judgments.

Any activity that is not appropriate for a bank (because regulators are

---

15. This discussion draws heavily on White (1996b); Shull and White (1998).

16. This concept of examinable and supervisable is consistent with the suggestions that bank deposits should be protected through a process of collateralization. In essence, the bank should always maintain a sufficient level of assets (collateral) to cover the deposits, with an appropriate "haircut" (that is, an extra amount of collateral) to cover uncertainties as to the value of the assets. But this haircut is the equivalent of the bank's capital in the discussion in the text, and a consideration of which assets are appropriate for this collateralization process (and what the appropriate haircuts for them should be) is equivalent to the concept of examinable and supervisable. If the bank chooses to fund itself partly with liabilities that are not deposits (which goes beyond the simple model of figures 1 and 2), then it can engage in other activities, so long as those liability holders understand that the depositors have the first claim on the examinable-and-supervisable collateral assets.

Figure 3. Stylized Structure of the Location of Appropriate Activities for a Bank and of Other Activities

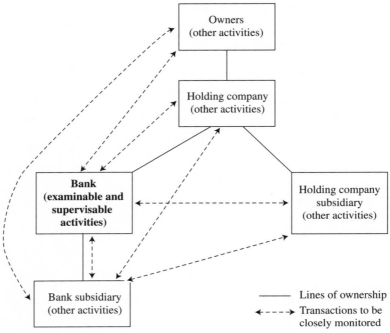

not able to set capital requirements or to judge managerial competence in the activity) should nevertheless be permitted for the owners of a bank, for a bank holding company, for an affiliate or subsidiary of the holding company, or for a bank subsidiary (so long as the bank cannot count the net worth of the subsidiary as an asset of the bank).[17] Figure 3 provides a highly stylized and condensed picture of the consequent structure of the location of appropriate and inappropriate activities for a bank.

As a practical matter, loans and loan-like products are highly likely to

17. This is frequently described as the subsidiary's being separately capitalized. If the bank could count the net worth of the subsidiary as an asset, then this is the equivalent of allowing the bank to undertake the activity directly. But, by assumption, the activity is not permitted in the bank because it is not examinable and supervisable. With the subsidiary's net worth not counting as an asset of the bank, the financial failure of the subsidiary would not directly affect the bank, but the bank could still take advantage of whatever organizational or legal advantages might apply to having the activity in the subsidiary.

be deemed appropriate for a bank. Regulators are familiar with them and believe that they can set appropriate capital requirements and judge managerial competence. What about the two financial services whose appropriateness for banks was at the center of two decades of contention in the United States—securities activities and insurance activities? The logic of the examinable-and-supervisable approach is that the placement of activities within a bank, or alternatively somewhere in a related entity, ought to be determined by the ability of bank regulators to set capital requirements and judge managerial competency.

And what if a bank decides that it wants to operate a delicatessen? Although bank regulators might be able to hire restaurant consultants who could provide advice as to appropriate levels of capital and ways of judging managerial competence, it seems likely that bank regulators would decide that this activity was not an area of their expertise and ought not to be permitted for a bank—but should be permitted for a bank's owners or for a bank's subsidiary.

Finally, even with activities sorted by examinable and supervisable criteria, the transactions (for example, loans or the sale or purchase of assets) between the bank and its owners, affiliates, and subsidiaries must be closely monitored, because they provide a ready means for siphoning resources from the bank. The bank may overpay for some services that it buys or undercharge for some services that it sells and thereby become insolvent.[18] There are also indirect ways that a bank can be weakened to the benefit of its owners. The bank may misprice transactions to friends of the owners, who in turn provide payment or favors to the owners. Or, in the context of a financial conglomerate, a bank may provide loans to a company whose equity shares are being underwritten by the conglomerate's securities affiliate. Although such loans may have a sound basis in the special information that the securities affiliate possesses and forwards

18. The bank subsidiary has an advantage over the bank holding company as a place for such activities. If the bank overpays for some services from its subsidiary (or undercharges for some services sold to the subsidiary), any dividends from the subsidiary to the bank's parent holding company would have to pass through the bank and thus can be trapped there by regulators to offset the inappropriate transaction. However, to the extent that the subsidiary is less than 100 percent owned by the bank, it becomes more like a part of the holding company and thus more susceptible to straight siphoning (Edwards 1979). Also, even with a subsidiary that is 100 percent owned by the bank, if that subsidiary transacts directly or indirectly with the owner, then the subsidiary can overpay or undercharge and still be a conduit for siphoning.

to the bank, the loans may instead be a way for the bank to provide risky support for the company so that the securities affiliate reaps benefits from the company through investment banking fees.[19]

Consequently, such direct and indirect transactions between the bank and its owners and affiliates must be on arm's-length terms and monitored closely, and penalties for violations must be severe.

The Similarities with Insurance Companies and Defined-Benefit Pension Funds

Part of the logic of the case for safety-and-soundness regulation extends to at least two other financial institutions: insurance companies and defined-benefit pension funds.[20] Figures 1 and 2 can be readily adapted to portray stylized versions of each. For either, the assets can be loans or other investments. Instead of deposit liabilities for banks, the insurance company would have the likely claims of its insureds as liabilities, and the pension fund would have the likely claims of its pensioners. An insolvency for either, along the lines of figure 2, would mean that the assets of the institution are inadequate to cover the claims.

Although neither type of institution is subject to the risk of runs that banks face, their claimants are likely to be poorly informed or in a poor position to protect themselves against actions that could put their claims at risk. Accordingly, it is not surprising that every state has a safety-and-soundness regime that applies to insurance companies and that all states have mutual guarantee funds that serve as a financial backup for a claimant whose insurance company has become insolvent. Similarly, since 1974 the claimants of defined-benefit pension funds have had recourse to guaranty coverage provided by the federal Pension Benefit Guaranty Corporation (PBGC), and the PBGC and the Department of Labor's Pension and Welfare Benefits Administration have safety-and-

---

19. There is also a converse possibility: the securities affiliate may tout and underwrite the equity shares of a weak company so that the commercial bank can have its loans repaid. Although this arrangement strengthens safety and soundness, it raises larger issues of investor deception that are addressed below.

20. A defined-benefit pension fund is one in which an employer has promised retirees a specified level of retirement benefit payments. By contrast, a defined-payment pension fund is one in which a retiree's receipts are linked to what the retiree (while employed) previously paid into the fund (along with any payments from the employer) and the subsequent investment performance of those paid-in funds.

soundness regulatory powers vis-à-vis defined-benefit pension plans and their corporate parents.[21]

Appropriate Disclosure to Regulators

The safety-and-soundness regulatory regimes that surround banks (and insurance companies and defined-benefit pension plans) need information about their regulated institutions. Since maintaining solvency is the primary goal of the regulation, I first focus on the representation of solvency: the balance sheet of figure 1.[22] I also discuss the riskiness of the balance sheet[23] and the special concern about transactions with affiliated parties.

Financial Statements

As briefly described above, a financial institution's balance sheet portrays the assets and liabilities of the institution at a specific point in time. The *system* for ascribing values for assets and liabilities and thus their portrayal on the balance sheet are crucial aspects of disclosure, as is the frequency with which the information is updated. I first address the issue of accounting systems and then discuss the frequency with which updated balance sheets should be issued. Finally, I contrast my recommended approaches with those of the Basel committee.

---

21. Beyond these two categories of institutions, the Securities Investor Protection Corporation (SIPC) provides insurance for investors who leave their securities with a brokerage firm that becomes bankrupt. This is seen as protection for the poorly informed small investor. And the Securities and Exchange Commission (SEC) imposes minimum capital requirements on securities broker-dealers, as a system or network protection for broker-dealers that transact with each other. (It is unclear, however, why the knowledgeable securities firms themselves cannot impose capital-solvency discipline by informing themselves as to which of their potential trading partners is skirting insolvency and thus should be shunned in any transaction that requires the extension of credit to that firm.) Finally, the Federal National Mortgage Association (Fannie Mae) and the Federal Home Loan Mortgage Corporation (Freddie Mac) are regulated for safety and soundness by the Office of Federal Housing Enterprise Oversight (OFHEO), because of the two companies' federal charters and special privileges and the financial markets' consequent perceptions that the U.S. government would cover their liabilities in the event of their financial difficulties.

22. Although our focus is primarily on the balance sheet, the profit-and-loss statement is inexorably linked to it, so our discussion implicitly covers that as well.

23. And thus limitations on activities are implicitly covered.

A MARKET VALUE ACCOUNTING APPROACH. Capital serves two important functions.[24] First, it is the direct indicator of solvency—the direct
buffer that protects depositors (or the deposit insurer) against a decline in
the value of the assets. Second, because capital is essentially the owners'
equity in the bank, greater capital is a disincentive to risk-taking, since
owners have a larger relative stake in the bank (which would be at risk).

The logic of these functions points strongly toward regulators' receiving balance sheet information that best represents this buffer and incen-
tive-disincentive. *This logic points to the use of market value accounting
(MVA), where market values are used wherever possible for asset and liability values.*[25]

Unfortunately, this is not the standard accounting system for financial
statements presented either to regulators or to the public. Instead, the
standard accounting system—generally accepted accounting principles
(GAAP)—is a backward-looking, historical cost-based system for
assigning values to assets and liabilities. Although GAAP does have
some elements that reflect current market values,[26] it is primarily based
on historical costs, and this perspective pervades standard accounting.

The drawback to GAAP for the purposes of safety-and-soundness regulation is straightforward. A bank's solvency, by definition, diminishes
as the value of its assets declines (or the value of its liabilities increases).
And it is just at the time of diminished solvency that the owners' incentives to take greater risks increase (since the owners have less to lose),
but the downside of that risk-taking means even greater losses and possible insolvency. Accordingly, bank regulators should want to know about
declines in asset values as rapidly as possible, so as to limit the risk-
taking behavior that might exacerbate those declines.[27] But GAAP, with
its historical orientation, is slow to recognize changes in the value of
assets, either down or up, and thus does not serve regulators well.

24. This section draws heavily on White (1991a, 1991b); see also Kaufman and others
(2000).

25. In the accounting literature, this is frequently described as fair value accounting.

26. For example, securities that are held in a held-for-sale account are marked to market; and where there is a clear diminished likelihood of repayment of a loan, the asset is
supposed to be written down. Nevertheless, GAAP is clearly oriented toward historical
costs rather than current values.

27. The incentives for risk-taking behavior are likely to be driven by owners' knowledge of the market value–based measurement of their net worth rather than by any GAAP-
based measure.

Although this slowness to recognize changes in asset value looks evenhanded, it is not. First, regulators have asymmetric concerns. They care much more about insolvency than about overly high levels of capital. Second, banks have a ready but dangerous strategy for circumventing GAAP's slowness to recognize asset gains: sell the assets that have embedded gains.[28] But banks can continue to hold assets that have declined in value and continue to account for them at the cost of acquisition. In essence, GAAP provides banks with a valuable option.

This strategy of selling "winners" to recognize gains (which can be sent, via dividends, to owners) while holding "losers" at historical cost can logically lead to a balance sheet with only overvalued assets, whose current (market) values are below their nominal values as listed on the balance sheet. This is not a recipe for maintaining the true solvency of a bank.[29]

It might appear that the numbers on the balance sheet do not matter, so long as regulators know the "true" value (that is, market value) of assets and liabilities. And GAAP (since the mid-1990s) has required a footnote statement of the market value of financial assets. But regulators are driven largely by what is represented on the balance sheet, not what is in the footnotes. The regulatory rules are written largely in terms of capital as reported on the balance sheet. The ability of regulators to restrict a bank's behavior is driven by the balance sheet's report of capital, as is the ability to appoint a receiver and thus wrest control from the owners.[30]

There are two main objections to a system of MVA.[31] First, opponents claim that it would introduce more volatility into banks' income statements. Support for this claim is sometimes provided by a "back casting"

---

28. Under some circumstances, financial institutions may not even have to sell the assets; they may be able simply to reclassify them within their portfolios from a hold-to-maturity account to a held-for-sale account; see Patrick Barta, "Fannie Mae Critics Pounce on Boost in Holder Equity," *Wall Street Journal (Eastern Edition),* October 25, 2002, p. A2.

29. Also GAAP's slowness to recognize gains can lead companies generally to engage in uneconomic behavior, such as a sale and the leaseback of a facility, just so the company can recognize the gain on its balance sheet.

30. During the period of the 1980s and early 1990s, when almost 1,500 commercial banks became insolvent and required regulatory action, bank regulators complained that they knew that some of these banks were in financial difficulties but that their apparently healthy (GAAP) balance sheets forestalled earlier preemptive action. See FDIC (1998).

31. See, for example, Engelke (1990) and Fisher (1992).

of historical bank experiences showing how their reported incomes would have been more volatile if an MVA framework had been in place. But this argument fails to acknowledge that volatility as measured by market values is what regulators should care about. Even more important, the backcasting exercise fails to recognize that banks would change their behavior if they knew that the MVA framework would be the standard for future reporting. To the extent that they care about reported volatility, banks would hedge and otherwise modify their behavior in ways that would reduce volatility as reported in the MVA framework. This additional hedging and other behavior modifications might be costly, but if market value reporting is what is important, this is the right framework within which the trade-offs between the smoothing of income flows and the costs of doing so should be considered.[32]

A second objection is that some assets and liabilities may have no ready markets for valuation purposes, and thus estimates would be required—opening the door to potential error and manipulation. This argument has gotten progressively weaker, as larger portions of banks' assets have become securitized or otherwise sellable. Further, significant parts of a bank's balance sheet already require estimates and judgments—for example, the life and depreciation of assets, the timing of when the value of an asset should be considered impaired and written down and the extent of the write-down, and the liability costs of the benefits of future retirees.

Still, even where there are no perfect substitutes that have market valuations, there may be close substitutes that, through modeling, can be related to the balance sheet assets in question. The modeling, of course, must be validated, first by the bank's auditor and ultimately by the regulator. But even imperfect modeling, if done and monitored responsibly,[33] is likely to be an improvement over the backward-looking focus of historical cost accounting. Only where market analogs and reliable modeling are not available ought historical costs to be the standard.

---

32. Similarly, the higher-volatility criticism of proposals that would place only some parts of the balance sheet on an MVA basis is misplaced. To the extent that banks care about reported volatility, they will modify their behavior. It is the trade-off between the increased costs of that behavior and the gains from the improved balance sheet information that should be weighed and argued.

33. This should rule out the wildly excessive optimism that apparently governed some of Enron's "mark-to-market" modeling and valuations.

The same general principles should apply to the valuation of liabilities as well.

THE FREQUENCY OF REPORTING. The current standard for frequency of reporting of financial statements is once a quarter, although regulators can require more frequent reports from banks that are of concern. This is far too infrequent. Banks do not slide into difficulties only at the end of a calendar quarter.

In an age when every bank is or should be wholly electronic in its financial accounts (and thus the marginal costs of frequent reporting ought to be quite small), more frequent reporting is both desirable and feasible. Weekly reporting should be the immediate goal, and daily reporting ought to be a near-term goal. Daily reporting is the standard for securities firms and investment banks. It should also be the standard for commercial banks and other depositories.

THE BASEL COMMITTEE'S APPROACH. Unfortunately, the Basel committee is hostile to MVA, embracing the historical cost orientation of GAAP. Although it acknowledges the problem of selling winners and holding losers, the committee is worried about increased volatility and imperfect estimates.[34] The committee has consequently greatly weakened the effectiveness of its capital standards.

The Basel committee's approach to frequency of reporting is one of silence as to specificity.[35] Again, this weakens the effectiveness of its capital standards.

Riskiness

Information about the riskiness of a financial conglomerate is only partially conveyed by the entries on its balance sheet. More information is needed. I first discuss the additional information that regulators should receive and then describe the Basel committee's approach.

THE NECESSARY INFORMATION. The primary regulatory approaches to riskiness are the insistence on adequate capital (for activities that are examinable and supervisable) and the exclusion of activities that are not examinable and supervisable. Essential to the determination of adequate levels of capital is a measure of the risk characteristics of the assets and

34. This hostility can be found in Basel Committee on Banking Supervision (1998b, 1999a, 2000b).
35. See Basel Committee on Banking Supervision (2001e).

liabilities, including any covariance effects. And essential to that determination are forward-looking stress tests that indicate how well the institution's capital (that is, the net arithmetic outcome of assets less liabilities) survives a variety of unfavorable macroeconomic scenarios. Further, of course, all such outcomes must be calculated in MVA terms.

Consequently, regulators need detailed information about the types, amounts, characteristics, and histories—including covariances—of all assets and liabilities of a bank. And they need a standardized stress test that is sufficiently comprehensive and detailed so as to be able to use all of the information to forecast outcomes.

Further, because transactions with owners and affiliates are potential vehicles for siphoning resources out of the bank, detailed information about such transactions is essential. In addition, information about indirect transactional advantages provided to owners or their affiliates is necessary.

Finally, a requirement that banks issue a tranche of tradable long-term subordinated debt as part of their required capital—say, equal to 2 percent of their assets—would provide regulators with an additional source of information from the capital markets.[36] The presence of subordinated debt would bring to the bank a group of stakeholders whose interests would be similar (though not identical) to those of the regulator, since the holders would not gain from the upside of risk-taking and would be the first parties affected by the downside after the owners' equity was erased. If issued as long-term debt with layered maturities, its holders could not all run on the bank simultaneously. The pricing of the debt would itself be an important source of information. And the layered maturities would mean that the bank would be rolling over and reissuing the debt at frequent intervals, providing an important additional source of information.

THE BASEL COMMITTEE'S APPROACH. The Basel committee has three alternative approaches to risk. First, and simplest, is its "standardized approach" to credit risk.[37] Similar to its 1988 capital standards, the standardized approach has a number of risk categories (buckets), with a capital requirement (risk weight) for each category. The standardized approach expands the number of buckets (as compared to the 1988 stan-

36. This argument is advanced forcefully by Calomiris and Litan (2000) and Kaufman and others (2000). See also Board of Governors of the Federal Reserve System and U.S. Department of the Treasury (2000).

37. See Basel Committee on Banking Supervision (2001h).

dards) and includes information on the bond ratings of any borrower that has rated debt.[38] However, it does not encompass an explicit forward-looking stress test;[39] it does not acknowledge covariances;[40] and it relies on GAAP rather than MVA for measurements of capital.

Second is the committee's "foundation internal ratings-based approach," whereby a bank can provide its own estimates of default probabilities.[41] The Basel II document provides the other components of risk, including loss in the event of default, exposure at default, and allowances for offsets. Forward-looking stress tests are expected to be part of the bank's estimation procedure. But the stress tests need not be conducted any more frequently than once every six months. Again, covariances are not explicitly acknowledged. And, again, all capital measurements rely on GAAP rather than MVA.

The third method is the committee's "advanced internal ratings-based approach," whereby a sufficiently sophisticated bank can provide its own estimates of the other components of risk. Otherwise it is similar to the second approach.

Further, the committee takes no specific stand on what activities are or are not appropriate for a bank, although it is suspicious of "significant" equity holdings in commercial enterprises,[42] and it recognizes the risks of transactions with affiliates.

The committee's concerns about special disclosure with respect to financial conglomerates appear to be focused largely on the risks of multistage financial leveraging or gearing.[43] This issue is readily demonstrated in a modification of figure 1, as shown in figure 4. Instead of all $100 of the top-tier bank's assets being devoted to loans, $8 is devoted to an equity investment in a subsidiary second-tier bank. With that $8 of equity, the subsidiary bank can attract $92 in deposits and make $100 in loans—or even itself set aside $8 for an equity investment in a third-tier bank. Thus, in principle, multitiering means that the original $8 of equity

38. For a critique of that inclusion, see White (2002a).

39. To the extent that companies' bond ratings are part of the process, forward-looking stress tests are present, since that is a component of bond ratings.

40. Except for explicit hedges and other offsets.

41. See Basel Committee on Banking Supervision (2001a).

42. The committee mandates that aggregate equity holdings in excess of 60 percent of the level of the bank's capital should not be counted as an asset for the bank. See Basel Committee on Banking Supervision (2001b).

43. See Basel Committee on Banking Supervision (1998c, 1999b).

Figure 4. Stylized Balance Sheet of the ABC Bank (Solvent, Multi-Tiered), as of December 31, 200Z

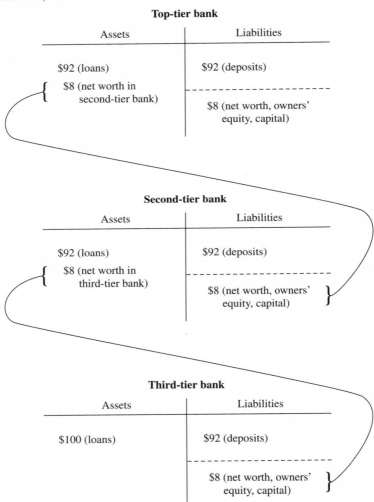

Top-tier bank

Assets	Liabilities
$92 (loans)	$92 (deposits)
$8 (net worth in second-tier bank)	$8 (net worth, owners' equity, capital)

Second-tier bank

Assets	Liabilities
$92 (loans)	$92 (deposits)
$8 (net worth in third-tier bank)	$8 (net worth, owners' equity, capital)

Third-tier bank

Assets	Liabilities
$100 (loans)	$92 (deposits)
	$8 (net worth, owners' equity, capital)

in the top-tier bank has achieved substantially greater leverage (and reduced protection for deposits) than the 12.5-to-1 capital-to-assets ratio of the simple bank of figure 1. The committee also points out that this multitiering could occur with an insurance company or a securities firm as the parent or the subsidiary.

The committee's approach to the multistage leveraging problem is to insist on consolidation at the parent level for the purposes of determining adequate capital—that is, ensuring adequate capital at the level of the parent bank so as to take into account the full leverage of the overall conglomerate. However, the committee fails to acknowledge explicitly that this multistage leveraging is a general problem that applies to any equity position taken by the bank.

Finally, the committee fails to endorse a requirement for the issuance of subordinated debt, a mechanism that (as argued above) would yield additional valuable information for regulators.

In sum, the Basel committee's approach falls substantially short of appropriate disclosure to regulators—in the accounting framework employed, the frequency of reporting, and the specifics of addressing risk.

Appropriate Disclosure to the Public

Appropriate public disclosure by publicly traded companies is a broad topic that extends considerably beyond the issues surrounding financial conglomerates. The Basel committee's interests in disclosure do not extend broadly, however. They are concerned solely with disclosure as the third pillar to support the safe-and-sound operation of banks. Nevertheless, the broader context is worth considering before focusing on the committee's concerns.

The Broad Issues

Generally, the extent to which regulatory involvement in public disclosure is required depends on one's view of investors. I offer two broad views in order to highlight the contrasts.[44]

---

44. This section draws heavily on White (2002b). See also Easterbrook and Fischel (1984); Diamond (1985); Fishman and Hagerty (1989); Diamond and Verrecchia (1991); Elliott and Jacobson (1994); Ball (2001).

THE ASYMMETRIC INFORMATION-AWARENESS MODEL. This approach starts by assuming that potential lenders and investors are aware of the asymmetric information problems that pervade finance. They realize that potential borrowers have more information about themselves and about their prospects for repayment than do the lenders and that actual borrowers may know more about their actions and the effects on repayment than do the lenders.[45] Lenders therefore recognize that they need to acquire information about prospective borrowers so as better to assess the riskiness of prospective borrowers, to decide to whom to make loans (and to whom to say no) and on what terms, and to monitor their actions after advancing a loan, so as to be able to intervene if circumstances warrant.

Here I describe the lenders-investors in this paradigm a bit more. They are *aware* of their informational limitations. Loosely, they *"know* that they don't know what they don't know." They may occasionally be fooled by deliberately misleading information, but they learn from this experience and move on. They rarely are fooled by vague or inadequate information. Because they are *risk averse* as well as *aware*, the presence of less (or inadequate) information about a prospective borrower causes the lenders to fear the worst about that borrower and to add a large risk premium in their consideration of whether to lend and on what terms.

In this context, financial statements provide an important source of information about enterprises that want to borrow, which helps the *aware* lenders to pierce the fog of asymmetric information in assessing prospective borrowers beforehand and in subsequently monitoring them. Equivalently, financial statements allow an enterprise to emerge from the fog of asymmetric information and better show its true prospects.

However, financial statements are not free; resources are required to gather, process, certify, and disseminate an enterprise's financial statements. Greater details and specificity of disclosure—although providing greater assurance to lenders—are generally more costly. Also an enterprise will be reluctant to reveal proprietary information that competitors may use to their own advantage and to the enterprise's disadvantage. Further, with respect to an enterprise's managers vis-à-vis its investors-shareholders-owners, the managers generally prefer to reveal less to the

---

45. In the interests of brevity, I describe the problem in terms of lenders and borrowers, but the same issues arise with equal force with respect to investors and seekers of equity finance.

shareholders, since revealing less information gives them greater flexibility of actions. But revealing more (useful) information helps to dispel the fog of asymmetric information for the investors and reduces the costs of equity capital to the enterprise.

Consequently, the enterprise tries to find the cost-minimizing point in the trade-off between the higher direct costs of greater information disclosure and the lower costs of capital from greater revelation. This cost-minimizing point should yield the most efficient financial statement disclosures for that enterprise.

With a multiplicity of enterprises in an economy, this quest for efficient disclosure appears to yield a multiplicity of formats and accounting systems—perhaps one for each enterprise. But the transactions costs for lenders and investors of translating the various firms' financial statements—in essence, the network aspects of financial reporting and the role of accounting—indicate that such a multitude of systems would itself be costly for enterprises and their lenders-investors, because of the incompatibility (comparison) costs. Accordingly, enterprises face a further set of trade-offs in disclosure—between the lower transactions costs of adhering to a more widely used accounting system and the higher costs of adhering to a less widely used system that is better at portraying a specific enterprise's information.

In this context, the role of government regulation with respect to disclosure is relatively modest. It consists primarily of policing fraudulent disclosure and helping firms and their investors-lenders to deal with the network aspects of disclosure. The latter would involve helping the system to decide whether one or a few accounting systems will be the basis for disclosure (as a template) by the enterprises that will be subject to the comparisons of the capital markets of an economy.[46]

---

46. As the number of accounting systems increases, the number of comparisons between systems increases more rapidly. If there are n systems (and one of them is considered to be the base system for comparisons), then there are $(n^2 - n) / 2$ potential comparisons; hence, an extra system—that is, $(n + 1)$ systems—yields $(n^2 + n) / 2$ comparisons. The difference between them is n. Thus each additional system adds ever-more comparisons and greater complexity and costs. For example, if we start with four systems, there are six comparisons; an additional system raises the number of comparisons to ten; an additional system after that (bringing the total to six) raises the number of comparisons to fifteen. White (1996a) points out that if each of the fifty states in the United States had its own GAAP, this would entail a potential for 1,225 comparisons between systems. On templates, see Sunder (2001); Dye and Sunder (2001).

THE INVESTOR PROTECTION MODEL. As compared with the awareness paradigm just described, an investor protection model entails more than just protecting investors from deliberately misleading information (that is, fraud) and helping them to navigate the network issues.[47] Instead, the lenders-investors in this model are not fully aware of their informational limitations. They can be fooled by vague or inadequate information; they do not realize that they need to pierce the fog of asymmetric information (or impose a large risk premium for remaining in the fog).

These lenders-investors need not be complete dupes; instead, they just cannot deal appropriately with vagueness.[48] Consequently, opportunistic corporate managers take advantage of this gullibility by remaining vague; some lenders-investors experience losses as a consequence; and rather than learning from their experience and moving on, the lenders-investors instead stay away from the securities markets (and tell their friends to do likewise), thereby reducing the liquidity and depth of the markets and raising the costs of capital.[49]

This paradigm calls for a much more active role for government regulation of disclosure, beyond policing fraud and dealing with network issues. Disclosure must be mandated, with extensive detail required.

Appropriate Disclosure

I now address the question of appropriate disclosure of financial conglomerates to the public. As a first approximation, requiring the same general framework of financial disclosure from financial conglomerates as from other publicly traded companies in the economy seems about right. After all, from the perspective of shareholders or of creditors (other

47. This model appears to drive the policies of the SEC and of Congress; see, for example, Sutton (1997); Levitt (1998).

48. "We [the SEC] pursue this mandate [to protect investors] not through merit regulation—allowing only 'healthy' companies to trade their securities—but by market regulation. . . . The goals of this approach are to prevent misleading *or incomplete* financial reporting and to facilitate informed decisions by investors" (Levitt 1998, p. 79; emphasis added).

49. In this model there can be politically charged distributional aspects. Lenders (bond buyers) and especially investors are "little guys" (or, perhaps, "widows and orphans") who are fooled by the vague claims of "corporations." But there is also a negative spillover effect. The "burned" lenders and investors (and their friends) exit from the capital markets, thereby raising the cost of capital in these markets.

than insured depositors), financial conglomerates are just another set of firms embedded in the fog of asymmetric information with which they must deal.

However, two qualifications to this position should be made. First, as argued above, banks (including, but not limited to, those that are part of a larger conglomerate structure) ought to be required to issue subordinated debt. The holders of this subordinated debt may well demand additional financial disclosure from banks. This is all to the good.

Second, because securities firms are at the center of the operations of the securities markets, their errant actions are more likely to yield negative externalities for the overall markets. Consequently, they should bear a higher responsibility for their disclosure concerning their activities.[50] Accordingly, when a securities firm is an affiliate of the bank, the customers of the securities firm should receive information about any connections among the securities affiliate's underwriting activities, its analysts' recommendations, and the bank's lending.

The Basel Committee's Approach

As noted, the Basel committee's approach to public disclosure for financial conglomerates is not rooted in concerns about disclosure in general. Instead, the committee envisions information disclosure as bolstering market discipline, which serves as the third pillar for safety and soundness in banking.

The committee's arguments in support of disclosure are surprisingly brief, consisting of about a page and a half in a supporting document.[51] In essence, the committee argues that the transactors with a bank can be a constraint on risk-taking by the bank if they are aware of the bank's actions and positions. With information revelation, the bank's creditors, counterparties, customers, suppliers, and so forth can find out about risk-taking earlier and can protect themselves earlier by ceasing their relationships with the banks or insisting on improved terms for continuing the

---

50. This would pertain, for example, to the disclosures that relate an analyst's recommendations to other aspects of the analyst and the securities firm. These disclosures could include the personal portfolio of the analyst, the past performance of the analyst, the past movement of the analyst's portfolio subsequent to a recommendation, and the securities firm's other relationships with the enterprise that is being recommended.

51. See Basel Committee on Banking Supervision (1998a, pp. 4–5).

relationship. These reactions, in turn, deter the bank's management from embarking on the course of risk-taking in the first place.

Consequently, the committee mandates an extensive menu of public disclosure for a bank. Indeed, it is difficult to distinguish between the committee's expectations for disclosure of information to regulators and its expectations for disclosure to the public. The former, of course, can be expected to remain as confidential information; the latter most certainly cannot. In that connection, the committee does not address the trade-offs between the short- and long-run efficiency consequences of the public disclosure of proprietary information and the potential benefits for transactors and ultimately for safety and soundness.

Further, the committee does not address how effective market discipline can be if the transactors with banks believe that governments will intervene and bail out the bank and its transactors (beyond the explicitly insured depositors). If the belief in bailouts is pervasive, then the disclosure is largely irrelevant, and market discipline is largely absent. In addition, the transactors are likely to be sophisticated parties (and would have to be, in order to be able to absorb and use the elaborate menu of information disclosures recommended by the committee). Why would they not be able to protect themselves by making their own demands for information (or declining to transact)?[52] Finally, by not endorsing the mandatory issuance of subordinated debt, the committee has forgone an important potential source of market discipline and of market pressures for information disclosure.[53]

In sum, although market discipline has a resounding ring, the committee's arguments for the disclosure of public information generally and for the disclosure of specific information are weak indeed. And the committee undermines its best opportunity for achieving market discipline by failing to endorse mandatory subordinated debt.

Conclusion

The appropriate information disclosure for financial conglomerates has been and will continue to be an important area for policy concern. As

52. Further, why might not the ratings provided by bond-rating firms provide the information that transactors need?
53. See Calomiris and Litan (2000).

this paper has argued, there are at least two audiences for information disclosure: bank regulators and the general public. They should be distinguished.

There is little doubt that the goals of Basel II—to improve the safety and soundness of banks—are worthy. The specific measures chosen, however, are more open to question. By turning its back on the three most important steps that could be taken to improve information disclosure—mandating market value accounting for banks' reports to regulators, aiming toward daily electronic submission of those reports, and requiring the issuance of subordinated debt—the Basel committee fundamentally undermines the achievement of those goals.

References

Ball, Ray. 2001. "Infrastructure Requirements for an Economically Efficient System of Public Financial Reporting and Disclosure." In Robert E. Litan and Richard Herring, eds., *Brookings-Wharton Papers on Financial Services 2001*, pp. 127–69. Brookings.

Basel Committee on Banking Supervision. 1998a. "Enhancing Bank Transparency." Basel: Bank for International Settlements, September.

———. 1998b. "Sound Practices for Loan Accounting, Credit Risk Disclosure, and Related Matters." Basel: Bank for International Settlements, October.

———. 1998c. "Supervision of Financial Conglomerates." Basel: Bank for International Settlements, February.

———. 1999a. "Sound Practices for Loan Accounting and Disclosure." Basel: Bank for International Settlements, July.

———. 1999b. "Supervision of Financial Conglomerates." Basel: Bank for International Settlements, February.

———. 2000a. "A New Capital Adequacy Framework: Pillar 3." Basel: Bank for International Settlements, January.

———. 2000b. "Report to G7 Finance Ministers and Central Bank Governors on International Accounting Standards." Basel: Bank for International Settlements, April.

———. 2001a. *The Internal Ratings-Based Approach.* Basel: Bank for International Settlements, January.

———. 2001b. *The New Basel Capital Accord.* Basel: Bank for International Settlements, January.

———. 2001c. *The New Basel Capital Accord: An Explanatory Note.* Basel: Bank for International Settlements, January.

———. 2001d. *Overview of the New Basel Capital Accord.* Basel: Bank for International Settlements, January.

———. 2001e. *Pillar 2 (Supervisory Review Process).* Basel: Bank for International Settlements, January.

———. 2001f. *Pillar 3 (Market Discipline).* Basel: Bank for International Settlements, January.

———. 2001g. "Pillar 3—Market Discipline." Working Paper. Basel: Bank for International Settlements, September.

———. 2001h. *The Standardized Approach to Credit Risk.* Basel: Bank for International Settlements, January.

Board of Governors of the Federal Reserve System and the U.S. Department of the Treasury. 2000. *The Feasibility and Desirability of Mandatory Subordinated Debt.* Washington, December.

Calomiris, Charles W., and Robert E. Litan. 2000. "Financial Regulation in a Global Marketplace." In Robert E. Litan and Anthony M. Santomero, eds., *Brookings-Wharton Papers on Financial Services 2000*, pp. 283–339. Brookings.

Chen, Yehning. 1999. "Banking Panics: The Role of the First-Come, First-Served Rule and Information Externalities." *Journal of Political Economy* 107 (October): 946–68.

Diamond, Douglas W. 1985. "Optimal Release of Information by Firms." *Journal of Finance* 40 (4, September): 1071–94.

Diamond, Douglas W., and Philip H. Dybvig. 1983. "Bank Runs, Deposit Insurance, and Liquidity." *Journal of Political Economy* 91 (3, June): 401–19.

Diamond, Douglas W., and Robert E. Verrecchia. 1991. "Disclosure, Liquidity, and the Cost of Capital." *Journal of Finance* 46 (4, September): 1325–59.

Dye, Ronald A., and Shyam Sunder. 2001. "Why Not Allow FASB and IASB Standards to Compete in the U.S.?" *Accounting Horizons* 15 (3, September): 257–71.

Easterbrook, Frank H., and Daniel R. Fischel. 1984. "Mandatory Disclosure and the Protection of Investors." *Virginia Law Review* 70 (May): 669–715.

Edwards, Franklin R. 1979. "Banks and Securities Activities: Legal and Economic Perspectives on the Glass-Steagall Act." In Lawrence G. Goldberg and Lawrence J. White, eds., *The Deregulation of the Banking and Securities Industries*, pp. 273–94. Lexington, Mass.: Heath.

Elliott, Robert K., and Peter D. Jacobson. 1994. "Costs and Benefits of Business Information Disclosure." *Accounting Horizons* 8 (December): 80–96.

Engelke, George L., Jr. 1990. "Mark-to-Market Accounting: What *Is* Real Value?" *Financial Managers' Statement* 12 (1, January-February): 33–34.

FDIC (Federal Deposit Insurance Corporation). 1998. *Managing the Crisis: The FDIC and the RTC Experience, 1980–1994.* Washington.

Fisher, Donna J. 1992. "Con: Market Value Accounting Boils Down to 'Trust Me' Values." *Journal of Corporate Accounting and Finance* 3 (3, Spring): 327–32.

Fishman, Michael J., and Kathleen M. Hagerty. 1989. "Disclosure Decisions by Firms and the Competition for Price Efficiency." *Journal of Finance* 44 (3, July): 633–46.

Kaufman, George B., and others. 2000. *Reforming Bank Capital Regulation: A Proposal by the U.S. Shadow Financial Regulatory Committee.* Washington: American Enterprise Institute.

Levitt, Arthur. 1998. "Commentary: The Importance of High Quality Accounting Standards." *Accounting Horizons* 12 (1, March): 79–82.

Morgan, Donald P. 2002. "Rating Banks: Risk and Uncertainty in an Opaque Industry." *American Economic Review* 92 (4, September): 874–88.

Postlewaite, Andrew, and Xavier Vives. 1987. "Bank Runs as an Equilibrium Phenomenon." *Journal of Political Economy* 95 (3, June): 485–91.

Shull, Bernard, and Lawrence J. White. 1998. "The Right Corporate Structure for Expanded Bank Activities." *Banking Law Journal* 115 (5, May): 446–76.

Sunder, Shyam. 2001. "Standards for Corporate Financial Reporting: Regulatory Competition within and across International Boundaries." Unpublished paper. New Haven, Conn.: Yale University, School of Management.

Sutton, Michael H. 1997. "Financial Reporting in U.S. Capital Markets: International Dimensions." *Accounting Horizons* 11 (June): 96–102.

White, Lawrence J. 1991a. *The S&L Debacle: Public Policy Lessons for Bank and Thrift Regulation.* New York: Oxford University Press.

————. 1991b. "The Value of Market Value Accounting for the Deposit Insurance System." *Journal of Accounting, Auditing, and Finance* 6 (April): 284–301.

————. 1996a. "Competition Versus Harmonization: An Overview of International Regulation of Financial Services." In Claude E. Barfield, ed., *International Trade in Financial Services,* pp. 5–48. Washington: American Enterprise Institute.

————. 1996b. "The Proper Structure of Universal Banking: Examinability and Supervisability." In Anthony Saunders and Ingo Walter, eds., *Universal Banking: Financial System Design Reconsidered,* pp. 682–95. Chicago: Irwin.

————. 2002a. "The Credit Rating Industry: An Industrial Organization Analysis." In Richard M. Levich, Giovanni Majnoni, and Carmen Reinhart, eds., *Ratings, Rating Agencies, and the Global Financial System,* pp. 41–63. Boston: Kluwer.

————. 2002b. "Globalized Securities Markets and Accounting: How Many Standards?" Paper presented at the conference Is GAAP Worth Fighting For? American Enterprise Institute, Washington, March 13.

Efficient Confidentiality for Privacy, Security, and Confidential Business Information

PETER P. SWIRE

T HIS PAPER IS, IN PART, about the efficiency of privacy protection within financial conglomerates. Addressing that topic, however, requires the analysis to go broader in three respects. First, the issues affecting privacy in financial conglomerates are fundamentally similar to privacy issues for other industries. Second, privacy issues have been so contentious in recent years that it helps our understanding to broaden the discussion to other settings where confidentiality may be appropriate. Third, the claims for the efficiency or inefficiency of financial privacy protections require a more probing examination of what the concept of "efficiency" means as applied to privacy and other confidentiality issues.

The paper begins with a brief background on recent developments in financial privacy. It then contrasts the history of widespread confidentiality in banking, a history that suggests the efficiency of the practice, with economists' views that confidentiality often makes a market less competitive and less efficient. To reconcile the contrasting stories, the paper then moves away from the privacy debate to analyze the efficiency of confidentiality in other settings. Notably, many people believe that confi-

My thanks for comments from participants at a workshop at the Moritz College of Law and at the Netherlands-United States Roundtable on Financial Services Conglomerates, hosted by the Brookings Institution, the Wharton School, and the Royal Netherlands Embassy. Thanks as well for research assistance from Cary Bishop and Aimee Kaplan.

dentiality aids efficiency in connection with security, confidential business information, account numbers, and other key data that can result in identity theft. The reasons supporting confidentiality in these other settings make it easier to see when confidentiality may be efficient in the handling of personal information. The paper then discusses a new study that gives evidence of a link between higher consumer trust in privacy and willingness to participate in other financial services. Based on the analysis, it proposes a general approach for assessing the efficiency of confidentiality. In doing so, it also highlights the particular ways in which economists have systematically given less weight to privacy protection than academics trained in other disciplines.

On the level of methodology, this paper specifically targets arguments about confidentiality from two groups that, in my experience, are most skeptical of privacy claims: economists and a regulated industry that prefers not to face greater regulation. By making arguments within the discourse of financial services and economics, I am not claiming that this is the best or the only approach to assessing the importance and desirability of privacy protections. Scholars trained in other disciplines have vigorously argued for privacy protection. These scholars have argued, for instance, that privacy protections foster autonomy,[1] develop and maintain desirable social norms,[2] encourage democracy,[3] prevent tyranny,[4] and serve other worthy goals.[5] This paper does not attempt to umpire among the competing perspectives on privacy protection. Instead, it primarily

1. See Cohen (2000) on values of protection of individual dignity, promotion of personal autonomy, and development for meaningful participation in the social and political life of the community; see Westin (1967) on the importance of privacy for protecting personal autonomy, enabling emotional release, and allowing self-evaluation and personal communications.

2. See Post (1989, 2001).

3. See Schwartz (1999), who argues that privacy is essential for self-development and essential for a democratic society.

4. See Swire (1999) and Solove (2001, p. 1393), who states that Kafka's novel *The Trial* "captures the sense of helplessness, frustration, and vulnerability one experiences when a large bureaucratic organization has control over a vast dossier of details about one's life."

5. According to Gavison (1980), we claim privacy to promote liberty, autonomy, selfhood, and human relations as well as to further the existence of a free society; Reiman (1984 p. 314) argues that privacy "protects the individual's interest in becoming, being, and remaining a person." Rosen (2000, p. 8) says, "Privacy protects us from being misdefined and judged out of context in a world of short attention spans, a world in which information can easily be confused with knowledge."

explores ways in which economic analysis to date has likely, in its own terms, undervalued the importance of privacy protection.[6] It then seeks to place the economic analysis of privacy and confidentiality more clearly within the broader debates about those important topics.

Bank Confidentiality Versus Economic Theory: Two Contrasting Stories

For a number of years I have done research on the topic of financial privacy as a lens for exploring more general issues of privacy, data protection, and information technology.[7] Along with this academic research, I have had the privilege of participating more directly in the development of law and policy in the area of financial privacy. From March 1999 until January 2001, I served as the Clinton administration's chief counselor for privacy in the U.S. Office of Management and Budget. In that role, I participated in what was likely the most intense political debate in U.S. history about the rules for financial privacy. In May 1999 President Clinton announced his support for significant financial privacy legislation, in what I believe was the first event by a U.S. president that focused on the topic of information privacy. That July the House of Representatives passed the Financial Services Reform Bill, with privacy as the most hotly contested issue in the floor debate. That November President Clinton signed the Financial Modernization Bill, after arduous negotiations on privacy and other issues and a threat to veto the bill if the privacy protections were not strong enough. The next spring, President Clinton proposed the Consumer Financial Privacy Act,[8] calling on Congress to

---

6. Previous articles that support privacy protections from within the economic paradigm notably include Murphy (1996); Schwartz (1997).

7. Swire (1997b) explores the extent to which even perfectly implemented technologies could create privacy protection; Swire (1997a) analyzes the conditions under which markets, self-regulation, and regulation are likely to be desirable. Swire (1999) studies the special concerns, including the risk of totalitarianism, that could arise if governments gained knowledge of every financial transaction that an individual had ever made; Swire and Litan (1998) focus on some of the possible inefficiencies of the European Union Data Protection Directive as applied to transborder flows in the financial sector; Swire (2002) describes the passage of financial privacy provisions in the Gramm-Leach-Bliley Act, with special focus on what to do next on the issues of affiliate sharing and notice to customers.

8. Consumer Financial Privacy Act, H.R. 4380, 106th Cong. (2000).

address the "unfinished business" of privacy protection that was not accomplished in the Gramm-Leach-Bliley Act.

The Gramm-Leach-Bliley Act, as enacted, was considerably weaker than privacy advocates had wished and considerably more regulatory than financial firms had hoped and expected. I have written elsewhere on what I consider the surprising virtues of the act's privacy provisions.[9] For purposes of this paper, I briefly summarize that law in terms of "fair information practices," as defined by the Federal Trade Commission and the U.S. Department of Commerce. On the issue of notice, the act requires a detailed annual notice to customers about sharing of personal information both to third parties and within a financial holding company. On the issue of choice, the most controversial part of the law, the act provides customers the right to opt out of many kinds of sharing with third parties but does not limit sharing within a holding company. On the issue of access, the law does not provide any new rights. On the issue of security, it provides for standards to be issued by the financial regulators. On the issue of enforcement, it gives regulators the ability to use their usual strict enforcement powers against institutions that violate their privacy promises. The act also provides that stricter financial privacy laws at the state level apply. This lack of preemption will become even more important in early 2004, when the preemption provision of the Fair Credit Reporting Act expires. At that point, stricter state laws could take effect for both credit reporting and other financial privacy issues. If a large state such as California passes a stricter law, and California has repeatedly come close to doing so, then financial institutions may have a powerful incentive to seek federal financial privacy legislation that includes preemption. The issues of financial privacy discussed in this paper may therefore have immediate as well as ongoing relevance to the policymaking process.

Is Confidentiality in Banking Outdated?

This history of recent American legislation provides the context for my first story. In July of 1999, just a few weeks after the House of Representatives surprised and angered many bankers by passing financial privacy rules, I boarded a plane to Colorado Springs to make what was pos-

9. Swire (2002).

sibly the most difficult public appearance of my time in government. The American Bankers Association had invited me to address their annual meeting, filled with several hundred bank chief executive officers and other senior managers. Many of these bankers had labored for more than a decade to support financial modernization legislation in Washington. Many of those same bankers now were concerned that the entire point of modernization would be negated by burdensome new privacy restrictions on how data could be shared in the new, supposedly modernized, financial holding companies.

My task as an administration official was to get out of Colorado Springs alive. It was bad enough that I worked for President Clinton, who had made the White House speech favoring privacy legislation. Even worse, as chief counselor for privacy, I personified a new government yoke being imposed on banks just as they were being unleashed from decades of excessive regulation.

Nothing sharpens the mind quite like the prospect of an execution. I cast about for some way to speak to this audience that would elicit a more thoughtful response. The best I could come up with was a story and a question, which I now discuss.

The story concerns my father-in-law, Ted Putney.[10] Ted is now retired. For most of his career, he was a successful banker in Albany, New York. For a number of years, he was head of the trust department of one of the larger banks in town. On occasion, while Ted was walking around town with my wife Anne and the rest of the family, some grown-up would approach Ted, and they would talk for a bit, perhaps in a way that showed that the person was a customer of the bank. Afterward, Ted would remind Anne and her little sisters that they were not supposed to talk about what they had heard in the conversation. As they grew older, my wife and her sisters did not need to be reminded to keep the names of customers confidential. They just knew that this was what bankers did.

The night before my speech in Colorado Springs, I told this story to the other bankers at my dinner table. A number of them nodded in recognition, saying that I indeed described the banking world in which they had worked. In the speech the next day, I included the story as the opening to the question I posed to the banking industry: Is confidentiality in

---

10. Both Ted and my wife Anne have given consent to tell the story.

banking outdated?[11] The speech made a number of points about the history and rhetoric within the industry of carefully safeguarding client information. For instance, individuals and businesses, when applying for a loan, do not expect the details they divulge to be told all over town or to their business competitors. Banks have always provided strictly confidential services to customers of their trust departments and private banking services. At a broader level, the central importance of "trust" has always included both trust that the bank is financially sound and also that the bank will safeguard the information about one's private business.

It would be pleasant to report that this speech to the American Bankers Association converted the listeners. In the movie version (never to be made), they would jump to their feet in wild applause. They would join in a common mission to reinvent confidentiality for the new age of financial modernization and information technology. That would not be true. At the end of the speech, there was polite applause (a bit better than I had feared), and the expected concerns about the costs of the proposed legislation emerged during the question-and-answer period.[12]

Nonetheless, the story of Ted Putney and the question of whether confidentiality in banking is outdated do stand for an important intellectual point. There is indeed a strong tradition of confidentiality within the financial services industry. The intellectual point is that this tradition, in order to survive for so long and in such diverse settings, must have important efficiency properties.[13] Looking ahead, I contend that an efficient financial services industry in the future will be characterized by confidentiality in a variety of respects.

Economists and the Free Flow of Information

There is a second story about efficiency, one that is deeply skeptical about confidentiality. My appreciation of this different view arose when I was in government, discussing privacy with people from many intellectual and political backgrounds. In these conversations, I came to believe

11. The PowerPoint slides for the speech are available at www.peterswire.net.

12. Some individuals did come up after the speech to say that they were glad to have the confidentiality tradition of the industry brought up in this way. A larger number, I recall, came up to argue that any privacy legislation would be unnecessary.

13. For one prominent scholar who explores the economic efficiency of institutional arrangements, see Williamson (1985).

that there was one important predictor of people who did not "get" the privacy issue. That predictor was having received graduate training in economics.[14] Again and again, I have been in meetings where the professional economists are outliers when regarding the importance of privacy. Although some economics-based writing argues for the importance of privacy protection, most of it does not.[15]

The reason for this, I believe, comes from the basic model of a competitive market. This model is inculcated into economics students with their first graphs on supply and demand. A competitive market is characterized by *perfect information*.[16] The closer a market comes to perfect information, the better can willing buyers and sellers find each other. With perfect information, buyers and sellers can make the bargains that maximize the gains from trade. In short, economists learn that competitive markets are efficient and that efficiency is enhanced the closer one gets to perfect information.

A simple example illustrates this point. Imagine a community where ten people wish to sell a house and ten wish to buy a house. Suppose, to begin, that yard signs are the principal way that sellers alert the market that a house is for sale. Buyer A may live close to a house that goes on the market and may therefore see the yard sign. Buyer A, after looking at the house, may offer $100,000. The seller, after considering the lack of other offers, may accept that price. Meanwhile, Buyer B never sees the yard sign. In fact, the house is perfect for Buyer B, and she would have

---

14. A second predictor of who would argue against the importance of privacy was being employed to lobby against privacy rules. Trade group and company representatives are paid to articulate the interests of their principals, and it is often rational for these employers to argue against stricter privacy laws. That said, my experience has been that the individuals employed by industry on privacy lobbying are quite diverse when they express their views in private. Some are attracted to the privacy issue because they think that privacy is important. Some believe that they can foster better privacy practices by working within industry for sensible reforms. Others have the opposite view and are personally committed to the benefits of the free flow of information. Others do not let down their guard in private, and I never learn their personal views. My experience, in short, is that the professional opponents of privacy legislation span the spectrum of views about the importance of privacy. By contrast, very few professional economists I have encountered believe that privacy is an important value.

15. For examples of the former, see Schwartz (1997); Murphy (1996).

16. For example, see Samuelson and Nordhaus (1985), who discuss important factors in perfect competition, including that the buyers and sellers are well informed about quality and about each other's prices.

offered up to $125,000 for the house, considerably more than Buyer A ever would have offered. In this low-information scenario we get an inefficient outcome. Better information would have matched the seller with Buyer B. The seller would have gotten a higher price, and the buyer who valued the house more would have bought it.

Now shift the example to a high-information setting. Suppose now that there is a listing service for all houses that go on the market. Suppose as well that the listing service gives detailed and accurate information about the characteristics of each house, such as the number of bedrooms, age of the house, photographs of the exterior and interior, and so forth. In this scenario, Buyer B would find out quickly when her dream house came on the market. If Buyer A made a low offer of $100,000, then an auction could easily develop, and Buyer B would win the auction and move into her dream house. The high-information scenario thus leads to a more efficient matching of buyers and sellers.[17]

Given this link among efficiency, competitive markets, and greater information, what is the value of privacy? The key insight for the economist is that privacy rules systematically reduce information flows. Privacy rules thus appear to reduce efficiency, and what could be worse than that for an economist? This skepticism about privacy is evident in the work of law and economics scholars such as Richard Posner and Richard Epstein.[18] Judge Posner, in particular, is prone to see a privacy claim as an attempt by individuals to hide embarrassing information and misrepresent themselves.

Returning to our housing market, suppose that some individuals argue that the home is the most private sanctum and that it should be contrary to privacy laws for the listing service to disclose intimate details about homes. This law, for instance, might say that only summary information

---

17. The example, of course, simplifies from actual housing markets in various ways. For instance, the efficiency argument assumes that the gains from efficient trade are greater than the cost of running the listing service. Concerning listing services, practice in the United States is that only licensed agents are allowed to see the Multiple Listing Service, which contains the most detailed information about many houses. The basic argument for the efficiency of the Multiple Listing Service is similar to the argument for the efficiency of intellectual property generally. Having limited access to the valuable information and charging for access to that information encourage investment in the Multiple Listing Service.

18. Posner (1978, 1979, 1995). See generally the *Journal of Legal Studies* issue devoted to the law and economics of privacy ("Symposium" 1980). Epstein (1980, 1994).

about the home can be listed. Such a privacy law, in the eyes of economists, would be clearly inefficient due to the loss of useful information in the market.

Suppose, next, that there is a milder privacy law where the default is to have only summary information. Sellers provide more detailed information about the house only if they opt in. This scenario raises the possibility of misrepresentation and strategic behavior that is of such concern to Judge Posner. A seller with an apparently wonderful house—many bedrooms, large lot, and so on—may decide to give only the summary information. (The seller might even tell the listing service that privacy is the reason for the small amount of disclosure.) Buyers may flock to an open house, only to discover a run-down interior or other undesirable features. The seller's lack of disclosure may successfully trick a buyer into making the costly drive out to the open house. A buyer, once in the house, might bid for it even though the buyer would have gone to a different open house if full information had been available. The seller's trick—appearing to offer a better house than is true with full information—thus might work.

The costs of strategic withholding of information are likely greater in other settings. For the sale of a house, the buyer usually will get very substantial disclosure before closing the deal. The effectiveness of withholding the data from the listing service is thus limited. Consider instead the plight of a credit card company in a world where privacy laws shield information about a borrower's credit history. Suppose, for instance, that privacy laws prevent the lender from learning about the borrower's bankruptcy or default on previous loans. In this setting, privacy laws can be very inefficient. The riskiest borrowers can now engage in a form of fraud—looking the same as good borrowers. The results for the system are more defaults on loans, higher interest rates to compensate for that risk, and less efficiency generally.[19]

19. In economic terms, there is a risk of adverse selection. If lenders cannot distinguish between high- and low-risk borrowers, then they cannot add an efficient risk premium to the high-risk loans. Low-risk borrowers will pay the same interest rate as high-risk borrowers. Some of the low-risk borrowers will drop out of the market rather than pay the excessive interest rates, thus forgoing efficient transactions that would have taken place if the interest rates had been priced based on actual risk.
Let me be clear that I am not claiming that the Fair Credit Reporting Act (FCRA) and similar laws are themselves inefficient. First, the FCRA was originally enacted based on evidence of widespread and material mistakes in individuals' credit histories. See Miller

The home buying and credit card examples are designed to help the (non-economist) reader think like an economist about privacy rules. Privacy rules are inefficient because they deviate from the fundamental principles of competitive markets. They reduce the free flow of information, make it more difficult for buyers and sellers to find each other, and prevent efficient transactions from taking place. Even worse, privacy rules promote strategic withholding of information and facilitate fraud. Scholars trained in other disciplines may think that privacy is a good thing. Economists are skeptical. In their most generous moments, they think that there is a heavy burden of persuasion on those who support privacy rules that reduce the flow of information.

Don't Hand Out the Combination to the Safe, for Security, Confidential Business Information, or Personal Information

Thus far this paper has developed two conflicting stories about the efficiency of having confidentiality in financial services. One story emphasizes the tradition of confidentiality in banking and related markets and the likely efficiency of this behavior over time. The other story relies on the model of perfect information and the competitive market that stands at the core of neoclassical economics. We thus see a paradox concerning confidentiality—greater efficiency with it, but greater efficiency without it. To resolve this paradox, this paper temporarily moves away from privacy rules to discuss other settings where confidentiality applies—security information and confidential business information. By developing our instincts for the efficiency of confidentiality in these settings, we can better understand the conditions under which confidentiality for privacy is likely to be efficient.

In considering the advantages and disadvantages of confidentiality in these settings, this paper does not focus on the important issue of what institutional approaches are best for achieving a given level of confiden-

---

(1971). The FCRA gives individuals the right to access their credit history and correct mistakes. These rights serve the efficiency goal of having loans made based on accurate information. My own sense is that the FCRA generally provides lenders with detailed enough information to permit efficient lending decisions. If the FCRA indeed promotes decisions based on more accurate information and provides lenders with enough data to make good loans, as I believe, then it enhances efficiency.

tiality. I have written elsewhere about how to select among market approaches, self-regulation, and government legislation.[20] In the discussion here, the focus instead is on what *level* of confidentiality is likely efficient, without specifying the institutions for ensuring that confidentiality.

Efficiency, Security, and Handing out Passwords, Combinations, and Keys

Probing the relationship between security and confidentiality leads us to examine two topics: the question of openness versus secrecy in bank security and the economic analysis of the efficiency of confidentiality in security.

OPENNESS AND SECRECY IN BANK SECURITY. Banks have always been experts on security. In the old story, the thief was asked why he robbed banks. He answered: "Because that's where the money is." In response, banks learned how to ensure physical security in their vaults and other operations. They learned how to ensure security in the work force so that tellers and other employees would not pocket cash. In recent years, banks have been leaders in computer security, as illustrated by the fact that the financial services sector was the first to have an operational information security and analysis center (ISAC) for industry-wide cyber threats.[21]

This history of bank leadership on security issues is related to confidentiality in the following way: When is it efficient for banks to be open about their security activities (to disclose them), and when is it efficient instead for them to use secrecy (confidentiality) in how their security is achieved? This question, in turn, is part of the more general inquiry about when to be open or secret in how security is achieved. Openness can lead to deterrence—if the robber sees formidable defenses, then the robber is likely to go elsewhere. Openness can also lead to improved security measures over time, as outside experts test and critique the security system and suggest improvements. The argument that openness can improve

---

20. Swire (1997a).

21. For information about the financial services ISAC, see www.fsisac.com. The use of ISACs is an important element of the strategy for cyberspace security of both the Clinton and Bush administrations. For the Clinton administration's plan, see White House (2000); for the Bush administration's draft plan, see President's Critical Infrastructure Protection Board (2002).

security has become widely accepted in many computer security settings, as reflected in the slogan: "There is no security through obscurity." Encryption researchers, for instance, do not trust encryption systems where the underlying mathematical algorithms have not been disclosed. For these security experts, a crucial test of a strong encryption system is the extent to which it resists attacks even when the underlying algorithm has been published. Only encryption systems that have been publicly scrutinized, and have withstood the test of time, can be considered secure.

In contrast to these ways that openness can improve security, many people believe that secrecy will help to improve security even more. For instance, a military base would not wish to reveal the precise location of the guns that guard the perimeter. More generally, defenders may wish to use traps and other surprises to catch an intruder, and these surprises just will not work well if they are broadcast in advance.

For the past two years I have been engaged in a broader research project about the conditions under which openness improves or reduces computer security. I have made available some preliminary views but have found the topic challenging enough that more time is needed to become confident in my overall findings.[22] With that said, this research has helped me to see one category of security information that almost always should be kept secret. That category consists of particularized information about how to gain entry to a secure area. For instance, it does not help security to tell everyone the combination to a safe. Similarly, it is a security breach to provide keys to a lock or to reveal a user password or personal identification number (PIN). A malicious outsider can use the combination, the key, the password, or the PIN to enter an area that is supposed to be secure.

Perhaps this point seems almost too obvious to mention. If you hand out the keys to a lock, the lock will be less effective. If you disclose the combination to a safe, then the money can be stolen. I make this obvious point, however, to show a situation where I believe everyone will agree that confidentiality is efficient. Even the computer experts who are most devoted to openness understand that keys should be kept private. For instance, public key encryption and other modern encryption systems

---

22. For a preliminary version of the research, see Swire (2001).

publicize the specifications about how the system operates.[23] These encryption systems, however, absolutely require that the user password stay secret. Otherwise, all of a user's communications can become easily readable to the outsider who knows the password.

ECONOMISTS AND THE EFFICIENCY OF CONFIDENTIALITY IN SECURITY. How might an economist, generally skeptical of confidentiality, analyze the efficiency of maintaining confidentiality for passwords, combinations, and other key information? I believe an economic analysis would support confidentiality, due to the low benefits and high costs of disclosure.

In looking at the benefits of disclosure, the important point is that disclosing passwords and the like does not improve the matching of willing sellers and buyers. Looking at the example of home sales, the efficiency of disclosure results from lower search costs and increased likelihood that a house will be purchased by the person who values it most. Looking at disclosure of user passwords, the disclosure actually *interferes* with the contracts between willing sellers and buyers. Instead, disclosure unfortunately matches an individual with a willing thief. The bank and its customers wish to carry out transactions with minimum risk and effort. The disclosure of the user password increases the risk, thereby reducing the overall benefits of the commercial relationship.

In looking at the costs of disclosure, the important point is that disclosing a user password or the combination to a safe creates harm. The thief gains access to the safe or to the user account. Theft is widely understood by economists to pose serious threats to efficiency.[24] In a world with high levels of theft, individuals and businesses have to expend scarce resources on protection—bars on the windows, bodyguards on the streets, and so on. Measures that reduce theft, such as strong safes and secure passwords, allow business to go forward without inefficiently high levels of spending on protection.

Measures that reduce theft have the additional efficiency advantage of avoiding the chilling of business activity. If the streets are full of muggers, for instance, then individuals are less likely to go shopping. If banks routinely lose the funds of customers, then customers are less likely to

---

23. This openness encourages critiques and allows users all over the world to set up the software on their own computer systems.

24. Posner (1986).

give banks the funds for safekeeping.[25] This "chilling effect" is the equivalent of saying that reducing theft will encourage investment in the economic activity.

In light of the efficiency of keeping the combination or password secret, the next issue is how to allocate the security task efficiently between the bank and its customers. Who can contribute to system security at least cost? The answer will clearly depend on the circumstances, but the bank is likely to be in the best position for many aspects of system security. The bank controls the physical safe or the customer cyber accounts. The bank (with other suppliers) designs and manages the system for Internet banking. In light of its far greater expertise in the workings of the system, the bank is likely the least-cost avoider for many security problems.[26]

The bank is even more likely to be the efficient place for many precautions because of its informational advantages. It is difficult for individual customers to detect and understand the level of security offered, for instance, by a bank's Internet banking system. Most customers are not as expert in security as the employees of the bank tasked with security. Even customers who are knowledgeable about security will likely find it difficult or impossible to assess how well the system is designed and implemented.[27] By contrast, the bank often receives helpful information about the security risks affecting individual customers. Hackers who masquerade as a customer may create "red flags," such as when access is made from an unusual location or the customer engages in out-of-pattern transactions. Because of this informational asymmetry, it is likely effi-

---

25. In the United States and other countries, agencies such as the Federal Deposit Insurance Corporation insure depositors' funds up to a certain level. Above that level, however, individuals may be at risk for losing funds given to the banks for safekeeping. Even if individuals eventually recover stolen funds, moreover, they may face significant time and trouble in proving their claims and securing reimbursement.

26. The idea of "least-cost avoider" or "cheapest-cost avoider" is familiar to the law academy from the work of Calabresi (1970). As used in the area of tort accidents, the burden of taking precautions will be done most efficiently by the party that minimizes the sum of accident costs (here, security breaches), prevention costs (here, the costs of building and maintaining the security system), and transaction costs (here, the costs of allocating burdens among the banks, customers, and other parties).

27. This asymmetry in information and monitoring was recognized by the U.S. Department of Health and Human Services in its cost-benefit assessment of the medical privacy rule under the Health Insurance Portability and Accountability Act of 1996. 65 Fed. Reg. 82462 (December 28, 2000).

cient for a majority of the security precautions to be taken by the bank. Indeed, this is the experience the banking industry has had under the federal banking laws that limit the loss of a credit card user to $50.[28] Banks have developed extensive antifraud programs that detect out-of-pattern purchases and otherwise reduce the system losses from credit card fraud. I am not aware of any serious suggestion that individuals could undertake these sorts of effective precautions on their own.[29]

To summarize this part, modern computer security practice reinforces our common sense. It is a security flaw to reveal the combination to a safe, hand a key to an outsider, or reveal a password or PIN. Straightforward efficiency arguments point toward the efficiency of confidentiality here, with the system owner such as a bank likely best placed to take the bulk of the security precautions.[30]

Trade Secrets, Confidential Business Information, and the Confidentiality of Keys and Combinations

Another area to examine for efficient confidentiality concerns disclosure of trade secrets and other confidential business information.[31] The term "trade secret" refers to the set of confidential information for which courts provide legal protection. The discussion here addresses trade secrets as well as the broader set of confidential business information for which it may be efficient for a bank or other recipient to keep the information confidential.

I suspect that most readers believe that it is efficient for a bank generally to keep confidential a significant amount of information that it learns from its borrowers and other business partners. A first category of confi-

---

28. 15 U.S.C. § 1693g.

29. In pointing out the likely efficiency of having the bank take the lead on security, I am not taking a position on the relative merits of relying on regulation or legislation compared with relying on market forces or self-regulation. This paper addresses the efficient level of confidentiality but not the institutional choices among market, self-regulatory, and regulatory solutions.

30. There will undoubtedly be efficient safeguards by individual consumers, such as keeping their wallets from being stolen or protecting their passwords. Even for protecting passwords, however, system owners have learned to take measures such as requiring harder-to-break passwords or mandating more frequent changes in individual passwords.

31. For insightful earlier discussions of the interaction of trade secrets, confidential business information, and privacy, see Samuelson (2000); Kitch (1980).

dential business information, and the most familiar sort of trade secret, is a secret process or other technical advantage that the company may have. At a linguistic level, the reasons for protecting this trade secret match well the reasons for maintaining confidentiality in security. A trade secret might be the "key" to a business, with disclosure reducing the company's value. As for the "combination" to the safe, the words invoke the combination of ingredients—the secret recipe—that constitutes the trade secrets for Coca Cola's recipe or the ingredients of many other products. For economists, the ability to protect these trade secrets encourages innovation in the secret process. Similarly, the legal ability to protect the trade secret encourages the company to share the data with a bank or other outside company where that sharing will assist a transaction.

A second category of confidential business information, "positional" information, is less often litigated but is perhaps more important in the business world. Many kinds of information improve the position of a company in a negotiating or other business setting. For instance, individuals when selling a house generally do not disclose their reservation price, the lowest price they are willing to accept. Companies presenting a sealed bid do not wish the amount to be known to competitors, who can then underbid by $1 and get the contract. Under game theory in general, there are many situations where keeping one's information and strategy secret will lead to a higher expected outcome.[32] In the business world, companies often wish to keep their competitive plans secret for as long as possible, such as their pricing plans or the date and nature of a new product announcement. For this positional information, the holder of the secret may rationally be reluctant to share information with a bank or other outsider unless there is a nondisclosure agreement or some other credible basis for believing that the secret will not be disclosed. Many economists and business people likely have a strong intuition that it is desirable and efficient in many bargaining and competitive situations to keep positional information secret and share it only with colleagues or others who have credibly promised not to disclose it.

In considering the costs and benefits of a financial institution keeping confidential business information confidential, I begin, as I did for security, with the possible benefits of disclosure. The first point is that in

---

32. Baird, Gertner, and Picker (1994).

some situations the overall benefits from disclosure may outweigh the costs. For instance, a borrower may have an expected gain of $1,000 if it keeps its production process or competitive plans secret. The bank, knowledgeable about the usefulness of that information for a wide range of clients, may know another company that would gain $5,000 if it had that information. Disclosure can match a willing seller (the bank) with the buyer who values the information most highly (the second company). In such an instance, the efficient action in the short term (considering only the usefulness of the existing information to the two companies) is for the bank to disclose the information to the second company.

To tell this story, however, is to expose the ephemeral nature of that efficiency gain. If borrowers learn that banks disclose their trade secrets or other confidential information, they are less willing to tell those secrets to the banks. Lenders do not learn as much as they used to about borrowers, increasing the risk of making loans and driving up the price. The one-time gain from disclosure is likely to be swamped by the long-term loss from loans that are never made or are made with inefficiently high risk premiums. In prisoner's dilemma terms, the defection in the first period is unlikely to be efficient.

While the benefits of disclosing confidential business information thus appear low, the costs appear to be considerable. As in the discussion of security, a higher risk of disclosure increases the rational level of protective measures against disclosure. In the security setting, a high crime rate leads to more bars on the windows. For confidential business information, the fear of disclosure may lead to more extreme measures to protect against disclosure by the financial institution or other company. For instance, the company may decide not to write down the sensitive information, even where it would otherwise be more efficient to do so. The company might insist on numbered copies of documents, invest in costly monitoring of those who know the secret, or take other measures that reduce business efficiency due to concerns about premature disclosure. With less trust, it becomes more important to have a formal nondisclosure agreement, with the attendant costs of drafting and enforcing it.

A greater cost of routine disclosure is the chilling effect on business activity. The literature on trade secrets is part of the broader literature on the efficiency of protecting intellectual property. Our legal regime principally protects trade secrets and other intellectual property in order to provide an incentive for companies to invest in new productive processes and other competitively useful information. Legal enforcement of nondisclosure agreements is provided for similar reasons.

In short, disclosure of confidential business information can reveal key information about the private workings of a company, including its technical secrets and the positional information so important to success against competitors. Banks and other institutions have long been under legal obligations in some settings not to disclose the confidential business information that comes into their possession.[33] Excessive disclosure can lead to costly efforts by borrowers and other business associates to hide information and can chill useful transactions before they take place.

Identity Theft and the Disclosure of Passwords

We next move from security and confidential business information to identity theft. Consider information that acts like a combination or key for a criminal. If a malicious person today learns my Social Security number, bank account number, and mother's maiden name, then that person has a good chance of impersonating me for financial gain. The set of identifying data acts like a key for unlocking my finances. Criminals who call my bank with this personal information can quite possibly transfer funds to their own accounts. The information is a password for the creation of new credit card accounts that can run up thousands of dollars in charges. The Social Security number, bank account number, and mother's maiden name can be used in combination to unlock other financial information, allowing the determined criminal to enter other financial accounts.

Studies have shown that identify fraud is a significant and growing phenomenon. Much of the identity fraud to date has occurred in low-tech ways, such as by stealing a credit card offer from a customer's mailbox and using that offer to establish a fraudulent charge account.[34] Even these apparently low-tech crimes, however, are based on the high-tech changes in financial services in recent years. As recently as a decade or two ago, there were strict federal and state limits on bank branching.[35] Opening a

33. For a discussion of legal obligations, see Fischer (1998).
34. For general information on identity theft, see the proceedings of the National Summit on Identity Theft of March 15, 2000, available at www.securityunit.com/other/nati-foc.htm. See also Beales (2002).
35. For the history, see Macey, Miller, and Carnell (2001).

charge account, making transfers among accounts, and undertaking other transactions were far more likely to be done in person, often by an employee who had past dealings with that customer. Today, as an enhancement of customer service, individuals do an increasing proportion of their personal financial business by mail, by phone, or over the Internet.[36] Bank employees are less likely to know an individual customer well enough to spot an imposter.

Bank security experts can readily imagine ways to allow Internet banking while minimizing the risk of identity fraud. For instance, online transactions might require a digital certificate that is essentially impossible for an imposter to forge.[37] Banks might require fingerprints or other biometric identifiers before authorizing a transaction.[38] Bank call centers might refuse to do transactions for customers who have "lost" their PIN or password.

Each of these potentially effective precautions, however, runs up against the realities of administering a mass-market business. Banks that wish to keep customers happy are in the business of facilitating transactions and not having security protocols that offend or overwhelm legitimate customers. For digital certificates, it has been far harder to implement large-scale systems than most proponents had expected.[39] For biometrics, the jury is still out regarding the extent to which the general public will accept fingerprints and eye scans in their daily transactions. Even if they do, the debates about a national identification system have highlighted the ease with which imposters can get "breeder" documents such as a birth certificate and then build up an entire fake identity.[40] As for the customers who forget their password, the bank faces a difficult cost-benefit trade-off between denying the transaction (and thus risking the anger of a legitimate customer) and asking for "secret facts" such as

36. For instance, the Online Banking Report finds that nearly 20 percent of U.S. households used online banking by early 2002, with projections of 33 percent within four years. See "Online Banking by the Numbers," summary information available at www.onlinebankingreport.com/resources/sr7.html [April 18, 2003].

37. Froomkin (1996).

38. Dean Narciso, "Without a Fingerprint, Police Won't Investigate," *Columbus Dispatch,* November 1, 2000, p. 1A; Peter Sinton, "Banks Use Fingerprint as an ID for Checks," *San Francisco Chronicle,* March 21, 1997, p. D1.

39. Hogan (2000).

40. For an excellent review of breeder documents and other challenges to implementing a national identification system, see Kent and Millett (2002).

mother's maiden name (and thus risking theft by a criminal who has already learned the secret fact).

Looking ahead, the trend will continue toward online and other transactions where no employee knows the customer well enough to spot an imposter. Under these conditions, the financial system will rely ever more on key information that is supposedly known to the bank and the customer, but not to the imposter. Identity fraud will flourish when this key information becomes available to outside parties.

To summarize on identity theft, the Social Security number and other key information acts in the same way as the combination to a safe or the key to a lock. There are likely efficiency gains from keeping this key information out of the hands of criminals. When the key does fall into the hands of a criminal, the criminal can gain unauthorized entry to steal funds and cause other harm.

Privacy and Disclosure of the Keys to the Heart

The next step is to consider disclosure by a financial institution of identifiable personal information. I have already discussed the harms that can come from disclosing the keys to the bank vault (security), to a business strategy (confidential business information), or to a customer account (identity fraud). The analogy is to consider the advantages and disadvantages of disclosing sensitive personal information, which might be considered the "keys to the heart."

The efficiency question arises where a financial institution possesses sensitive information about an individual customer and is considering whether to use that information for its own purposes or to disclose the information to another entity for that entity's purposes. As a straightforward application of economic theory, the efficient outcome depends on the total utility from using or disclosing the information versus the total utility from keeping the information confidential. For instance, suppose the bank expects to benefit by one dollar if it sells a customer's name for telemarketing purposes.[41] If the customer would suffer ten dollars of disutility from the disclosure, then it is inefficient to disclose. If the customer would suffer only ten cents, then the disclosure is worth making.

---

41. More precisely, suppose that the one dollar of total utility is gained by the bank, the telemarketer, and any others who benefit from the sharing of the information.

The great difficulty, of course, is learning the degree of harm caused by the disclosure, what economists would call the "taste" for keeping the information confidential. Privacy supporters tend to believe there is a strong taste for privacy, as evidenced by numerous polls that show overwhelming support for keeping financial and other sensitive information confidential.[42] Economists, however, are often skeptical of such polls. They prefer to look at the actual behavior, or "revealed preferences," of consumers. When economists see consumers actually disclosing information in the marketplace or responding positively to telemarketing calls, then they are inclined to believe that the behavior of consumers reveals fewer concerns about privacy than the polls would suggest.

I offer six points in response to the skepticism about the stated preferences for privacy shown in polls. First, a new study on revealed preferences supports a link between greater trust in privacy and greater participation in some financial services. Second, it is possible that economists underestimate other people's taste for privacy. Many polls have shown a split in the population among "privacy fundamentalists," who care strongly about the issue, "privacy unconcerned," who do not care much if their information is revealed, and "privacy pragmatics," who have differing views depending on the context.[43] In my experience, economists are largely privacy skeptics and therefore may misgauge the intensity and range of preferences held by other people.

Third, economists engaged in cost-benefit analysis are likely prone to what has been called the "dwarfing of soft variables."[44] A variable such as the taste for privacy is "soft" in the sense that it is difficult to quantify. In any quantitative estimates of costs and benefits, the soft variables can readily be excluded from the main analysis. Even important variables can thus be treated as an afterthought when they do not fit neatly into the analytic structure. The disutility caused by privacy invasions, because it is so difficult to quantify, can thus be systematically undervalued in economic analysis.

---

42. For a collection of polling information on privacy issues, see www.epic.org. In the United States, polling shows that the most sensitive categories are financial information, medical information, and information collected about children. Privacy laws were enacted in each of these areas in the late 1990s.

43. The terms come from polling and studies led by Allen Westin, of the Center for Social and Legal Research. For example, see Westin (1999).

44. Tribe (1973, p. 622).

A fourth point, about which I have written elsewhere, is a discontinuity between many people's short-run and long-run tastes for privacy.[45] In the short run, faced with a modest advantage in convenience or cost, individuals are often willing to disclose a modest amount of personal information. In the long run, many individuals strongly prefer a society characterized by significant privacy compared with a society characterized by pervasive disclosure and lack of privacy. To simplify the point, individuals who are willing to share their personal information in some transactions do not generally favor a Big Brother society. A *Wall Street Journal* poll in late 1999 asked Americans what they feared most in the coming century. Among a dozen answers, such as nuclear holocaust and global terrorism, the most frequent answer was "erosion of personal privacy."[46] This intensity of support for privacy, in my view, shows long-run support for a society that fundamentally honors the privacy of the individual. Specific issues in the short term, such as willingness to share information in one particular setting, must be placed in the longer-term context in order to understand the nature of the preferences.

The fifth point about preferences concerns a likely market failure that has not received sufficient attention to date. Consider telemarketing calls or other selling techniques based on the sharing of personal information. One market-based defense of such activities is that telemarketers only continue to make such calls because consumers respond positively to them, making the sales activity profitable. On this view, the tastes of consumers are once again revealed by their actions (buying from telemarketers) rather than their polling responses (objecting to telemarketing).

This presumed efficiency, however, ignores likely harms to other persons. Consider a simple example in which a telemarketing firm calls 100 consumers. Suppose that the firm has a typical response rate for a successful product, with three out of the 100 deciding to buy the product. Suppose further that seventeen of the consumers receive the call but do not mind it—they are truly indifferent to having received the call. Now suppose, consistent with polling data, that eighty of the consumers have

---

45. See Swire (1999).

46. Christy Harvey, "American Opinion (A Special Report): Optimism Outduels Pessimism," *Wall Street Journal,* September 16, 1999, p. A10.

"negative utility" from receiving the call.[47] In assessing the efficiency of the telemarketing campaign, the correct analysis is to add the producer surplus (profit by the selling company) and the consumer surplus (utility for the three who bought the product). In a static analysis (ignoring for the time being any longer-term effects on industry and consumer behavior), the efficiency question is whether the sum of producer and consumer surplus is greater than the disutility suffered by the eighty persons who are unhappy about receiving the call. The telemarketing company here can take advantage of an externality because it does not have to pay for the disutility suffered by those eighty persons. In the scenario where some of the eighty persons object strongly to the calls and suffer significant disutility, it is clearly possible for the telemarketing company to make money while the overall societal effect is a loss of efficiency. The importance of this market failure is probably even more convincing for junk faxes or unsolicited commercial e-mail ("spam"). It may be profitable for the seller to clog your fax with unwanted phone calls or your in-box with a flood of e-mails. Many people, however, can see the disutility caused by a jammed phone line or an e-mail system that requires time-consuming deletions by users seeking the e-mails they actually wish to read. These market failures are in addition to other market failures that other scholars and I have discussed in connection with privacy.[48]

Sixth, the possibility of an inefficient result is even greater when one moves to a dynamic analysis, considering the effect over time of having greater use or disclosure of information than consumers would wish. One response to objectionable telemarketing calls is to become less willing to accept phone calls generally. One might simply choose not to answer phone calls during dinnertime, might screen calls on the answering machine before picking up (even though some desirable calls will

47. According to a major study funded by industry, "Nearly all consumers consider telemarketing calls 'intrusions,' and the majority would opt out of receiving such calls if given the chance. When asked to characterize the telephone calls they receive at their home from companies wanting to sell them products and services, the majority of consumers (79 percent) say these calls are either 'always' (47 percent) or 'mostly' (32 percent) intrusions. It is not surprising, then, that 68 percent of consumers also say that if their local telephone company gave them the opportunity to opt out or decline to receive telemarketing calls about offers of new telecommunications products and services, they would exercise that option" Westin (1998).

48. See Swire (1997a); Schwartz (1997); Murphy (1996).

thereby be lost), or might switch to an unlisted number. These and similar defensive mechanisms reduce the overall usefulness of a home telephone number. Communications between a willing caller and a willing recipient do not take place or take place at higher cost, due to fear that the ringing phone is from an objectionable source.[49]

More generally, individuals who fear disclosure of sensitive data might refuse to enter into a range of transactions. In its cost-benefit analysis of the medical privacy rule, the U.S. Department of Health and Human Services estimates that billions of dollars of medical procedures would not be undertaken in the absence of effective confidentiality protections.[50] These forgone transactions are directly analogous to the forgone transactions by companies that fear disclosure of their confidential business information or lack trust in the security measures taken by a financial institution. Excess disclosure has a chilling effect on the willingness of companies to enter into transactions; equivalently, individuals and businesses are less likely to invest in the activity given the risk of disclosure.

Similarly, individuals might take a range of other costly measures to prevent disclosure of their sensitive information. I have mentioned the inefficiency of placing bars on the windows or hiring bodyguards when walking the streets. In the privacy context, individuals who lack trust in privacy protections might take many actions to make disclosure less likely. They might pay cash for psychiatric, HIV, or other sensitive medical care. They might monitor their banks or other institutions to try to ensure against excessive disclosures. They might refuse to answer phone calls due to concerns about telemarketing. And so on.

The public concern for privacy has grown during a period where financial and other institutions have amassed far more detailed information about individuals' activities. Under Secretary of the Treasury Gary Gensler explained the problem in testimony in the summer of 1999:

49. This concern about unwanted phone calls may be a reason why the United States has not developed an effective directory system for cellular telephones, even as a growing portion of the population relies on such phones for their business and personal calls. Under the current billing system, the cellular phone recipient of the call must pay for the minutes of connection. If there were an effective directory system for cellular telephones, then telemarketers could easily call people on those telephones, imposing the external costs not only of the recipients' time but also of their costly minutes.

50. Health and Human Services acknowledged that dollar estimates in this area were difficult to document. 65 Fed. Reg. 82462, 82776–82779 (December 28, 2000).

> The credit card records of 1999 . . . can list each and every purchase ever made by that customer, sorted by date, location, and other details. Furthermore, if credit card companies work together with merchants, then the level of detail can become even more refined—each dish ordered at a restaurant or each book title bought at a store.[51]

The greater detail in the databases means that the risk facing the individual has changed: "A generation ago, financial privacy meant keeping private your salary, your bank balances, and your net worth. Today, financial privacy means keeping secret your entire way of life."[52] In the terms used in this paper, we have seen the risks created by disclosure of the keys to the safe (security), the keys to the business (confidential business information), and the keys to a customer account (identity theft). The analogy for privacy, I suggest, is disclosing the keys to the heart. The risk is that unauthorized persons will gain access to the secure, confidential area. Faced with that risk, individuals will be chilled from participating in activities. They will take action to cloak their sensitive activities.[53] They will seek a long-run regime that respects an autonomous, private sphere and does not subject the individual to distasteful surveillance. And they will suffer disutility—heartburn, if you will—if their sensitive information is disclosed or they fear it will be disclosed.

New Evidence Supporting the Efficiency of Effective Privacy Protections in Financial Services

The gap between revealed preferences and poll results has narrowed as a result of a large new study by the Ponemon Institute about privacy in U.S. banking institutions. The institute's director, Larry Ponemon, has given permission to share highlights from this September 2002 survey of 2,930 customers of the twenty-five largest U.S. retail banks.[54] The study

51. Gensler (2000).
52. Gensler (2000).
53. On the issue of hiding sensitive activities, I find the analysis of Richard McAdams (1997) convincing concerning likely inefficiencies in how norms are enforced. Individuals thus may often have a rational basis for hiding information even when the information, if known in full detail to all concerned, would not need to be hidden.
54. The median age of respondents was 40.4 years. Median household income was $84,000. Median education was 13.6 years. Gender was 53 percent female and 47 percent male. Internet access was 55 percent.

has a cluster of findings about the positive correlation between trust in the privacy practices of banks and customer willingness to engage in additional banking activities. The findings given here are statistically significant to the 5 percent level or better, with a margin of error of 3 percent.

The survey finds consistent information that the top group of banks (top five of the twenty-five in the survey on an overall privacy rating) gets significantly different responses than the bottom group of banks (bottom five). For customers of the top group, there is far greater awareness of privacy policies. One question asked: "Did your bank send a privacy notice or privacy policy to you in the past year?" Such a notice is required under the Gramm-Leach-Bliley Act. For the top group, 74 percent of customers answered yes and 19 percent answered no. For the bottom group, the answer was only 46 percent yes and 43 percent no. Similarly, the survey asked: "Did you read the privacy notice or privacy policy sent by your bank?" For the top group, 55 percent of customers answered yes and 26 percent answered no, with only 33 percent answering yes and 43 percent answering no for the bottom group.

Customers in the top group have a stronger belief in their bank's commitment to privacy. The survey asked: "Do you understand your bank's commitment concerning how your personal information is being used?" For customers of the top group, 55 percent answered yes and 25 percent answered no, while the numbers were reversed for those of the bottom group, with 23 percent answering yes and 47 percent answering no.[55] This understanding is linked to greater confidence: "How confident are you that your primary bank is honoring its commitment to protect your privacy?" Customers of the top group answered 64 percent "confident" or "very confident," compared with only 31 percent of customers of the bottom group. The confidence extends to customer access to their personal information: "If you wanted to see the actual data the bank collected about you, do you believe that you would be able to access your personal information from your bank?" The top five once again are strikingly different from the bottom five, with 63 percent of customers

---

55. Similarly, a question asked: "Do you understand your bank's privacy commitment to protecting your personal information?" Customers of the top five answered 69 percent yes and 17 percent no, while customers of the bottom five answered 29 percent yes and 50 percent no.

answering yes for the top compared to 22 percent for the bottom and with 14 percent answering no for the top group compared to 53 percent for the bottom.

These findings show a strong correlation between good privacy practices, such as clear notices that are understood by customers, and greater customer trust, such as confidence that the bank would honor its privacy commitments and give access to a customer's data. The most interesting results, however, are likely the correlation between customer trust and customer actions.

The first action item concerns the customers' actual efforts to block information sharing. One might suppose that the banks that communicate more clearly the customer's right to opt out would experience a higher rate of such requests. On this theory, a bank that wants to use customer information intensively might try to hide the opt-out right, such as by making the privacy policy or the opt-out box hard to find for the customer. In my experience, some financial institutions have gone down this path. An interesting result of this survey, however, is that stronger privacy practices are correlated with a *lower* likelihood of blocking data sharing. For the top five banks, where customers reported a much higher awareness of the privacy policy, only 8 percent said yes to the question "Did you ever request that your bank stop using or sharing your personal information for certain reasons?" By contrast, for the bottom five banks, where relatively few customers are aware of the privacy policies, 14 percent of customers sought to stop data sharing. Although the gap between 14 and 8 percent is not as statistically robust as some of the other findings, the survey suggests that clearer communication on privacy is linked to fewer customer efforts to prevent the bank from using and sharing data.

The single most notable finding of the study, however, is evidence that good privacy practices pay off by encouraging customers to engage more intensively in banking activities. The survey asked: "Do you ever use online banking?" For the top five trusted institutions, the answer was a resounding yes, by 65 to 29 percent. For the bottom five institutions, 45 percent said yes and the same percentage said no. The overall average of the twenty-five institutions was in between, with 54 percent answering yes and 42 percent answering no.

More research should be done on this intriguing finding. It is possible, for instance, that the banks that created trust on privacy just happened to have excellent online banking offerings. That said, participation in online banking would seem like good evidence of overall trust in a financial institution. Security and privacy fears are likely at their peak when a customer uses the Internet as the basis for financial transactions rather than having a teller or other person involved in the transaction.

For purposes of this paper, the finding about online banking provides new evidence of a link between greater customer trust and greater customer willingness to engage in banking activities. The top five banks consistently scored much better on privacy measures such as awareness of privacy policies and belief in the bank's commitment to honor privacy promises. These same banks also scored much better at getting customers to engage in online banking, an activity that depends on trust.

Seen in the context of the debate about revealed preferences, the new study supplies information about actual consumer behavior as it relates to privacy and trust in the financial institution.[56] The revealed preferences, as shown by the study, indicate greater participation in financial services by customers who have higher trust in the bank's privacy practices. This is one study, and we should not read too much into any single empirical result, but the study is one intriguing instance where actual practices appear to match the repeated poll findings that individuals value the privacy of their sensitive personal information.

Toward a Theory of Efficient Confidentiality

The discussion thus far has prepared the way for a more general discussion of when it is efficient to keep information confidential. This section provides a template for discussing the efficiency of confidentiality in diverse settings.

---

56. It is true that the study relies on self-reporting about whether individuals have used online banking, rather than directly observing how often they have used online banking. My own belief is that individuals likely report pretty accurately their participation in online banking. The fact is easy to remember and does not seem especially sensitive. Even if there is some gap between individuals' actual participation and reported participation in online banking, it is hard to see why customers of some banks would report so differently on the same question compared to customers of other banks. In short, I take the survey results about participation in online banking as a good proxy for actual participation.

A Template for Assessing the Efficiency of Confidentiality

The template has four parts. First, the static analysis looks at the allocational efficiency—the direct benefits—from a given instance of disclosure. As discussed, these benefits occur largely from the matching of willing buyers and sellers. Those efficiency gains may be offset by the efficiency losses or direct costs from the disclosure. These may occur, for instance, due to individuals' taste for privacy—their disutility from having the information disclosed.

The second step shifts to dynamic analysis, looking at the level of investment in the activity over time by seller and buyer. Will economic activity be chilled due to fears of disclosure? Will economic activity instead be increased due to the business made possible by the sharing of information? The Ponemon study provides evidence that consumers are more likely to buy certain financial services where they have a higher level of trust in the seller. Holders of confidential business information are similarly more likely to share that information with a seller when they believe there will be no disclosure. On the seller side, the level of investment in an activity will depend on the trade-off between the advantages of developing a reputation for trust versus the advantages of using the information for other purposes.

The third step, also part of the dynamic analysis, is to look at the measures taken by parties to get around the default level of confidentiality. On the buyer side, there may be cloaking activities, as the buyer hides information and makes other efforts to prevent disclosure. On the seller side, there may be efforts to learn information even where the usual practice would not provide that information. Hiring private investigators would be one example.

Next, the efficient level of confidentiality needs to be achieved in some institutional setting. As previously stated, this paper has focused on the level of confidentiality rather than doing comparative institutional analysis. The overall assessment of efficient confidentiality, however, needs to look at the relative costs and benefits of achieving confidentiality through market, self-regulatory, or government-mandated approaches.

Putting these pieces together, estimating the efficiency of a certain regime for confidentiality depends on analysis of the following: the static benefits from disclosure, the static costs from disclosure, the benefits derived from investment by sellers in the activity, the benefits derived from investment by buyers in the activity, the information-gathering investments by sellers, and the cloaking investments by buyers. The efficient outcome will be reached subject to the relative costs and benefits of different institutional approaches.

Efficiency in the Context of Other Approaches to Privacy

Identifying the components of efficient confidentiality does not dictate any particular outcome for the efficiency analysis. An accurate economic analysis depends on the empirical data found for each component in the list. That said, this paper has explained that the ideals of perfect competition and perfect information are so fundamental for many economists that they have a strong intuition that confidentiality measures generally move the market away from efficiency.

In partial response, this paper has developed a counterintuition that disclosure of confidential information often leads to misallocation of resources. Disclosing key information can lead to harm for security (aiding theft from the bank), for confidential business information (disclosure of important information to a competitor), for identity theft, or for privacy (the keys to the heart). For each of these areas, the static analysis shows a societal loss when the transfer goes from someone who on average values it more (the bank, the company, the account holder, the consumer) to someone who values it less (the bank thief, the competitor who steals the bid information, the identity thief, the entity that uses the sensitive personal information).

This static analysis, however, reminds us of something important about economic theory. Under the utilitarian approach of economics, the utility gain for the thief (perhaps stealing money to feed a starving family) may exceed the utility loss for the rightful owner (perhaps a rich person or company who will not even notice the loss of money). The static analysis concludes that utility will actually increase if the person taking the information derives a higher marginal utility than the person whose information is taken. To the extent the theft is inefficient, the economic analysis of crime will depend primarily on dynamic effects over time, such as the high expense of paying for bodyguards or the chilling effect on investment if crime is common.

In the privacy area, Judge Posner has indirectly acknowledged the weakness of the economic argument by suggesting that certain tastes should be left out of the efficiency analysis of privacy protection.[57] Notably, given his concern that individuals will use privacy rules to misrepresent themselves, he wishes to eliminate from consideration the utility gained by individuals seeking confidentiality and hiding information from others. This suggestion would be equivalent to discounting the utility gained by the thief. In both instances, there would be a decision that someone is engaged in conduct that should be unlawful (theft or fraud) and that the utility gained from the unlawful conduct should not count for the efficiency analysis.

In response, I point out, first, that it is a departure from the standard utilitarianism of economic analysis to pick and choose which tastes should "count." If an economist wishes to eliminate certain categories of utility from the cost-benefit analysis, then everyone should recognize that something special is going on. That economist is making a different sort of argument from the usual cost-benefit argument and is doing so in a way that necessarily leads that economist to value privacy less than individuals actually do.

Second, I suggest that Judge Posner's argument may arise in part from a debatable way of merging the long-run (dynamic) and short-run (static) arguments. It is clearly desirable in the long run—creates a better overall society—to have a low level of theft and other crime. In recognizing the importance of this goal, one might be tempted to argue that the utility gained by the criminals should be left out of the cost-benefit analysis. Similarly, Judge Posner emphasizes the desirability in the long run of having more accuracy in information and less fraud. Judge Posner thus might conclude that the utility gained by those committing what he considers fraud—concealing information—should be excluded from consideration. This approach, however, elevates the long-term goal of avoiding fraud (and an exaggerated version of fraud at that) over other important long-term goals.[58] Notably, it avoids any consideration of ways in which

---

57. Posner (1978).

58. A valid common-law action for fraud had to meet a number of quite strict requirements, such as knowledge of falseness, reliance by the person defrauded, and materiality of the misstatement. Many misstatements thus did not rise to the level of actionable fraud. In addition, individuals only rarely had an affirmative duty to speak. Individuals thus kept the option of staying silent (keeping information confidential) in many settings. In light of these many limitations on an action for fraud, it was consistent with the common law to keep personal information confidential in most settings.

it is desirable in the long run—creates a better overall society—to retain a space for personal autonomy and freedom from surveillance. To the extent that Judge Posner seeks to justify excluding the taste for privacy based on the long-run advantages of avoiding fraud, there logically should be a similar consideration of the long-run advantages of protecting privacy.

Even if an economist disagrees with Judge Posner's argument about the taste for privacy, and agrees to count such tastes fully in the analysis, economic analysis still systematically gives less weight to privacy concerns than many competing theoretical perspectives. Consider once again the economic analysis of crime, which seeks to reduce unlawful behavior principally in order to reduce defensive expenses (bars on the windows) and to avoid a chilling effect on economic activity (fear of shopping due to muggers). In the eyes of any child learning right from wrong, and almost any theorist of criminal law, this economic approach is perhaps interesting but distinctly narrow in its viewpoint. Much of the criminal law has to do with right and wrong, retribution, the moral imperative of providing safety to the community, and so on. No complex analysis is needed to compare the utility of the thief with the utility of the victim.[59] The crime violates important rights of the victim, and those rights should be upheld.

Similarly, for privacy, major legal systems support a "right of privacy." In the United States, this right is most clearly applied in cases involving bodily autonomy,[60] but the Supreme Court has also stated that the right applies in some settings to information about the individual.[61] In Europe, "the right to respect for his private and family life, his home, and his correspondence" is enshrined in Article 8 of the Council of Europe Convention for the Protection of Human Rights and Fundamental Freedoms.[62] Scholars who write about privacy often emphasize the role that the right of privacy plays in achieving goals such as maintaining individ-

---

59. Returning to the situation of the thief and the starving family, rights theorists face the difficult issue of defining what circumstances will excuse a crime, as famously illustrated by Victor Hugo's novel *Les Miserables*.

60. *Roe* v. *Wade*, 410 U.S. 113 (1973); *Eisenstadt* v. *Baird*, 405 U.S. 438 (1972); *Griswold* v. *Connecticut*, 381 U.S. 479 (1965).

61. *Whalen* v. *Roe*, 429 U.S. 589 (1977).

62. For discussion of the text and case law under Article 8, see Solove and Rotenberg (2003, p. 693).

ual autonomy, promoting democracy, reducing the risk of tyranny, and achieving other societal goals.

None of these goals, however, is easy to fit within economic analysis. Consider, for instance, the role that a system of privacy protection might play in reducing the risk of tyranny—a Big Brother society—over time. I myself am concerned that a system of pervasive surveillance and information sharing can infringe seriously on individual freedoms over time, weakening the checks and balances of a society against entrenched authority. The *Wall Street Journal* poll, showing intense worries about "the erosion of personal privacy" in the coming century, suggests that others share this concern.

Putting this concern into a cost-benefit analysis, however, is an odd proposition, to say the least. Roughly speaking, one would try to find the discounted present value of the efficiency losses that would occur under the totalitarian regime and multiply that by the probability that a particular disclosure rule would affect the likelihood of producing such a regime. To state the cost-benefit analysis, however, is to show how difficult it is to give significant weight to the long-run fears. Measuring the marginal likelihood of the bad event is impossible. If the bad event happens in fifty or 100 years, the discounted present value today will be minimal. It is difficult to imagine trained economists who would shift the outcome of a cost-benefit analysis due to such uncertain and long-run costs. Yet some of the most compelling arguments for protecting privacy may indeed depend on creating an overall structure of rules and practices that effectively guards against a slippery slope into a qualitatively less desirable society.

To summarize this discussion, the efficiency analysis of standard economic theory is impoverished compared to the concerns considered by other approaches. Economists often do not recognize an individual's right to privacy of personal information.[63] Even where they do, the mere

---

63. Under the standard Coasian approach, rights are only assigned after an analysis of the most efficient starting point for bargaining to an efficient outcome. A separate, lengthy discussion would be needed to complete an economic analysis of the extent to which the rights in information should "belong" to the seller or the individual. In this article, I point out simply that human rights approaches usually find that the individual should have a strong right over the information. Economists, perhaps influenced by their pro-disclosure intuitions, are more likely to think that the information "belongs" to the bank or other selling institution. Any such analysis of how to allocate property rights in information, more-

violation of a right, in the eyes of the economist, does not generally change the utilitarian calculus. There is no moral condemnation about the taking of property or information. The focus instead is on the costs over time of coping with the theft. The efficiency analysis leaves out much of what people actually fear in the area of privacy protection.

Conclusion

Earlier in the paper, I stated that, based on my experience in government service, graduate training in economics is an important predictor that someone will not "get" the issue of privacy protection. This paper sought to clarify our understanding of this phenomenon. Trained economists, in my view, are powerfully affected by the model of perfect information and perfect competition. Any rules limiting the free flow of information, therefore, are deeply suspect.

This paper, in response, has put forward diverse reasons within economic theory for believing that confidentiality is more often efficient than the perfect information model would suggest. First, the long-standing history of confidentiality in financial services suggests that confidentiality is adaptive and efficient in a range of settings. Second, the importance of keeping passwords, PINs, and other key information confidential should at least open the door a crack to the idea that confidentiality is efficient in some settings. Those inclined to be skeptical about the efficiency of confidentiality should ponder why they favor it in at least some settings.

Third, many economists systematically undervalue the harms from unwanted disclosure of information. Economists, who themselves on average appear to care little about privacy, may misgauge the tastes of other people. The paper explains a significant market failure that may lead to inefficiently high use of telemarketing and other business activities that rely on information sharing. Certain sorts of harms, including

---

over, would need to account for numerous specialized situations. This complexity is illustrated by the medical privacy rule in the United States, on which I worked extensively while in government. The rule assigns significant rights to the individual patient but also has numerous specific provisions tailored to research, judicial proceedings, and many other settings. 45 C.F.R. 164.512.

long-run societal harm from lack of privacy, have perhaps not received full weight.

Fourth, the Ponemon Institute study provides evidence about revealed behavior, and not simply about poll responses, when it comes to financial services and privacy. The most significant finding is that customers who trust their financial institution on privacy are substantially more likely to engage in online banking. Additional research would be helpful, but these data support the possibility that individuals will participate more in some financial services where confidentiality is ensured.

Examination of confidentiality in a range of settings sets the stage for a fuller discussion of when confidentiality is efficient. The discussion here shows the importance of considering both the static effects (the costs and benefits from a particular disclosure) and the dynamic effects (the level of investment in the activity in the future and the steps taken over time to find or conceal information).

The paper also places the economic efficiency analysis into broader debates about the desirability of privacy protection. The European and American legal systems and scholars from fields other than economics have stressed the violations of rights that occur when important data about individuals are disclosed without their agreement. Economic analysis gives no independent weight to the violation of rights. Although violation of rights often leads to moral outrage and legal claims, these sorts of concerns are generally external to the views of economists.

In conclusion, the perfect competition model pushes economists to believe that confidentiality rules are inefficient. This article presents reasons from within economics for believing that confidentiality is often efficient. It also shows how many of the strongest arguments from non-economists are essentially ignored by traditional economic analysis. By recognizing how these arguments fit together, we all might better understand why economists have been outliers in debates about privacy protection. And perhaps the economists among us, or the economist within each of us, will be challenged to think again about when confidentiality is efficient or otherwise desirable.

References

Baird, Douglas G., Robert H. Gertner, and Randal C. Picker. 1994. *Game Theory and the Law*. Harvard University Press.

Beales, J. Howard. 2002. "Testimony [given on March 20, 2002] of J. Howard Beales before the Subcommittee on Technology, Terrorism, and Government of the Senate Judiciary Committee." Available at www.ftc.gov/os/2002/03/idthefttest.htm [April 18, 2003].

Calabresi, Guido. 1970. *The Cost of Accidents: A Legal and Economic Analysis*. Yale University Press.

Cohen, Julie E. 2000. "Examined Lives: Informational Privacy and the Subject as Object." *Stanford Law Review* 52 (May): 1373–438.

Epstein, Richard A. 1980. "A Taste for Privacy? Evolution and the Emergence of a Naturalist Ethics." *Journal of Legal Studies* 9 (January): 665–81.

———. 1994. "The Legal Regulation of Genetic Discrimination: Old Responses to New Technology." *Boston University Law Review* 74 (January): 1–23 .

Fischer, L. Richard. 1998. *The Law of Financial Privacy*, 3d ed. Arlington, Va.: Warren, Gorham, and Lamont Banking, A. S. Pratt and Sons Group.

Froomkin, A. Michael. 1996. "The Essential Role of Trusted Third Parties in Electronic Commerce." *Oregon Law Review* 75 (Spring): 49–115.

Gavison, Ruth. 1980. "Privacy and the Limits of the Law." *Yale Law Journal* 89 (January): 421–71.

Gensler, Gary. 2000. "Testimony of Under Secretary of the Treasury Gary Gensler, June 14, 2000." Available at www.privacy2000.org/archives/Treasury_6-14-00Gensler testimony percent20_on_hr4585.htm.

Hogan, Tara C. 2000. "Now That the Floodgates Have Been Opened, Why Haven't Banks Rushed into the Certification Authority Business?" *North Carolina Banking Institute* 4 (April): 417–42.

Kent, Stephen T., and Lynette I. Millett, eds. 2002. *IDs—Not That Easy: Questions about Nationwide Identity Systems*. Washington: National Academy of Sciences and National Research Council, Committee on Authentication Technologies and Their Privacy Implications. Available at www.nap.edu/catalog/10346.html [April 18, 2003].

Kitch, Edmund W. 1980. "The Law and Economics of Rights in Valuable Information." *Journal of Legal Studies* 9 (January): 683–723.

Macey, Jonathan R., Geoffrey P. Miller, and Richard Scott Carnell. 2001. *Banking Law and Regulation*, 3d ed. Gaithersburg, Md.: Aspen Law and Business.

McAdams, Richard H. 1997. "The Origin, Development, and Regulation of Norms." *Michigan Law Review* 96 (November): 338–433.

Miller, Arthur R. 1971. *The Assault on Privacy: Computers, Data Banks, and Dossiers*. University of Michigan Press.

Murphy, Richard S. 1996. "Property Rights in Personal Information: An Economic Defense of Privacy." *Georgetown Law Journal* 84 (July): 2381–417.

Posner, Richard A. 1978. "The Right of Privacy." *Georgia Law Review* 12 (Spring): 393–422.

———. 1979. "Privacy, Secrecy, and Reputation." *Buffalo Law Review* 28 (Winter): 1–55.

———. 1986. *Economic Analysis of Law,* 3d ed. Boston: Little, Brown.

———. 1995. *Overcoming Law.* Harvard University Press.

Post, Robert C. 1989. "The Social Foundations of Privacy: Community and Self in the Common Law Tort." *California Law Review* 77 (October): 957–1010.

———. 2001. "Three Concepts of Privacy." *Georgetown Law Journal* 89 (June): 2087–101.

President's Critical Infrastructure Protection Board. 2002. "The National Strategy to Secure Cyberspace." Unpublished manuscript. Available at www. whitehouse.gov/pcipb/ [April 18, 2003].

Reiman, Jeffrey H. 1984. "Privacy, Intimacy, and Personhood." In Ferdinand David Schoeman, ed., *Philosophical Dimensions of Privacy: An Anthology.* Cambridge University Press.

Rosen, Jeffrey. 2000. *The Unwanted Gaze: The Destruction of Privacy in America.* New York: Random House.

Samuelson, Pamela. 2000. "Privacy as Intellectual Property?" *Stanford Law Review* 52 (May): 1125–73.

Samuelson, Paul A., and William D. Nordhaus. 1985. *Economics,* 12th ed. McGraw-Hill.

Schwartz, Paul M. 1997. "Privacy and the Economics of Personal Health Care Information." *Texas Law Review* 76 (November): 1–75.

———. 1999. "Privacy and Democracy in Cyberspace." *Vanderbilt Law Review* 52 (November): 1609–702.

Solove, Daniel J. 2001. "Privacy and Power: Computer Databases and Metaphors for Information Privacy." *Stanford Law Review* 53 (July): 1393–462.

Solove, Daniel J., and Marc Rotenberg. 2003. *Information Privacy Law.* New York: Aspen Publishers.

Swire, Peter P. 1997a. "Markets, Self-Regulation, and Government Enforcement in the Protection of Personal Information." In *Privacy and Self-Regulation in the Information Age.* Washington: U.S. Department of Commerce.

———. 1997b. "The Uses and Limits of Financial Cryptography: A Law Professor's Perspective." Available at www.peterswire.net/pscrypto.html [April 18, 2003].

———. 1999. "Financial Privacy and the Theory of High-Tech Government Surveillance." *Washington University Law Quarterly* 77 (Summer): 461–517.

———. 2001. "What Should Be Hidden or Open in Computer Security: Lessons on Deception, the Art of War, Law, and Economic Theory." Unpublished manuscript. Available at www.peterswire.net.

———. 2002. "The Surprising Virtues of the New Financial Privacy Law." *Minnesota Law Review* 86 (June): 1263–323.

Swire, Peter P., and Robert E. Litan. 1998. *None of Your Business: World Data Flows, Electronic Commerce, and the European Privacy Directive.* Brookings.

"Symposium: The Law and Economics of Privacy." 1980. *Journal of Legal Studies* 9 (January).

Tribe, Laurence H. 1973. "Technology Assessment and the Fourth Discontinuity: The Limits of Instrumental Rationality." *Southern California Law Review* 46 (1973): 617–60.

Westin, Alan. 1967. *Privacy and Freedom*. New York: Atheneum.

———. 1998. "The Era of Consensual Marketing Is Coming." Available at www.privacyexchange.org/iss/surveys/1298essay.html [April 18, 2003].

———. 1999. "'Freebies' and Privacy: What Net Users Think." Available at www.privacyexchange.org/iss/surveys/sr990714.html [April 18, 2003].

White House. 2000. *National Plan for Information Systems Protection: Invitation to a Dialogue*. Available at clinton4.nara.gov/media/pdf/npisp-fullreport-000112.pdf [March 10, 2003].

Williamson, Oliver E. 1985. *The Economic Institutions of Capitalism: Firms, Markets, Relational Contracting*. Free Press.